THE COMPLETE GUIDE TO
HORSE
BREEDS

THE COMPLETE GUIDE TO

HORSE BREEDS

Bounty Books

AN OCEANA BOOK

This edition published in 2005 by
Bounty Books, a division of
Octopus Publishing Group Ltd
2-4 Heron Quays
London E14 4JP

ISBN 0 7537 1239 3
ISBN13 9780753712399

QUMTIE2

This book is produced by
Quantum Publishing Ltd.
6 Blundell Street
London N7 9BH

Manufactured in Singapore by
Pica Digital Pte. Ltd.
Printed in China by
CT Printing Ltd

CONTENTS

INTRODUCTION

The horse as we know it today is the product of a long evolutionary chain stretching back for literally thousands of years. Before the end of the Ice Age, some 12,000 to 15,000 years ago, the ancestors of present-day Equus Caballos *roamed the world's grassy plains. These, in turn, emerged as a result of a process spanning some 55 million years of geological time.*

The earliest ancestor

The first of these ancestors was *Eohippus* or *Hyracotherium* (the latter is the accepted scientific name), which flourished from some 55 to 38 million years ago and is considered the first distinct horse. This breed was small in stature – about the size of a fox terrier – but was a notable advance over its own condylarth ancestors. The chief difference was the number of digits in each foot – *Hyracotherium* had four on the fore feet and three on the hind, as opposed to the five of the condylarths. Its legs were also longer, while the animal's teeth, jaws and skull were deeper and longer than those of its predecessors, making it more suited to grazing. Longer limbs, for their part, meant that *Hyracotherium*'s pace was increased, an especially important factor in its battle for survival against its various predator enemies. In addition, recent research has shown that the brains of *Hyracotherium* and other early horses were progressive in their evolution, when compared with other primitive mammals, such as their condylarth relatives.

Hyracotherium was also geographically widespread; traces of it have been found in both the New and the Old Worlds.

From four toes to three

About 38 million years ago, the first three-toed horses emerged, developing from one strain of *Hyracotherium* as the others died out. There were two groups of these; primitive browsers, feeding on leafy vegetation, and advanced grazers, feeding on grass. The browsers emerged first – they became extinct about 11 million years ago – to be followed later by the grazers.

Both groups were bigger than *Hyracotherium*; both had longer legs; and both had even more effective means of eating. Like *Hyracotherium*, too, they spread widely, starting in North America to reach the Old World some 20 million years ago. Yet, it was the development of the grazers as an independent entity that made this period an especially important one in horse history, for the change represented an important diversification of feeding habits in the evolutionary process. Specialized grazing meant that teeth, skull and jaws had to adapt to cope with the increased wear and tear of chewing abrasive grasses; accordingly all of them became deeper as time went by.

The main home of these grazers was in North America, though one group – the Hipparions – successfully migrated from the New World to the Old some 10 to 11 million years ago. It was on the grassy plains of North America, too, that the first one-toed horses emerged around 15 million years ago.

The emergence of *Equus*

The first one-toed horses were grazers, like their three-toed ancestors, though they apparently emerged from only one type in North America. This transition from three toes to one was a natural evolutionary consequence, as the size of the side digits gradually became smaller until only the central one played any

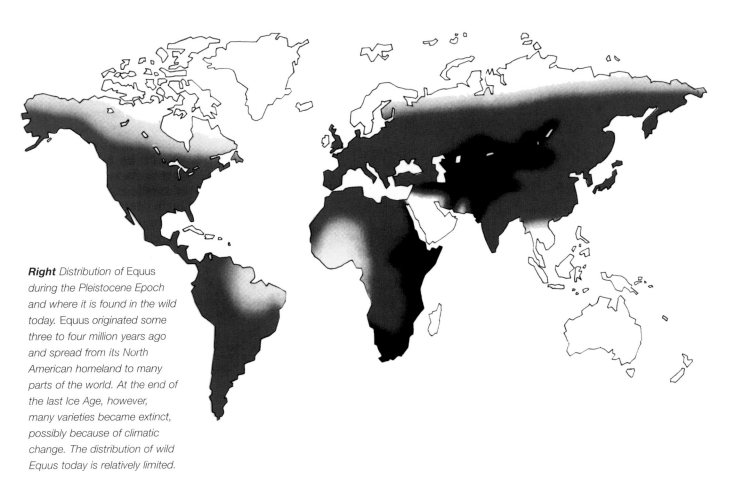

Right *Distribution of* Equus *during the Pleistocene Epoch and where it is found in the wild today.* Equus *originated some three to four million years ago and spread from its North American homeland to many parts of the world. At the end of the last Ice Age, however, many varieties became extinct, possibly because of climatic change. The distribution of wild* Equus *today is relatively limited.*

part in running. On the whole, these horses were bigger bodied than their predecessors, while their molars, skull and jaws were also enlarged.

Most of these one-toed horses were located in Central and North America and it was in the American north that the first representatives of *Equus* developed. These were descended from the one-toed *Dinohippus* and emerged between three and four million years ago. They spread quickly, becoming the most geographically diverse of of all ancestral horses; North, Central and South America, Asia, Europe and Africa all had their colonies. They also consisted of many different species, though, in common with many other large mammals, most of these became extinct by the end of the last Ice Age, about 12,000 to 15,000 years ago.

The reasons for this sudden drastic decline are obscure. Some experts think it was due to the change in climate or the influence of man, while others suggest a combination of these, or still more factors. Whatever the cause, the process was severe – particularly in America, the ancestral home of Equus. There, horses totally vanished from the scene; they were not to reappear until the Spanish conquistadores landed in Mexico in the early 16th century AD.

From the wild to domestication

By the end of this period, *Equus* had reached a recognizably modern form. During this long evolutionary progress, several trends had become apparent – all a direct result of the constant battle for survival in a sometimes hostile environment. On the whole, horses gradually increased in size, though there were times when some remained the same size or even grew smaller. Changes in skull and limbs also took place, as horses adapted to better suit themselves for grazing and running.

The next major step was the work of an external force – that of man. In around 3000 BC, probably in Asiatic Russia, the horse was first domesticated. The only major area of controversy here is whether a single type of horse was involved or whether several types were domesticated at the same time. Some experts believe that two distinct kinds – the now extinct tarpan and Przewalski's horse – were involved, but others argue that the one is related to the other.

In any event, what is certain is that, from there, the knowledge of domestication spread rapidly and widely.

The source of knowledge

The evolution of the horse is a fascinating and complex subject that today attracts scientists all over the world. The major source of knowledge is based on the rich fossil deposits of western North America – though the first description of *Hyracotherium* was in fact based on the finds made in the marshes around London in 1839. The discovery, made by the British paleontologist Sir Richard Owen, did much to inspire the work of successors in the field, particularly in the USA.

Chief amongst these scientists was O.C. Marsh, the Professor of Paleontology at Yale University in the mid-nineteenth century. It was Marsh who discovered

Eohippus – the 'dawn horse' – the oldest horse in North America. And it was on his work that others built to create much of the knowledge that we possess today.

The Exmoor Pony

The Exmoor Pony (*right*) is thought to have existed in south-west England since prehistoric times. It is believed to be descended from the original Celtic pony of western Europe. The

brefd has
remained very
pure, and is
thought to
have changed
little since primitive
times.

Below Eohippus *(far left) also known as* Hyracotherium, *is one of the earliest equine ancestors. It lived around 50 million years ago.* Dinohippus *(centre), a descendant of* Eohippus, *first appeared about 15 million years ago. Early* Equus *(right) evolved from* Dinohippus.

THE FAMILY TREE OF THE HORSE

This family tree shows the horse's evolutionary development since the emergence of Hyracotherium, *the ancestral four-toed horse, in the Eocene Epoch some 55 million years ago. As the diagram shows, the evolutionary path was by no means straightforward; during the Miocene Epoch in particular, there were many divergences from it.*

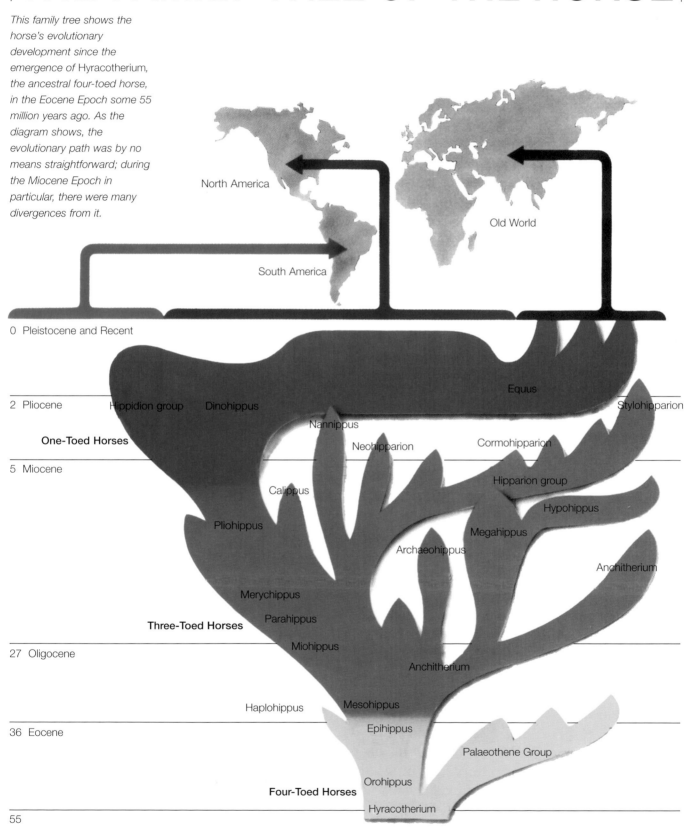

North America

Old World

South America

0 Pleistocene and Recent

Equus

2 Pliocene   Hippidion group   Dinohippus   Stylohipparion

Nannippus

One-Toed Horses   Neohipparion   Cormohipparion

5 Miocene   Hipparion group

Calippus   Hypohippus

Pliohippus   Megahippus

Archaeohippus

Anchitherium

Merychippus

Parahippus

Three-Toed Horses

Miohippus

27 Oligocene   Anchitherium

Haplohippus   Mesohippus

36 Eocene   Epihippus

Palaeothene Group

Orohippus

Four-Toed Horses

Hyracotherium

55

DOMESTICATION OF THE HORSE

It is generally accepted that the horse was the last animal to be successfully and widely domesticated, probably because it is highly strung, nervous and aggressive until tamed. There is no way of knowing exactly where and when horses were first domesticated, but it is believed to have been in the Far or Middle East.

Although the time of its general domestication is usually considered to have been between 5,000 and 6,000 years ago, there are cave paintings and rock carvings in Eurasia from before this time which seem to portray horses wearing simple harnesses.

Before the horse was used as a beast of burden, it was a prey animal for man. Horses would be used for hide, milk, blood, hair and bone. Early man would follow or herd his horses and other grazing animals, and eventually they became semi-domesticated with the increase of sedentary agriculture. It was probably at this time that the potential usefulness of the horse's attributes of speed and strength became appreciated. They were used in much the same way as oxen and reindeer for carrying loads such as sledges and wheeled vehicles. Probably the first horse riders were the sick, injured and elderly, who were hoisted up onto the beasts of burden.

Horses at war

Early horses were usually much smaller than today's. It is only during the last couple of hundred years that riding horses over 15hh have become widespread. These smaller horses were better suited to pulling chariots than to riding. The speed and strength of horses when combined with wheeled vehicles for military purposes proved crucial to the dominance of some empires and civilizations. The horse is unique among domesticated animals in the influence it had on warfare.

Unco-operative cousins

Man has tried his hand at domesticating most potentially useful species during his brief history on Earth. Not all have proved as amenable as expected. The onager (*Equus hemionus onager*) or half-ass was domesticated by the Sumerians, Egyptians, and Romans among others, but never successfully. This animal is unco-operative and habitually bites and kicks, unlike the African domestic ass or donkey (*Equus asinus*), which is domesticated almost the world over. Similarly unsuccessful attempts have been made to domesticate zebras.

Horses played an important part in the early Olympic Games in ancient Greece

The undomesticated zebra

Horse power in the fields and on the roads

In agriculture the heavy jobs of working the land were originally done by the less valuable and more numerous oxen and donkeys. During the 19th century in Europe, however, faster and more efficient ploughs were drawn by the heavy horse, which possessed more power than donkeys and more speed than oxen. With the development of improved road surfaces, too, faster horse-drawn vehicles became possible.

Horses and industry

Like mankind, horses first became acquainted with industry on a large scale in about the middle of the 18th century. Since Biblical times they had been used to operate wine and olive presses and to grind corn, while for hundreds of years they had powered windlasses at mine pitheads and worked ore-crushing machinery. Pit ponies, however, were not used until the 19th century, when the first horizontal drifts or galleries were constructed in coal mines; the last pit ponies working in a major coal mine in the United Kingdom went into honourable retirement in 1972.

Probably the first major equine contribution to the Industrial Revolution was in canal transport, which for 50 years before the coming of the railways was the fastest possible means of moving raw materials and finished goods between market, port and factory. Barges worked most efficiently at high speeds, with their noses lifted on to their own bow waves; to achieve this, relays of draught horses were stationed along towpaths. The horses moved at a fast trot between one stage and the next, never pausing, except at the locks.

The advent of the railways and the growth of industry actually raised the demand for workhorses to an unprecedented peak. As coaching companies went gradually out of business and the canals silted up, more and more horses were drafted into the cities, where, indeed, the railway companies were among their biggest employers. Teams of two or four hauled heavy wagons between factory, dock and railhead; well within living memory, it was possible to see apparently endless queues of patient Shires and Clydesdales waiting outside dock gates in the rain, as their drivers muffled in sacking and tarpaulins against the weather.

ANATOMY OF THE HORSE

Right *Points of the horse. Most occupations and hobbies have their own jargon, and horse-keeping is no exception. The terms used to describe different parts of the equine anatomy, and the names of many of the diseases which affect them, have evolved during thousands of years' close contact between humans and horses – and for that reason the origin of many of these words is obscure. Nevertheless, although some of the disease names – used in the past to intimidate the uninitiated – are disappearing in favour of more scientific terminology (generally providing a more accurate description of the cause of a problem), the names in common use for the external features of the horse's anatomy – the points of the horse (see diagram) – have remained unchanged for centuries.*

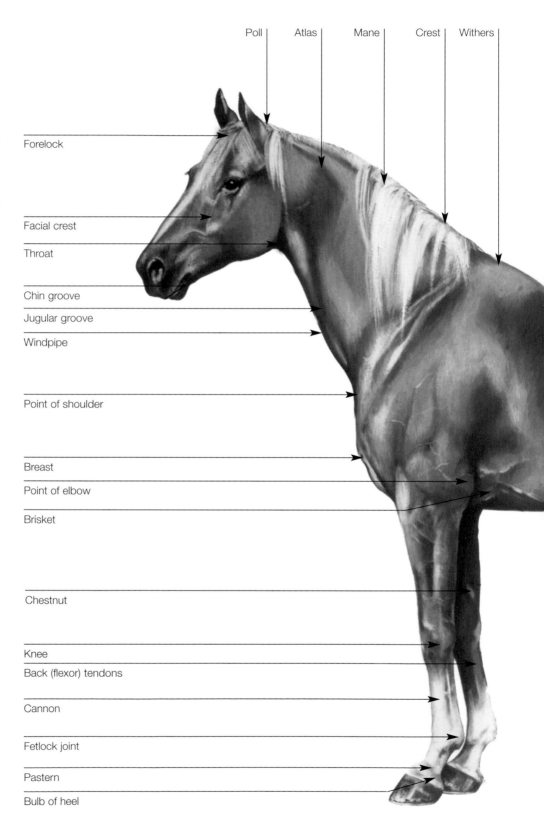

Poll | Atlas | Mane | Crest | Withers

Forelock

Facial crest

Throat

Chin groove

Jugular groove

Windpipe

Point of shoulder

Breast

Point of elbow

Brisket

Chestnut

Knee

Back (flexor) tendons

Cannon

Fetlock joint

Pastern

Bulb of heel

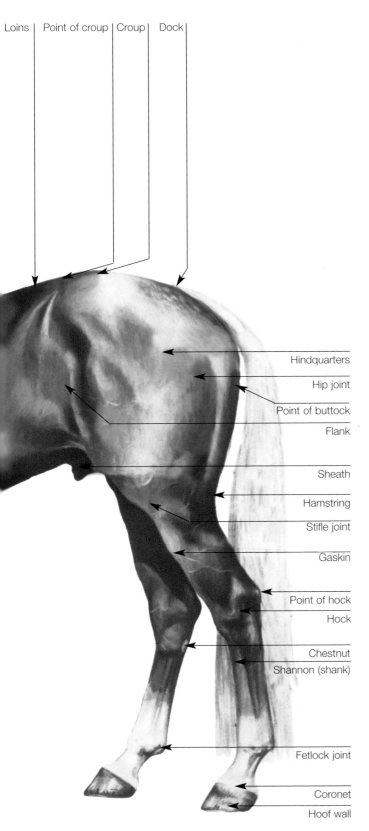

Loins | Point of croup | Croup | Dock

Hindquarters
Hip joint
Point of buttock
Flank
Sheath
Hamstring
Stifle joint
Gaskin
Point of hock
Hock
Chestnut
Shannon (shank)
Fetlock joint
Coronet
Hoof wall

The most striking feature of the horse is that it can perform the many tasks asked of it by man, though its physical make-up is in many ways unsuited to such demands. In its main period of evolution, the horse developed from a four or even five-toed marsh dweller to take the basic form it has today at a relatively early date; and even though it has somewhat changed its shape and improved its performance, the basic working mechanism remains the same.

Such basic physical facts should always colour the rider's attitude to the horse, and what he or she expects of it. With a basic understanding of the so-called points of the horse, it should be possible, for example, to go some way towards lessening the risk of muscular strains. These are all too common and, in extreme cases, can lead to a horse having to rest for weeks, if not months. More important still, knowledge of these points acts as a valuable guide in deciding what is a suitable or unsuitable horse for the prospective rider. The most vital attribute of any riding horse is depth of girth, which denotes toughness and strength. Tall, leggy horses invariably lack stamina. Short legs and a deep body, with plenty of heart room, are the signs to look for.

The most important points of the horse are its limbs and feet. Both in the wild and in domesticity, the horse depends on its means of locomotion for survival.

Feet and legs require, therefore, to be as correctly conformed as possible, if the horse is to remain sound and mobile. Correct conformation is, indeed, the most valuable asset any horse can possess.

The hind leg

Experts differ as to whether the most important single asset is a good hind leg or a good foreleg. As the hind leg is the propelling force, it is usually given priority. At the point where it emerges from the body the stifle joint is situated. This corresponds to the human knee and is similarly equipped with a patella, or kneecap. This acts like a pulley block to give added strength to the muscles extending the stifle.

The stifle itself is synchronized in its movements with the hock, as it is controlled by the same muscles and ligaments. As one flexes, so does the other. Then comes the gaskin, or second thigh. This should be muscular and well-developed enough to stand up to the work and strain demanded of it. This runs down into the hock – probably the most important part of the leg as the main propelling agent which enables the horse to gallop and jump.

The hock is made up of a whole series of joints, tightly bound together by ligaments. It articulates directly with the tibia (another vital bone) only through one bone – the astralagus. The feature as a whole should be big, flat and free from unsightly lumps, bumps or swellings. These can be indications of various types of unsoundness, such as curbs, spavins or thoroughpins.

The hock should also be near to the ground; short cannon bones from hock to fetlock and from knee to fetlock are a sign of strength. The tendons should stand out sharply, and there should be no thickening of the lower leg.

The fetlock joint should also be well-defined and not puffy – a puffy fetlock resembles a human swollen ankle. This leads on to the pastern, which should be of medium length and slope. Very short pasterns cannot fulfil one of their main tasks – absorbing the concussion produced by movement. Though over-long pasterns give a springy, comfortable ride, they, too, are a sign of weakness that could lead to future trouble.

The foot

The size of foot varies with the type of horse. Thoroughbreds usually have small, rounded feet and, often, low heels. Heavy breeds, such as Clydesdales, Shires and Percherons, have larger, flatter feet.

The foot should be wide and open, not narrow, 'boxy' and contracted. The horn should look healthy and be free from unsightly cracks or ridges. Under it lie the sensitive laminae.

When the foot is lifted up, a well-developed frog should be visible on the underside. Starting at the bulbs of the heel and running upwards to end in a point near

White face

Blaze

Snip

Stripe

Star

Above *The size and shape of the markings on the horse's face are a means of identification used when describing individual horses. Some of the more common ones are shown above. The size and position of a star, and whether a stripe is narrow or broad, should be stated. A star followed by a stripe is usually described as a disjointed stripe.*

the toe, the frog acts as an anti-slip device and also helps to absorb concussion.

Each hoof is surmounted by the coronary band, which lies between the foot and the pastern.

Proper care of the feet is vital. In jumping, for instance, one forefoot has to take the whole weight of both horse and rider at the moment of landing. Good shoeing is therefore essential, or lameness will result. A young horse, too, can develop a form of lameness called pedal ostitis, caused by an excess of pressure on the sensitive sole of the foot by the os pedis – the terminal bone. This comes about largely through overwork, particularly in jumping.

The foreleg

The unique feature of the horse's foreleg is that it is attached to the upper part of the body by nothing more than muscle and ligamentous tissue. The horse has no equivalent to the human clavicle, or collar bone. The chief advantage of this is that the muscle is able to absorb a great deal of the concussion that would otherwise be transmitted to the spine. However, if undue strain is placed on the muscle, the horse can easily break down. This is particularly the case in race horses – often because the horse is what is known as 'back at the knee' (the shape is concave rather than convex).

The foreleg extends from the body below the point of the shoulder. The forearm runs down into the knee, which, like the hock, should be big, flat and prominent. Then the cannon bone, with tendons standing out clear and hard, runs down into the fetlock. The pastern separates this from the foot.

The legs have one final individual feature – the horny growths inside the legs above the knees. These are called chestnuts, and are, like fingerprints, completely individual. They are thought to be the remains of a digit.

The body

The shoulder runs from the withers – the bony prominence dividing the neck from the back and the highest part of the dorsal spine – down to the point of the shoulder. The shoulder itself should be long and

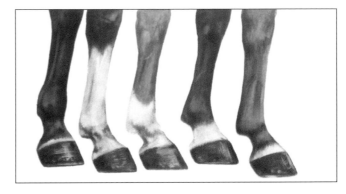

Above *White leg markings are also an important means of identification. A sock covers the fetlock and part of the cannon, while a stocking extends to the knee or hock. Other marks take the name of their site.*

sloping, especially at the upper end. An upright shoulder reduces endurance, as the horse has to do more work to cover the ground, and it cannot help to reduce concussion, which instead is passed on to the rider, making the horse uncomfortable to ride. This is particularly the case if the horse is ridden downhill.

The breast lies to the front of the shoulder, between the forelegs. It should be broad and muscular; narrow-breasted horses are weak and lack stamina. The underside of the neck should be concave and not unduly muscular.

The jaws run down to the muzzle. Well-defined, slightly distended nostrils and large, generous eyes are a sign of quality and good breeding. So are alert, well-pricked ears, which should not be too large. Between them lie the poll, leading to the top of neck and the crest, which runs down to the withers and back. The back consists of about 11 of the 18 dorsal vertebrae, as well as the arches of the corresponding ribs. Behind it lie the loins, which should be strong and well-muscled. These extend to the croup, or rump, which runs down to the tail and its underside, the dock.

Standing behind the horse, the points of the hip can be seen projecting outwards on either side of the backbone, above the flanks. This outwards projection means that they can easily be injured.

Just below the loins, a triangular depression, known as the 'hollow of the flank', is located. This is the highest point of the flank, which stretches downwards from the lumbar spine. The condition of the flank often acts as a guide to the health of the horse; if the horse is sick, it may well be 'tucked up' or distended.

Coat colours

Coat colour and markings developed over millions of years to give the animal the best possible camouflage for the area in which it lived. The more closely it resembled its background, the less likelihood there was of its being spotted by a predator.

One of the most primitive horse and pony colours is dun (a yellowy beige) with black points (the points being mane, forelock, tail and the lower legs). In a woodland background or plains environment where by no means everything is a lush green, duns are extremely well camouflaged.

Old stories abound of good and bad colours in horses. Chestnut horses were supposedly hot tempered, black nasty tempered and lacking in stamina, bay and brown dependable, and so on. The truth is that colour has no bearing whatsoever on temperament or performance ability.

The only exceptions to this are horses who have pink skin under white hair (and some white-haired horses have dark skin underneath). These horses are much more susceptible to the weather than others, because pink skin lacks the strengthening substance melanin, which is responsible for skin and hair colour. The pink hue comes from blood circulating through colourless skin. Because this skin is less resistant to sun and wet, and hence bacteria, it becomes more easily infected with skin diseases, sunburn and allergies.

The varieties of horse colours which abound today are the result of domesticated breeding, and bear no relation to camouflage. Some horses, such as palaminos, paints and pintos (piebalds, skewbalds and odd-coloured horses) are bred for special colours, and during the last century the German royal stud bred cremello (cream) horses for carriage-work.

Above ALBINO
White markings are areas with no pigment, and such markings do not appear to have existed in primitive and early strains. Albino horses with white coats, pink skin and red eyes have no melanin at all. The skin under white hair is often susceptible to diseases such as mud fever, grease or scratches, and to rain rash and sunburn. These conditions, however, are controllable with good management. White (creamy-yellow) hooves are no softer than dark ones.

Zebra marks, horizontal stripes found on the legs (darker than the coat colour) and sometimes on the neck, withers or quarters, are sometimes found on horses. Some pony breeds have a dark stripe running down the spine called a dorsal, or sometimes an eel, stripe. A few ponies and more donkeys have a further stripe running across this at the withers.

Foals change colour

When foals lose their foal coat in their first autumn it is quite common for them to change colour, their adult colour emerging underneath the fluffy foal hair as it falls out in patches. They look quite moth-eaten at this time. Chestnut foals will turn grey if they have one grey parent, and dun foals often turn bay.

Albinos

True albinos have no colouring agent in their bodies. They have pink skin, white hair and pink eyes, like albino rabbits. Some so-called albinos have blue eyes, but this is not true albinism, as blue is a colouring matter. Blue eyes are not all that common in horses, however; and where it does occur often only one eye is blue, called a wall eye. There is no evidence that wall eyes see less well than dark eyes, but albinos with pink eyes (due to the blood circulating through an uncoloured iris) are known to have poorer sight.

Appaloosa

Appaloosa patterning is found in a number of different breeds and there are four basic patterns:

Blanket: A coloured horse with a white area over the hips, sometimes extending onto the back and sides.

Leopard: A white horse with coloured spots all over.

Varnish roan: This is like regular roan, with two exceptions: the roaning extends onto the head of the horse, and there are coloured (non-roan) patches on certain parts of the head and body.

Snowflake: This is a coloured horse with white spots in random places on the body.

All of these factors, and others which alter the appearance of the horse, are inherited separately, so a horse can display more than one, such as varnish roan with a blanket. Appaloosas also often have vertically striped hooves, mottled pink-and-black skin, and visible sclera on the eyes.

Skewbald

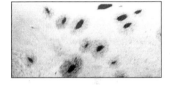

Leopard Appaloosa

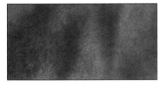

Black

Dark liver

Dappled beige dun

Dappled brown

Liver chestnut

Duy

Dappled chestnut

Cream

Red chestnut

Red dun

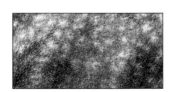

Palomino

Dappled grey

Rose roan

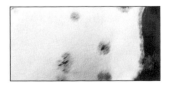

Piebald

Fleabitten grey

Grey

Below The skeleton of a normal adult horse consists of 205 bones, plus small amounts of cartilage. They are articulated at the joints, spanned and held together by ligaments. The larger bones form a scaffolding to which the muscles are attached. As well as the supporting framework for the body, the skeletal bones are a storehouse for calcium and phosphorus. Certain bones also produce red and white blood corpuscles in the marrow.

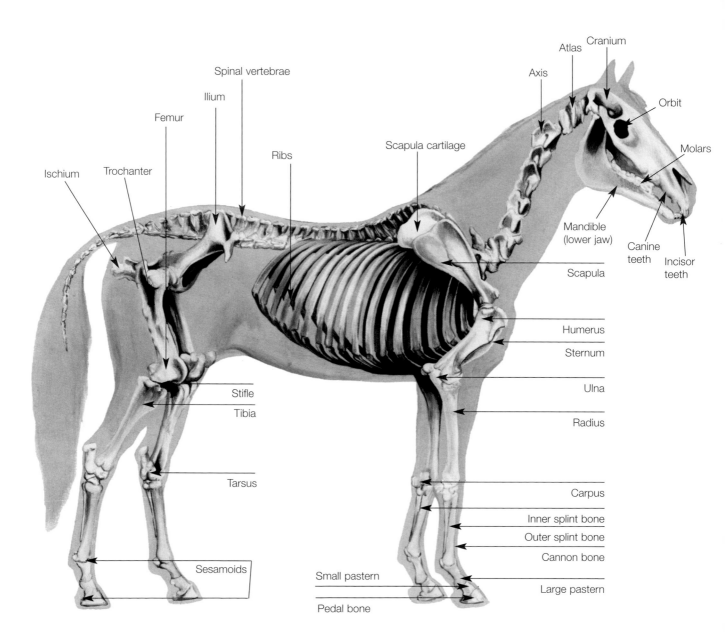

The skeleton of a horse can be divided into two main sections, the axial skeleton which is made up of the skull, spine, ribcage and pelvis and the appendicular skeleton which is made up of the bones of the limbs.

The skeleton has several examples of nature's way of adapting structure to meet particular requirements of function. The broad flat surface of the scapula or shoulder blade and the transverse processes of the lumbar vertebrae provide ample space for the attachment of powerful muscles required to move the fore and hind limbs. The special features of the skull are the relatively elongated face providing space for the teeth and their roots; and the orbits housing the eyes which are placed well above ground level when the horse is grazing. These provide it with a greater area of vision to look for impending danger.

The parts of the skeleton which have particular importance for horse owners are:

The splint bones, on either side of the cannon bones, which are remnants of the digits lost during evolution. These bones are bound to the cannon bone by ligaments. It is a fracture of the shaft of this bone, or inflammation of the ligament which binds it to the cannon bone, that causes the painful enlargements known as 'splints'.

Other small bones which are sometimes troublesome, are the sesamoids. These are two small bones forming the back of the fetlock joint, and the navicular bone below the pedal bone.

The internal organs

Most of the horse's internal organs work in the same way as those of other mammals, but both the digestive and respiratory systems are features of interest. In the digestive system, in particular, there are three unique features which distinguish the horse from other mammals. These are that the greatest volume of the alimentary tract is at the rear, where the major digestive processes take place; that the stomach is very small for the animal's size; and that there is no gall bladder. The reason for that is probably because the animal needs a constant supply of bile, as it is a continuous feeder.

Three points about the respiratory system are worth noting, since they are connected with the risk of illness or injury. The guttural pouches of the head, for instance, can be infected or become the site of bleeding, while the larynx can become paralysed on one side. This paralysis obstructs the intake of air and leads to the condition known as roaring. This is particularly noticeable at speed. So, too, is the condition known as broken wind, which is involved with the bronchioles and the alveoli in the lungs.

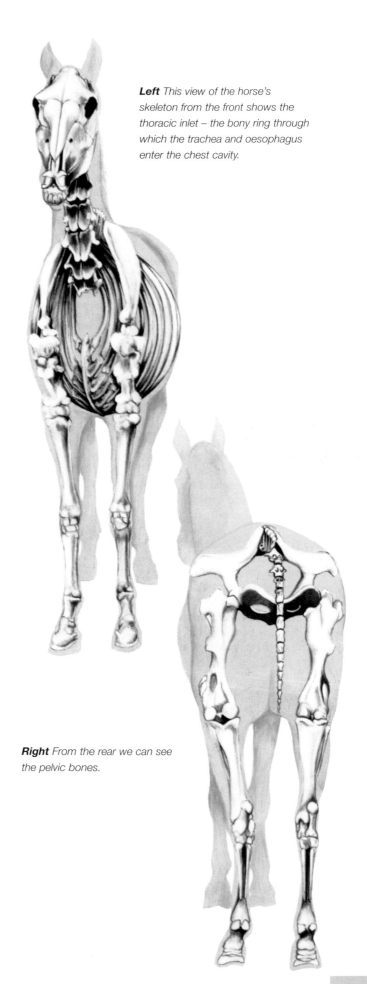

Left *This view of the horse's skeleton from the front shows the thoracic inlet – the bony ring through which the trachea and oesophagus enter the chest cavity.*

Right *From the rear we can see the pelvic bones.*

19

Teeth and age

The age of a horse is determined by an examination of the six incisor (tearing) teeth in each jaw. In common with other mammals, the horse has two sets of teeth during its life; the first deciduous, or milk, teeth are replaced by permanent teeth as the animal matures, the process usually starting at the age of three and being completed by the age of five. The central teeth erupt first, followed by the laterals and finally by the corners.

The two central incisors are cut when the foal is only four weeks old – they may even be present at birth – and are followed by the laterals and corners at six week and six to nine month intervals respectively. The milk teeth are white, as opposed to the yellow of the permanent teeth, and taper towards the base.

With the complete emergence of the permanent teeth, other considerations have to be taken into account when determining age. By six, the corner incisors will have worn level; by the age of seven, they will have developed a hook shape – the 'seven year hook'. This disappears by the age of eight. At seven, too, the dark line known as the dental star begins to develop; by nine, this is visible on the biting edges of the teeth.

It is now that Galvayne's groove, a longitudinal furrow, appears on the upper corner incisors near the gum. The growth of this groove serves as one indication of increasing age; another is the increasing slope of the teeth, which reaches its climax between the ages of 20 and 25. By the age of 15, Galvayne's groove will be halfway down the tooth, while, at 20, it should have reached the lower edge. From this time onwards, however, it starts to disappear at the same speed as it first appeared. By the age of 30, it will have vanished completely.

All these points make it possible to determine the age of a horse with reasonable accuracy. However, after the age of eight – when the horse is said to be aged – these methods are not always certain; this is particularly the case after 15.

The adult horse has a total of 40 teeth – three incisors, one canine (in colts and geldings) and six cheek teeth (three pre-molars and three molars) on the left and right sides of the upper and lower jaws. The chisel-like front teeth work with the animal's mobile lips when grazing; the back teeth, with their flat top surface criss-crossed with sharp enamel ridges, are ideally suited to grinding the food down.

Horses have particularly big, strong teeth, much more so in proportion to their size than in humans. This is due to their diets, which cause them to need efficient mastication (chewing) to break the foods up so the digestive juices can process the nutrients which can then be absorbed by the horse.

Domesticated horses need regular dental care to maintain proper chewing and comfort in their mouth, and this is because the upper jaw is larger than the lower which makes their teeth wear on a slant.

Constant grinding of foods can cause the back teeth to become very sharp and irritate the inner cheeks. Also, hooks can form on the front and back of the rows of molars which, if not removed, can result in the horse not being able to close its mouth. The vet can file or rasp the sharp edges off. This might need to be done twice a year, and therefore a regular series of checkups should be carried out.

A horse's teeth continue to erupt from their sockets throughout its life. The length of the crown in the gum shortens and the roots develop with age, and only a small amount of tooth is left by the time a horse becomes elderly (see below).

5 years   10 years   18 years

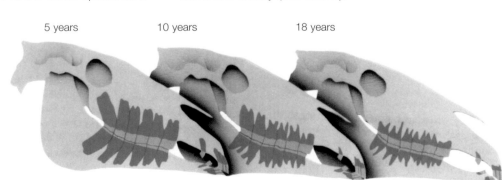

Changes in dentition used to estimate the age of a horse

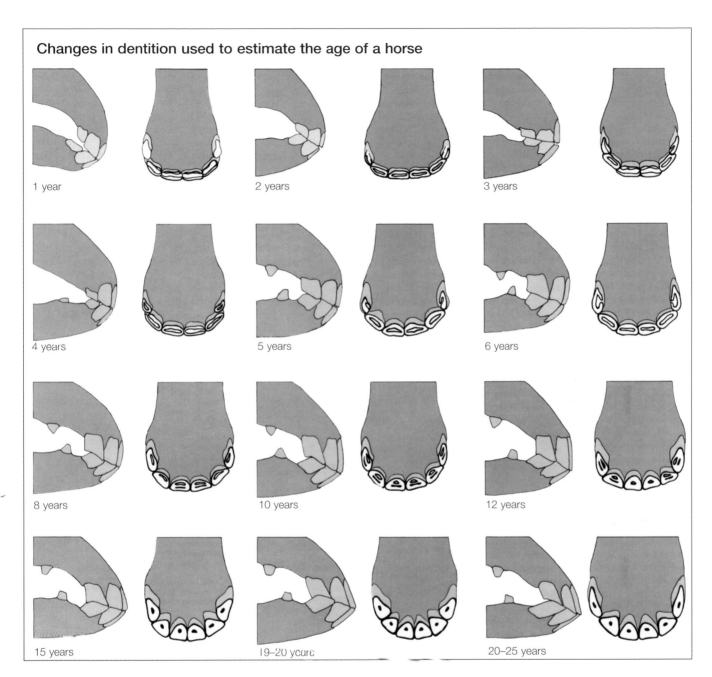

1 year

2 years

3 years

4 years

5 years

6 years

8 years

10 years

12 years

15 years

19–20 years

20–25 years

Hooves

The horse's hooves are extremely complex structures, very sensitive to stress and pressure and with an excellent blood and nerve supply. On the outside and underneath, they are protected by horn (a form of modified, hardened skin) which grows down from the coronet band, a fleshy ridge around the top of the hoof, equivalent to the cuticle on human nails. Inside the hoof, the horny outer structures are tightly bonded to the sensitive ones by means of leaves of horn and flesh (called laminae) which interlock around the wall of the hoof. The sensitive structures themselves surround the bones of the foot.

When weight is put on the foot it flattens and expands slightly, squashing the sensitive tissues and their blood vessels between the horn outside and the bones inside. The blood is squeezed out up the leg into the veins, which have valves stopping the blood running back again. When the weight is removed, fresh blood rushes back into the tiny vessels (called capillaries) and so the process goes on.

It was thought until very recently that it was almost entirely pressure on the frog which pumped the blood around like this, but recent research has shown that, although the frog plays a part, it is the expansion of the whole foot which is important. The frog, together with the plantar cushion inside the heels, mainly helps reduce concussion on the foot.

The need for shoes

The hoof horn grows all the time but is worn away very quickly in a horse working on a hard surface. Horses are shod with metal shoes to prevent them becoming footsore, but this prevents the horn being worn down, so the farrier has to trim away excess horn at each shoeing before refitting or replacing the shoes (approximately every four to eight weeks, depending on the rate of wear and growth).

It takes a horse an average of six months to grow a complete new hoof. Existing horn quality cannot be improved. However, new horn can be improved by a diet containing methionine, biotin and other substances, on which your vet can advise you.

Conformation

Conformation is a horse's make and shape, which depends on its skeleton. There is a great variety of conformation in the horse world, but within each breed and type there is a common basic blueprint of shape.

The most important factor overall is balance. The lines of the body should flow and have a pleasing symmetry. All the horse's parts should seem to fit well together.

Horses with good conformation can be quite different shapes, even though they may be the same height. The Thoroughbred, at one extreme, has a light, sleek frame, long legs in relation to its trunk, a sloped shoulder for speed and a comfortable ride, and a long neck. The heavy draft horse, at the other end of the spectrum, has a much deeper trunk and shorter legs in proportion to its height; an 'upright' shoulder to allow it to lift its knees and lean into a collar for pulling; a shorter, thicker neck; and a bigger head. Its limbs are generally much thicker than those of the Thoroughbred, and its hindquarters often slope down to the tail. There are many horses in between these two types. Competition warmbloods, for example, have a base of 'heavy' blood plus Thoroughbred blood.

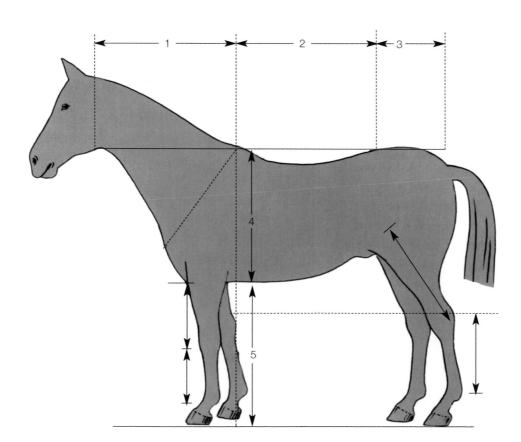

GOOD CONFORMATION
A basic method of gauging a horse's conformation is to compare sections of the body. Distances 1, 2, 4 and 5 should be about the same, with 3 about half of any of them. The distance from the point of the shoulder to the knee should be more than from the knee to the ground. The points of the hocks should be no higher than the front chestnuts.

In riding breeds, the angle of the shoulder should be about 45° to the vertical, with the front hoof wall/pastern angle the same. The hind hoof wall/pastern angle can be slightly more upright. Harness breeds may have slightly more upright shoulders and pasterns.

How the horse moves

The horse has four basic, natural gaits – the walk, the trot or jog, the canter or lope, and the gallop. However, there are other paces which seem to come naturally to some breeds and are developed by man through selective breeding and training. These are, among others, the pace (most useful in harness-racers as it is faster than the trot), the *tølt* in Icelandic ponies, and the gaits shown by American five-gaited saddle-horses, the normal walk, trot and canter plus the slow gait and the rack.

WALK This is the slowest gait. Horses always start a stride, in any gait, with a hind leg. The sequence for walk may be near (left) hind, near fore, off (right) hind, off fore, in a regular, four-beat rhythm, although some horses delay very slightly in the middle of the sequence. There is no moment of suspension in walk.

TROT An active, two-beat gait, the legs moving in diagonal pairs, the horse springing from one pair to another, with a moment of suspension when the horse has all four feet off the ground.

CANTER This is a three-beat gait, with a moment of suspension at the end of each stride, a stride being regarded as one full sequence. The horse may appear to 'lead' or 'point the way' with either foreleg. The sequence for off fore leading is near hind, off hind and near fore together, off fore, suspension.

GALLOP A very fast four-beat gait which is a natural extension of the canter. The sequence for off fore leading is near hind, off hind, near fore, and off fore, suspension.

HORSE BEHAVIOUR

Equine behaviour has fascinated horsemen and women for thousands of years and can be one of the most fascinating aspects of our involvement with horses. It is very important to understand how a horse 'thinks', in times of both health and sickness, so that we, as handlers, can learn to interact with the animal. Of course our perception of something is totally different to that of a horse, which makes it difficult for us not to think 'for' them and put our own interpretation on a situation.

Horses and ponies are by nature highly strung and reactive. It comes down to evolution. Horses evolved as prey animals and had to be constantly on the look out for predators. Their natural habitat of steppes and grassy plains provides little or no cover, so the instinct to run at the first sign of danger developed as a defence.

This instinct for flight has been changed little by 5,000 years of domestication. Even the most 'bomb-proof' children's pony and the most obedient police horse will succumb to its instinct to run when frightened. This means that a rider must learn to be calm and quiet around horses.

The herd instinct

Horses live in herds as a form of defence. A lone animal is much more vulnerable to predators. Within the herd there is a strict but flexible hierarchy, although animals form strong individual friendships with each other which may complicate the picture. For example, a small animal low down the hierarchy may form a strong bond with a dominant animal. Different animals may be dominant in different facets of herd life. For example, one individual may be dominant over grazing, one over shelter.

Fighting in established herds is rare. Not all horses crave close company, but they are usually friendly and tolerant towards each other and even those of other species – which is one reason for their successful domestication.

Equine communication Horses communicate with each other, and with other animals and people, mainly by body language and facial expressions. They do, though, also use their voices.

Anger, dislike, or threat towards a particular individual is shown by the head outstretched, ears flat back, eyes angry, nostrils drawn back and wrinkled, and perhaps the teeth being bared ready to bite or warn.

Interest is shown by ears pricked (pointed) towards the interesting object or person, the eyes alert, the head held high if the object is distant or more flexed inwards if it is near, and the nostrils open (flared) and perhaps quivering if the horse is near enough to smell the object or person.

Fear is shown by the ears being directed towards whatever the horse is afraid of. The eyes will look wide and alarmed, the nostrils will be wide open, and the skin

Reacting to a threat

1 Startle response
2 Aggressive head thrust
3 Moving to attack
4 'Bottoms up' action – warning
5 Fighting

will appear tightly drawn across the face. A sign of submission in youngsters is the head outstretched and held fairly low, with the front teeth being gently snapped repeatedly together. This is called 'mouthing'.

The attitude of 'flehmen' is when a horse is closely examining an odour. It breathes in the smell, then raises its head and turns its upper lip up to hold the smell in its air passages where the sensory Jacobsen's organ analyses the smell.

Stallions herd their mares and offspring with a peculiar 'snaking' motion. The head and neck are outstretched and held low as he goes along, usually at a trot, snaking his head and neck from side to side.

The senses

Horses have a highly developed sense of hearing. They also have extremely mobile ears which can move independently, rotating through an angle of 360 degrees; without moving, a horse can thus pick up sounds from all directions. Horses can also hear sounds of a pitch too high to be audible to the human ear, and are able to distinguish specific words rather than the tone in which they are spoken; they are additionally much better able to judge the location of the source of a sound than humans. For this reason it is important to talk to horses when moving around the stable or approaching them, because they are using mostly sound, rather than eyesight, to detect your whereabouts.

Horses have the largest eyes of any land animal except for the ostrich. A horse's eyes can move independently of each other in a half circle, meaning that a horse can look forwards with one eye and backwards with the other. Because of the position of the eyes, a horse must turn its head to see objects a short distance in front of it. Horses' eyes take a fairly long time to adjust to changes in light, which can make them nervous until they get used to it.

The horse has an extremely well-developed sense of smell. They have large nostrils which can detect scents from a very long distance.

BREEDS OF THE WORLD

There are literally hundreds of breeds of horse in the world today and their number and composition are constantly changing. There are many reasons for this; a breed can die out because the environment changes, for instance, or because it is no longer useful to man. The latter fate now threatens many of the breeds of heavy horses, whose work is now largely done by machine.

This decline, however, has been partly compensated for by growth in other parts of the horse world. With the great increase in the number of people riding for pleasure in the last 20 years, many countries have started stud books for riding horses to meet the growing demand. These books are divided into two main types. Many are 'open' – that is, the stallion and mare concerned need not be necessarily of the same breed, though they must both be pedigree stock. Others are 'closed'. This means that the offspring can only be registered if the parents are both members of the same breed.

A further means of definition is whether an animal is classed as a hotblood, warmblood, coldblood or pony. Hotbloods are pure-bred, fiery pedigree horses – the English Thoroughbred is a good example. Coldbloods are the heavy horses, the work horses of the world. The warmbloods are lighter animals, usually riding horses, which frequently have both coldblood and warmblood ancestry. Ponies are the small breeds – those which are under 14.2 hands in height – and are the particular favourites of children.

There are, however, certain anomalies within the system. Types, such as Hunter, Hack and Cob, are not registered in the stud books, though a registered Thoroughbred can, of course, be a Hunter. Horses such as the Australian feral Brumby, too, are difficult to place. The Brumby is not a recognized breed – nor is it a type – yet it has been crossbred with domestic stock to produce recognized offspring.

Middle East and Africa

Two of the most influential horses in the world – the Arab and the Barb – originated in these two areas. Though there is some dispute over the Arab's exact origins, the majority opinion is that it first ran wild in the Yemen in the Arabian peninsula. These early horses proved prepotent – that is, they passed their classic qualities of speed, toughness and stamina on from one generation to the next – and today Arab breeding is a world-wide industry. In the Middle East, the most important are the Persian and the Egyptian; the former plays an important role in Iran's horse-breeding programme, which also utilizes imported Thoroughbreds and native Turkomans. Most other Iranian strains are covered under one stud book, that of the Plateau Persian. Neighbouring Turkey, too, at one time produced fine Arabs, but a decline in quality meant the importation of the Nonius from Hungary to improve them and breed the Karacabey.

The Barb comes from North Africa. It is distinguished from the Arab by the different appearance of its head, the lower set of its tail and its more fiery temperament. Frequent crossing over the centuries, however, means that few pure-bred Barbs survive today. In South Africa, there is only one native horse – the Basuto Pony.

Australia and East Asia

Australia's domestic horses are all descended from ones brought to the country by the first British settlers in the 1790s (the Brumby is descended from some which escaped to roam wild). The first major native breed was the Waler, so-called because it was first bred in New South Wales. Formed by crossing Arab, Thoroughbred and Anglo-Arab stallions with local mares and cobs, the breed was the chief source of remounts for the British army in India in the 19th century; however, it was not until 1971 that a stud book was finally formed. The animal was then renamed the Australian Stock Horse. The Australian Pony's stud book was started in 1929. In addition to these, many Thoroughbreds, Trotters and Arabs are bred.

This activity is all part and parcel of Australia's flourishing horse industry. From the start, the country proved to be an excellent one for rearing horses, as New Zealand did later. Today, from originally having been importers, both nations are now major exporters.

Throughout East Asia, there are many exotic breeds. These include the Indian Manipur (a type rather than a true breed), which was the first polo pony when the game was taken up by Europeans. China is the home of the oldest surviving breed of horse – the Mongolian Wild Horse, discovered by Colonel Przewalski in 1881 – while among Indonesia's ponies is the romantic Sumba. This is bred as a dancing pony.

Russia

It was in about 3000 BC that the horse was first domesticated – this momentous event taking place within the boundaries of the USSR, present-day Russia. Since that time, horses have played a major role in the region's development. Because of the vast geographic area involved, many different types and breeds have evolved – the Arab having the chief influence in the west and the Mongolian Wild Horse to the east. Today the state authority recognizes 40 breeds and breed groups.

Two of the most important of those are the Akhal Teké and the Orlov Trotter. The Akhal Teké is descended from the ancient Turkoman horses and is noted for its powers of endurance. The Orlov Trotter is of more recent origin. It was first bred in 1877 by Count Orlov by crossing an Arab stallion with a Dutch/Danish mare. The product was later refined to produce the Russian Trotter.

This process of refinement is now official breeding policy and is carried out by crossing existing stock with outside breeds. The Don, for example, has had Thoroughbred and Arab blood added; and was used to toughen other breeds.

In addition, new breeds have been developed, while, at the same time, some of the celebrated 19th-century

breeds have been allowed to die out – though not before being used as foundation stock for their replacements. Thus the Strelets (a large Arab) was used as a basis for the Tersky (established 1948), and the Klepper (a tough preponent pony) for the Toric and Viatka.

Eastern Europe

Out of all the countries in Europe, Poland has the largest horse population; today it stands at about three million. Over the centuries, many different types of horse have been bred for a variety of uses, but a constant factor has been the influence of Arab blood. The Wielkopolski, for instance, has Arab, Thoroughbred and Trakehner ancestry. It is one of the many products of the state studs, whose other successes include the world-famous Polish Arab.

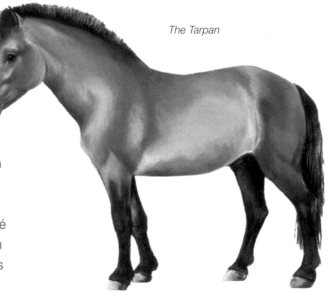

The Tarpan

The oldest surviving native pony is the Tarpan (*above*), whose origins go back to the Ice Age. However, the modern Tarpan is an act of skilful recreation. Its influence is also seen in the Hugul and the Konik, the latter being the foundation stock for many other breeds. Hungary's horse-breeding history, too, shows Arab influence. The tough horses of the early Magyars were later cross-bred with Arabs to produce many famous types, the most celebrated being the

Shagya. This, in turn, played a vital part in the foundation of the Lipizzaner. Other major influences were the British Thoroughbreds which were used in the founding of the Furioso strain. A French stallion produced the Nonius. Czech Republic (former Czechoslovakia) and Bulgaria are also important horse centres. The former has the oldest operational stud in the world at Kladruby, where the white Kladrubers (*below*) are bred. Bulgaria produces three well-known half-breds – the Pleven, the Danubian and the East Bulgarian while Yugoslavia's (now Serbia and Montenegro) most important native product is the Bosnian pony.

Scandinavia

The demands of war played a part in the development of two of Denmark's best-known horses. The Jutland – today a work horse – carried many medieval knights into battle; the Frederiksborg, bred from a mixture of Andalusian, Neapolitan, Arab and British blood in the 16th century, similarly served as a charger. Other Danish horses are the Fjord Pony and a relatively recent innovation, the Danish Sports Horse.

Sweden has the Swedish Halfbred – a good dressage and eventing horse – the Swedish Ardennes as a work horse and the Gotland as its native pony. The Norwegian pony is the Norwegian Fjord, while the country also produces the Døle and the Døle Trotter. Finland has the Finnish Horse and Iceland the Icelandic Pony.

Switzerland, Austria, Belgium and Holland

The most celebrated Austrian horse is without question the Lipizzaner, the world-famous mount used by the Spanish Riding School in Vienna. Spanish blood, too, played a major part in the founding of the breed; it was

first bred at the stud founded by the Archduke Charles in 1580 at Lipizza near Trieste. The horse's present breeding centre is at Piber in south Austria.

The other noted Austrian horses are the Halflinger and the Noriker. The latter was originally bred by the Romans. Home-produced half-breds, Hanoverians and Trakeheners are used to breed the Austrian Riding Horse.

The Belgian and the Ardennes, are Belgium's chief work horses. The former is a direct descendant of the medieval Flanders Horse. The Belgium Warmblood is a more recent innovation. Neighbouring Holland has three native breeds – the Gelderland, the Gronigen and the Friesland – as well as stud books for Arabs, Hackneys, Dutch Warmbloods, Trotters, Racehorses and five pony breeds.

The Kladruber

Switzerland's two historic horses are the Einsielder and the Freiberger. Since the 1960s, they have been joined by the Swiss Halfbred.

Germany

The western part of Germany is particularly noted for its fine riding horses, the best known of which are the

Hanoverian, the Trakehner and the Holstein. The Hanoverian owes a great deal of its success to the English Thoroughbred blood introduced between 1714 and 1837. Its great rival, the Trakehner, had its original home in East Prussia, where the founding stud was established in 1732. In 1944, however, the advancing Soviet armies forced evacuation; 700 mares and a handful of stallions reached the West to form the nucleus of the present breed. The Holstein, for its part, has been bred in Schleswig-Holstein since the 14th century.

All other German warmbloods have used these three breeds as foundation stock, with other blood being added if necessary. Germany's heavy horses, the Rhineland and the Schleswig Heavy Draught, similarly owe a debt to imported stock.

The former East Germany's two leading breeds are the Mecklenburg and the East Frisian; they are closely related to the Hanoverian and the Oldenburg respectively.

France

More than in any other Western country, the state dominates horse-breeding in France through the Service des Havas, which is responsible for the industry. The Service runs 23 stallion depots, which, in the best breeding areas, such as Normandy, house as many as 200 stallions.

The main competition horse is the Selle Francais, an amalgamation of 45 different breed groups founded in 1965. Of these, the Anglo Norman and Anglo-Arab were the most influential – Arabs, indeed, are the ancestors of all French breeds and are still extensively used for cross-breeding.

French Thoroughbreds and Trotters are world-famous, while the Percheron is the best-known heavy horse. Ponies include the Camargue, the Basque and the Landais.

Southern Europe

Italy's most famous horse was the medieval Neapolitan, which found its way into the royal courts of Europe as a high school horse and also became the foundation stock for many breeds. So, too, did the Andalusian, the most important of the horses of Spain. Nowadays, however, imported breeds dominate the Italian scene and native riding horses, such as the Murghese and Calabrese, are on the decline.

Portugal's breeds – the Altér-Real and the Lusitano – have close links with the Andalusian, as they have similar Arab and Barb ancestry. So, too, has the Minho pony; the other native Portuguese breed is the tough Sorraia. Greece's native stock consists of three ponies – the Peneia, Pindos and Skyros.

South America

The Criollo, the horse of the Argentinian *gaucho* (cowboy), is descended from a group of Andalusian horses brought by the Spanish to the New World, which escaped to roam wild. The Argentinian polo pony is a cross between it and the Thoroughbred, while Brazil's Crioulo is a smaller version of the Criollo. Other Brazilian horses of note are the Mangalarga and the Campolino, the latter being selectively bred from the former. Peru's Steeping Horse, with its unique lateral gait, gave rise to Puerto Rico's Paso Fino. Venezuela, like most South American countries, has its own version of the Criollo – the Llanero.

North America

Though North America was the original home of *Equus caballos*, horses died out there at the end of the Ice Age, not to reappear until the Spanish landed there in 1511. Some of these escaped to give the Indians their Mustangs, but the only Indian horse to be recognized as a breed is the Appaloosa. This was first bred by the Nez Perce tribe at the end of the 18th century.

Later colonists also brought horses with them and it was from these that the first native breeds emerged. The earliest of these was the Narrangansett Pacer; it was followed by the Quarter Horse, the oldest surviving US breed. Its name comes from the test of quality instituted by its Virginian breeders – racing it over a quarter of a mile. An all-purpose animal, it proved suited to many tasks, chief amongst these being its use as a cow pony. It is also used in rodeos, for riding, racing and in shows. Another old-established US breed is the Morgan, so-called because its founding sire was owned by an inn keeper, Justin Morgan.

With the Thoroughbred and the Narrangansett Pacer, the Morgan was also the foundation stock for the Saddlebred, a spectacular horse with three or five smooth gaits. The Tennessee Walking Horse, officially recognized in 1935, has even smoother paces.

In more recent times, the US has defined breeds that do not, as yet, breed true on the basis of colour. One such breed is the Palomino; others are the Indian Pinto and the Albino. The US native pony is the Pony of the Americas, developed in the 1960s. Imported horses, particularly Thoroughbreds, also play an extremely important role on the American scene.

Canada has no native horse breed, the Canadian Cutting Horse being defined as a type.

Britain and Ireland

Britain and Ireland have bred some of the finest horses in the world. The UK's greatest contribution has been the Thoroughbred, the world's fastest and most valuable breed, whose origins date back to the 17th and 18th centuries. Starting from around 1660, more than 200 Arab-type horses were imported to improve the native British racing stock. It is still uncertain whether these imported horses were crossed with native racing mares – the now extinct Galloway ponies – or whether the foundations were purely Oriental. There is no question, however, that the three greatest influences were the stallions Darley Arabian, Byerley Turk and Godolphin Barb. The first was the originator of the Blandford, Phalaris, Gainsborough, Son in Law and St Simon lines, the second of the Herod line and the third of the Matcham line.

Arab blood, too, has played an important part in the development of the Welsh Mountain Pony, which is officially described as 'an Arab in miniature'. Similarly, the eye-catching Hackney Horse, with its spectacular high-stepping trot, combines Yorkshire Hackney and Arab blood. There are also traces of the now extinct Norfolk Trotter in its ancestry.

The Hackney

The UK's other main contribution to the horse world has been its native ponies. These have a long history, dating back to the original wild stock that roamed moor, forest and fell.

Nine native breeds of pony now exist, of which the Exmoor is probably the oldest. Its presence is recorded in the Domesday Book, but its origins go back much further – to prehistoric times when the remote ancestors of the Exmoors crossed the land bridge that then linked Britain and the Continent. Its neighbour, the Dartmoor, is bigger and not as pure bred. Further to the east, the New Forest Pony has had additions of Arab, Thoroughbred and Galloway blood. Among the donors of Arabs was Queen Victoria, who in 1852 lent a stallion to improve the breed. This ran wild with the mares for eight years and was followed by two more – also donated by the Queen – in 1885. The result was a well - proportioned, sure-footed riding pony, standing about 14hh, with an easy action and a good temperament.

The Pennines are the home of the Fell Pony; its neighbour to the east – the Dale – is the largest of Britain's native pony breeds. Across the border in Scotland, the Highland shares a common ancestry with the Fell and the Dale. However, additions of Arab and French blood have led to the emergence of two quite distinct varieties – the Highland Pony and the Highland Garron. The latter is bigger and stronger than the former.

Even further to the north lies the island home of the Shetland Pony. The ancestry of the small but sturdy breed dates back to around 500 BC, when ponies were introduced to the Shetlands from Scandinavia. Subsequently, these ponies were probably crossed with animals brought from the mainland by the Celts.

The only recognized British riding/driving horse is the Cleveland Bay, which has been bred in Yorkshire for over 200 years. The largest British horse is the Shire, which is probably a descendant of the medieval Great Horse. So, too, is the Scottish Clydesdale. The slightly smaller Suffolk Punch originated in the 1760s.

Ireland's horse industry plays a major part in the country's economic life and many of the horses bred there become world-beaters, particularly in the racing field. On the west coast, the tough, handsome Connemara Pony still roams wild, as it has done for centuries. In origin, it probably has the same ancestry as the Highland; the chief difference lies in the injection of Spanish blood the Connemara received from the horses and ponies that swam ashore after the shipwreck of the Spanish Armada in 1588.

In the wild, coping with a background of bog and moor studded with rocky outcrops, the Connemara pony developed remarkable qualities of hardiness, sagacity and agility.

ENCYCLOPAEDIA OF HORSE BREEDS

BRITAIN AND IRELAND

DALES
CONNEMARA
DARTMOOR
SHETLAND
EXMOOR
SHIRE
HACKNEY
HIGHLAND
SUFFOLK PUNCH
THOROUGHBRED
WELSH PONY
CLEVELAND BAY
ANGLO-ARAB
IRISH DRAUGHT
IRISH HALFBRED

DALES (Pony)

Height 13.2–14.2 hands.

Colour black or brown with white star permitted.

Physique neat head, strong neck, powerful compact body, short legs, thick mane and tail with feathering on the feet.

Features strong (can pull 1 ton), sure-footed.

Temperament sensible, quiet and hard-working.

Use riding, agricultural work and trekking.

THE DALES PONY is the one native British breed which has never been truly wild. Although descended from the primitive Celtic Pony, it has received infusions of other blood.

The Dales Pony hails from the Yorkshire hills and dales on the eastern side of the Pennine hills which run down the northern half of Britain. In the past, Dales Ponies were known as superb trotting ponies and also for their ability to carry and pull enormous amounts of weight. They have been used by the military for transporting ammunition, by farmers as all-round mounts, and for surface work in the coal-mining and lead-mining industries.

The ponies could cover 1.6km (1 mile) in three minutes, and could carry weights of up to 100kg (220lb), carried in a pannier on each side of their body. As pannier ponies, they went loose, supervised by a single rider known as a jagger.

Today, the Dales is coming into its own as a trekking and competition driving pony. They are tough and hardy with particularly strong feet and legs.

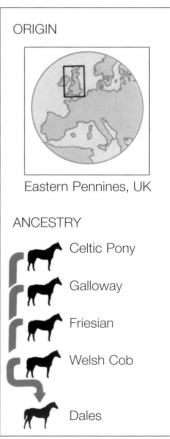

ORIGIN

Eastern Pennines, UK

ANCESTRY

Celtic Pony

Galloway

Friesian

Welsh Cob

Dales

CONNEMARA (Pony)

Height 13–14 hands.
Colour usually grey, but can be black, brown or bay.
Physique compact, intelligent head, crested neck, sloping shoulder and deep, strong, sloping hindquarters.
Features sure-footed, hardy and a good jumper.
Temperament intelligent, tractable and kind, good with children.
Use riding and driving.

THE CONNEMARA is the only native pony breed of Ireland. it is an ancient breed, and has run free in the mountains of the west coast since prehistoric times. Over the centuries in the ruggedness of its western Irish environment, the Connemara developed its prized qualities of hardiness, agility and extraordinary jumping ability.

The Connemara's origins go back some 2,500 years to the time when Celtic warriors brought their dun - coloured ponies onto the island of Ireland and used them to draw war chariots and carts along the beaches and river plains of their new found home. Mythology tells us that the tribes of western Ireland were mounted. Legend has it that when the Spanish Armada sank off the Connemara coast in the 16th century, the horses swam to shore and bred with the native ponies running wild in the mountains. They learned to live on the tough vegetation and survive the hardships of their habitat, as a misplaced step could send a pony crashing to its death.

The largest display of the finest Connemara Ponies in the world takes place in Clifden, Connemara, Ireland, on the third Thursday of August every year. The Show has been organized by the Connemara Pony Breeders Society since 1924 and over 400 ponies travel from all over the country to take part in this unique event.

It is a huge gathering from home and abroad, attended by the International Societies, overseas breeders, and friends. Foreign breeders have the opportunity to meet Irish breeders and mingle in the exciting atmosphere where ponies are judged and sold. The finest specimens of the breed, including young foals, stallions, young stock, aged brood mares and, of course, ridden ponies compete in over 20 classes.

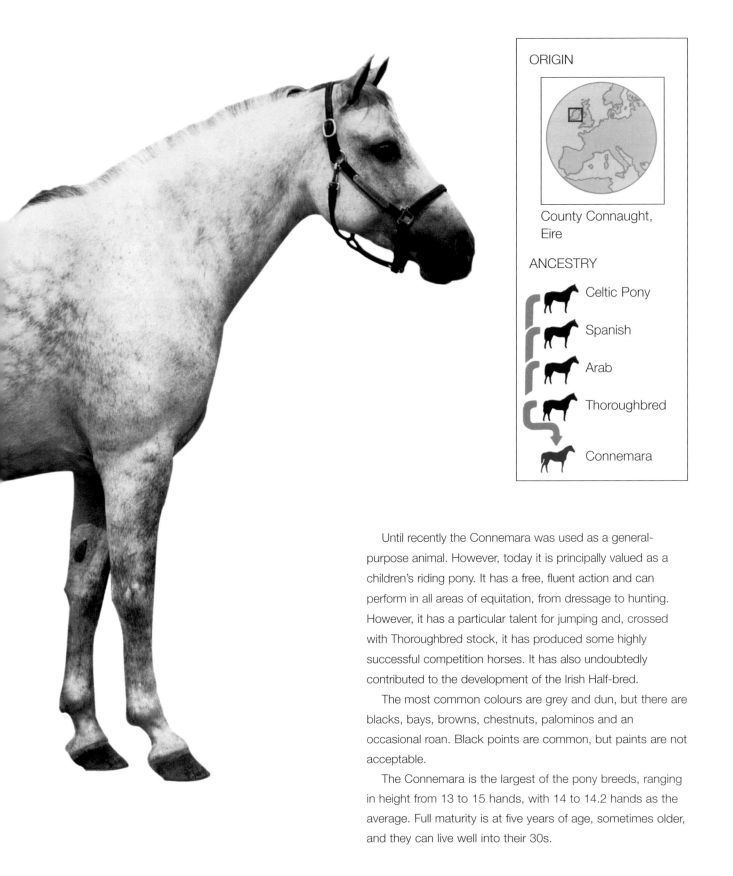

ORIGIN

County Connaught, Eire

ANCESTRY

Celtic Pony

Spanish

Arab

Thoroughbred

Connemara

Until recently the Connemara was used as a general-purpose animal. However, today it is principally valued as a children's riding pony. It has a free, fluent action and can perform in all areas of equitation, from dressage to hunting. However, it has a particular talent for jumping and, crossed with Thoroughbred stock, it has produced some highly successful competition horses. It has also undoubtedly contributed to the development of the Irish Half-bred.

The most common colours are grey and dun, but there are blacks, bays, browns, chestnuts, palominos and an occasional roan. Black points are common, but paints are not acceptable.

The Connemara is the largest of the pony breeds, ranging in height from 13 to 15 hands, with 14 to 14.2 hands as the average. Full maturity is at five years of age, sometimes older, and they can live well into their 30s.

DARTMOOR (Pony)

Height up to 12.2 hands.

Colour brown and bay are most common, black, excessive white markings on legs and head discouraged.

Physique small head, very small ears, strong neck, shoulders set well back, strong hindquarters, high-set full tail, slim, hard legs.

Features long-lived, sure-footed and tough.

Temperament quiet, reliable, kind and sensible.

Use excellent child's first pony.

ORIGIN

Dartmoor, Devon, UK

ANCESTRY

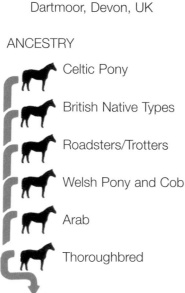

Celtic Pony

British Native Types

Roadsters/Trotters

Welsh Pony and Cob

Arab

Thoroughbred

Dartmoor Pony

BOTH GEOGRAPHICALLY and genetically, the Dartmoor Pony is a close neighbour of the Exmoor Pony, but there are obvious differences in both appearance and history which have produced two obviously different types of pony.

Exmoor is on the 'arch' of the south-western 'foot' of England while Dartmoor is in the 'heel'. Both bleak and unforgiving, Dartmoor has higher tors or hills. The Dartmoor Pony has been subjected to many 'improvements' over the centuries, made possible by the easier accessibility of Dartmoor than Exmoor, and today's pony can hardly be called either natural or indigenous since it has had so many infusions of various blood. However, the formation of a breed society, and the setting down of entry requirements, at the end of the 19th century have gone a long way towards stabilizing the breed. It is now considered to be a superb example of a riding pony, and comes recommended as a child's first pony. It is extremely reliable and sensible and exceptionally versatile. It goes well over jumps and can also be used for hunting and in harness.

The Dartmoor Pony's habitat is wild and harsh, for the thin, acid soil which covers the elevated block of granite which forms Dartmoor supports only poor vegetation and scrub. The native pony is therefore tough and hardy, but even so, requires hay if it is to do well in the wild over winter. During World War II, Dartmoor was closed off except to troops, and the pony population was decimated by the severe climate over those years, only two stallions and twelve mares being found at the end of the War for inspection and registration. Since then, selective breeding and careful nurturing of the ponies have brought the Dartmoor back from danger and its future now seems assured.

SHETLAND (Pony)

THE SHETLAND PONY from the islands of the same name in the far north of Scotland is a prime example of how a cold climate and appalling keep created a small, tough pony with all the features of coldblooded animals adept at reducing heat loss from their bodies. The Shetland Islands are truly bleak and treeless, with a thin, acid soil which supports poor grasses and heather. Shetland Ponies are animals which have evolved to live off them, despite these deprivations, Shetlands have always been long-lived ponies, often being good for riding at 24 years of age. The Shetland Pony (formerly called the Zetland) has been exported all over the world and, even when kept in an environment very like its homeland, always seems to lose type very quickly when bred elsewhere. Of particular note in this respect is the American Shetland Pony, which has so developed that it hardly looks like its forebear at all.

The Shetland's strength in relation to its diminutive body size (averaging 9 or 10hh, or 90 –106cm (36 – 40in) as the Shetland is usually measured in inches, not hands) is truly phenomenal. It has been said that a pony which a man could lift up in his arms could, in turn, carry him on a journey of 16km (10 miles) and back. One pony of 91cm (36in) in height is reported to have carried a man of 76kg (168lb) a distance of 64km (40 miles) in one day.

The origins of the Shetland Pony are obscure and subject to differences of opinion. Some believe that they came over from Scandinavia before the ice sheets retreated, others that they crossed the English Channel area before the British Isles became isolated from the rest of Europe. It is certain, however, that they have been present on their native islands for many thousands of years. There is archaeological evidence of their existence there as far back as 500 BC.

The Shetlands' uses traditionally have been as pack, harness and riding ponies. They have been used in their islands' agriculture, principally for carting seaweed in huge panniers to spread on the poor land as fertilizer, carrying peat for kitchen fires in the same way, carrying people around the islands, and pulling carts and other vehicles. As the coal industry burgeoned in the 19th century, word of these immensely strong and tiny ponies spread, and most of the best stock was taken to work down in the mines, many never seeing daylight again.

Their character is not always trustworthy. They can be domineering, independent and headstrong. Not always docile, their occasional inclination to bite makes not all of them entirely suitable for children. However, when one of good temperament is found (and there are plenty), they make good children's mounts and family pets.

SHETLAND (Pony)

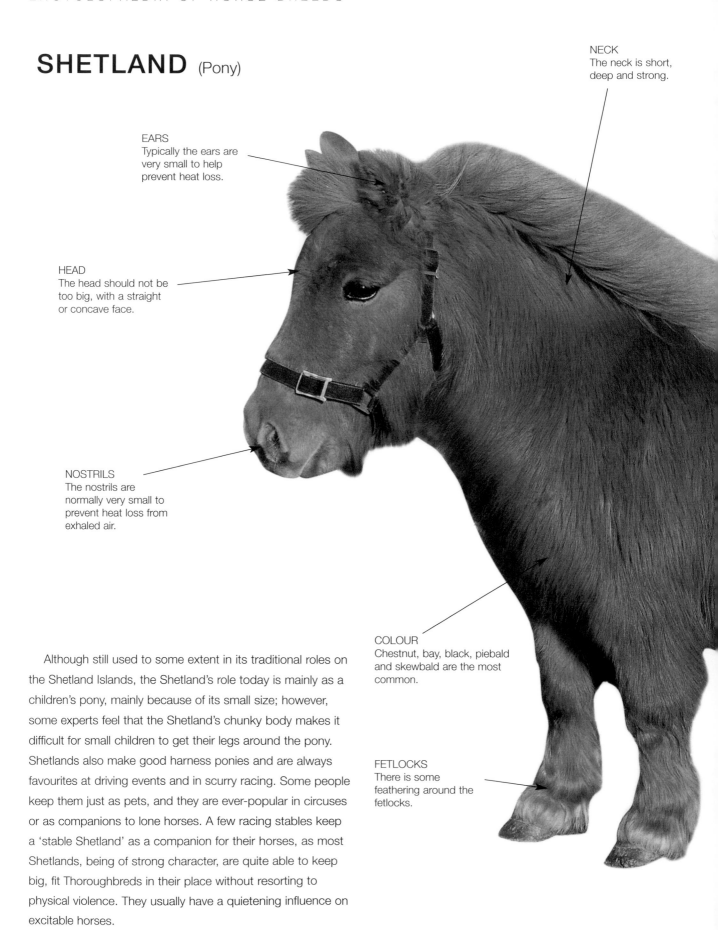

NECK
The neck is short, deep and strong.

EARS
Typically the ears are very small to help prevent heat loss.

HEAD
The head should not be too big, with a straight or concave face.

NOSTRILS
The nostrils are normally very small to prevent heat loss from exhaled air.

COLOUR
Chestnut, bay, black, piebald and skewbald are the most common.

FETLOCKS
There is some feathering around the fetlocks.

Although still used to some extent in its traditional roles on the Shetland Islands, the Shetland's role today is mainly as a children's pony, mainly because of its small size; however, some experts feel that the Shetland's chunky body makes it difficult for small children to get their legs around the pony. Shetlands also make good harness ponies and are always favourites at driving events and in scurry racing. Some people keep them just as pets, and they are ever-popular in circuses or as companions to lone horses. A few racing stables keep a 'stable Shetland' as a companion for their horses, as most Shetlands, being of strong character, are quite able to keep big, fit Thoroughbreds in their place without resorting to physical violence. They usually have a quietening influence on excitable horses.

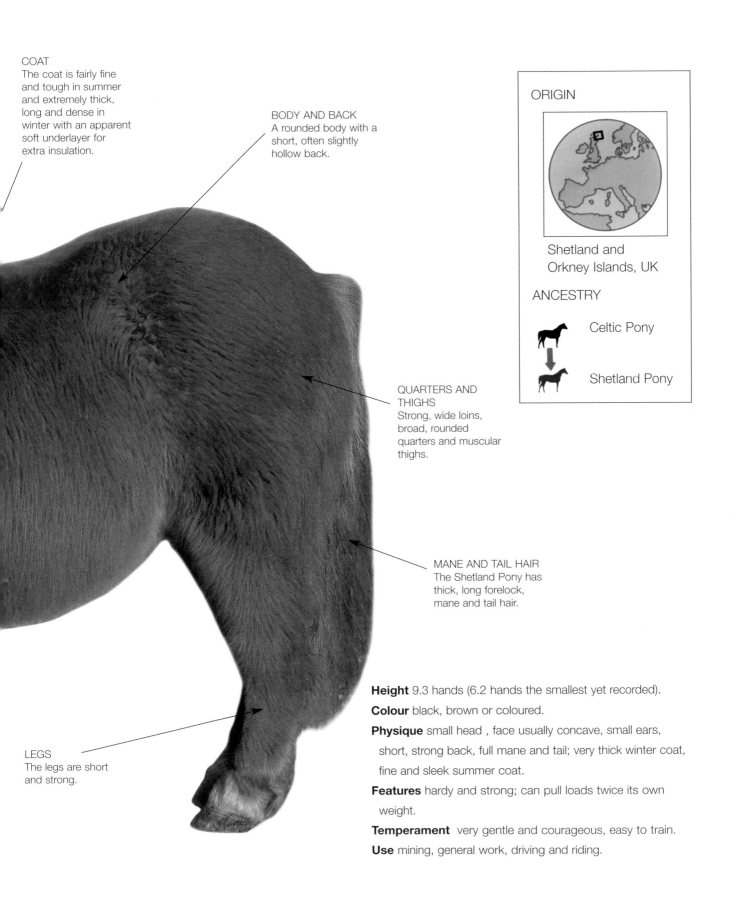

COAT
The coat is fairly fine and tough in summer and extremely thick, long and dense in winter with an apparent soft underlayer for extra insulation.

BODY AND BACK
A rounded body with a short, often slightly hollow back.

ORIGIN

Shetland and
Orkney Islands, UK

ANCESTRY

Celtic Pony

Shetland Pony

QUARTERS AND THIGHS
Strong, wide loins, broad, rounded quarters and muscular thighs.

MANE AND TAIL HAIR
The Shetland Pony has thick, long forelock, mane and tail hair.

LEGS
The legs are short and strong.

Height 9.3 hands (6.2 hands the smallest yet recorded).

Colour black, brown or coloured.

Physique small head , face usually concave, small ears, short, strong back, full mane and tail; very thick winter coat, fine and sleek summer coat.

Features hardy and strong; can pull loads twice its own weight.

Temperament very gentle and courageous, easy to train.

Use mining, general work, driving and riding.

EXMOOR (Pony)

Height mares up to 12.2 hands; stallions and geldings up to
12.3 hands.

Colour bay, brown or mouse dun; mealy muzzle; must not
include white.

Physique broad forehead, prominent 'toad' eyes, thick neck,
deep chest, short clean legs and hard feet. Thick, springy
coat with no bloom in winter.

Features strength and endurance.

Temperament intelligent, quick-witted, alert and kind.

Use riding, foundation stock.

ORIGIN

Dartmoor, Devon, UK

ANCESTRY

Ancient Celtic
Pony type

Exmoor Pony

THE EXMOOR PONY is one of the most individual, ancient,
and pure pony breeds. Its origins have been traced from a
prehistoric pre-Ice Age type of pony whose bones and fossils
have been found in Alaska. The climate, coupled with danger
from many predators, forged a tough, wild pony. As the Ice
Age ended, this pony migrated across the Bering land bridge
to Siberia, through the Urals and westwards through Europe.
The pony crossed the land mass which has now become the
English Channel and arrived in southern England.

The Exmoor is a neighbour of the Dartmoor in south-
western England and is just as wild. From the 11th century,
Exmoor has been marked as a Royal Forest, used for hunting
by royalty and the aristocracy. At one time the ponies
belonged solely to the Crown, but now belong to the
wardens, local farmers and others.

Exmoor Ponies have been subject to little outside blood.
Some Welsh blood was introduced, which began a
deterioration in some stock, but the effects were not long
lasting.

World War II decimated Exmoor Pony numbers as many
were slaughtered to feed the soldiers camped on the moor.
After the War, restoration of the breed and numbers began.
Some wild herds do still roam Exmoor, but most ponies are
now bred on farms and private studs.

Exmoors are tough and hardy with a willing and hard-
working nature – provided they are caught and broken in
whilst they are still young.

SHIRE (Coldblood)

THE SHIRE is the greatest of the heavy horse breeds, standing at up to 18hh, and weighing approximately 1,000 kg (over a ton). The breed is probably descended from the Great Horses and Old English Blacks that were ridden into battle by the medieval knights. The ancestry of these breeds is uncertain but probably stems in part from the Friesian and Flanders horses of northern Europe.

The Old English Black was a popular draught horse, especially in the midland counties of England, in the 18th and 19th centuries. It was particularly in demand for transporting the raw materials and products of the Industrial Revolution.

During the mid-19th century indiscriminate breeding to fill the demand for draught horses led to a deterioration in the quality of the breed, and in 1878 the Shire Horse Society (at first known as the Cart-Horse Society) was formed in order to raise and maintain standards again.

These marvellous, aristocratic horses are a pleasure to work with. Their popularity and ability to draw large crowds at shows have ensured the breed's survival despite the fact that it is no longer in demand as a working horse.

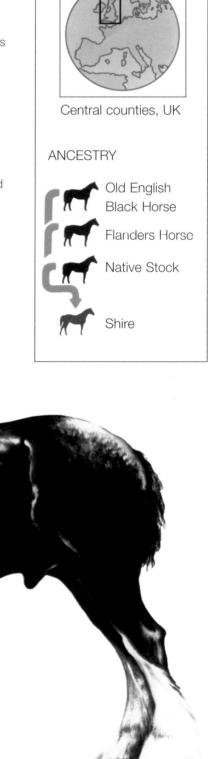

ORIGIN

Central counties, UK

ANCESTRY

Old English Black Horse

Flanders Horse

Native Stock

Shire

Height 17 hands.

Colour dark with white markings.

Physique slightly convex profile, broad forehead, long, crested neck, broad back, sloping croup and much fine silky feather.

Features strength, the tallest breed in the world.

Temperament docile and gentle, active, industrious and adaptable.

Use pack, agricultural work and riding.

HACKNEY (Warmblood and Pony)

Height 14–15.3 hands (horse), under 14 hands (pony).

Colour bay, dark brown and black.

Physique small head with convex face, long neck, compact body with deep chest, short legs with strong hocks, tails set and carried high, fine silky coat.

Features high stepping action.

Temperament spirited, alert and vigorous.

Uses driving.

ORIGIN

UK

ANCESTRY

Norfolk Roadster

Thoroughbred

Hackney Horse

Hackney Horse

Fell

Dales

Hackney Pony

HACKNEY-TYPE HORSES and ponies were used in Britain in the Middle Ages, when they were equally at home under saddle or between the shafts. Their name is probably derived from the French *haquenée*, in turn derived from *haque* (meaning a riding horse, usually a gelding), from which comes the English term 'hack', describing a riding horse. The Hackney's main gait was the trot, the gait both speedy for the rider and energy-efficient for the horse.

The modern Hackney Horse traces back to the Yorkshire and Norfolk Trotters of the 18th century. The Norfolk Trotter (or Roadster) may descend from the Danish horses brought to

England by King Canute in the 11th century. The related Hackney Pony is also based on trotting blood plus Fell and Welsh Mountain blood. The Hackney Horse Society, which also registers Hackney Ponies, has administered the British stud book since 1883.

The Hackney Horse and Hackney Pony are spirited and energetic animals, not suited to novice handlers. They have great stamina at a fast trot and require expertise in their handling. These days, Hackneys are almost exclusively used in the show ring, where their speed and stamina is seldom displayed or tested. Some Hackneys have been used in competitive carriage-driving and show jumping.

HIGHLAND (Pony)

ORIGIN

Western Isles and
Scottish Mainland

ANCESTRY

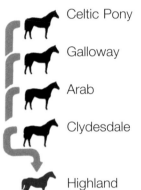

Celtic Pony

Galloway

Arab

Clydesdale

Highland

Height 13–14.2 hands.

Colour dun ranging from golden-blue to silver-blue with dorsal stripe; sometimes black, grey-black or brown.

Physique neat head, solid deep body, short strong legs and well-shaped hard hooves.

Features good action.

Temperament docile, intelligent, sensitive and trusting.

Use riding and trekking.

OF ALL BRITAIN's native mountain and moorland ponies, the Scottish Highland Pony has the most amiable temperament, possibly because for many hundreds of years it has lived in closer contact with people than most of the other native breeds. Apart from in the Highlands themselves, types of Highland Pony are also present on the islands of Skye, Jura, Uist, Barra, Harris, Tiree, Lewis, Arran, Rhum, Islay and Mull – and in each of these different locations, a slightly different type of Highland pony can be found. Historically, the ponies have been made into what the local people wanted and needed at the time.

Traditionally, there have been two main types of Highland Pony, a small island type and a larger, heavier mainland type known as a Garron. Today, the Highland Pony Society recognizes only one pony, and interbreeding has largely done away with the two main types, though both small and larger Highlands can now be found. Highland Ponies have long been used as general farm and estate ponies, and they have also been extensively used in Scottish military service.

SUFFOLK PUNCH (Coldblood)

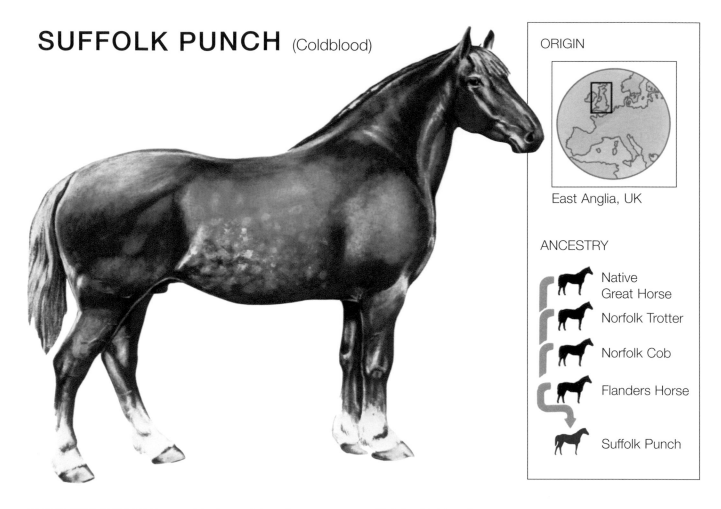

ORIGIN

East Anglia, UK

ANCESTRY

Native Great Horse

Norfolk Trotter

Norfolk Cob

Flanders Horse

Suffolk Punch

THE SUFFOLK PUNCH is surprisingly small for a heavy horse, standing at an average of I6hh. It is very heavily muscled and compact, and low to the ground for its body type. It takes its name from the county of Suffolk, East Anglia, in the east of England, and from the old word Punch, meaning short and fat (muscle!).

The earliest written reference appears to be in 1506; it was possibly created in the 13th century by crossing heavy mares native to the east of England with imported French Norman horses. Norfolk Roadsters/Trotters (cob types) and the imported Flanders horses were also probably used. Some Thoroughbred blood was added in the 18th and 19th centuries.

The need for a smaller but agile heavy horse, with 'clean' legs for working in the clay, and for better handiness around towns and cities brought the Suffolk Punch into being. The breed is renowned for working long hours with little refreshment or rest.

All present-day Suffolks descend from one nameless horse, believed to be a trotter foaled in 1768, and owned by

Height 16.1 hands.
Colour chestnut, with no white markings.
Physique short clean legs, massive neck and shoulders, square body.
Features good action, frugal and long lived.
Temperament kind, active and intelligent.
Use draught.

Mr Thomas Crisp of Ufford (Orford), near Woodbridge, Suffolk. Some authorities also cite a horse called Blake's Farmer, foaled in 1760, as being an ancestor of all today's Suffolks. Both these horses were chestnut and seem to be responsible for passing on this colour to all Suffolk Punches.

Suffolk Punches are tough, well-balanced, and extremely powerful, smaller-sized heavy horses. They are able to thrive on moderate rations, begin work at two years of age and work well into their 20s. They have, on the whole, kind natures and are willing workers.

THOROUGHBRED (Thoroughbred)

THE THOROUGHBRED can rightly be said to be the most important modern breed of horse. Its development over the last 250 years has been phenomenal. It was initially bred entirely for racing for the amusement of the British royalty, aristocracy and gentry, but the popularity of the sport among the general public and the lure of gambling led to the spread of Thoroughbred racing and breeding to every continent of the world.

The most rapid development of the breed to its present levels of performance and recognizable characteristics took place mainly during the 19th century and the early part of the 20th century. Recently, a distinctive American type of Thoroughbred has emerged which is a horse with a high croup (with quarters higher than withers) and a longer hindleg which often swings slightly outwards in action to create a longer stride.

The origins of the horse are in the Middle East, but it is generally accepted that the Thoroughbred breed stems from three Arab stallions imported into England – namely the Darley Arabian, the Godolphin Arab (or Barb) and the Byerley Turk. Of these three initial ancestors, probably only the Darley Arabian was a true Arab. The Godolphin was almost surely a Barb, and the Byerley Turk was almost certainly a Turkmene type.

Further importations of Oriental horses, largely Arabs, firmly established the Eastern-blood basis for the breed which, when mated with native British horses and ponies of colder blood and obviously different type, produced a horse of larger size, longer stride, more scope and more speed.

In temperament the Thoroughbred is not as consistent or amenable as its ancestor, the Arab, and needs very sensitive, skilled handling. In type it is variable, too; some individuals show coldblooded features such as rather large, plain heads and coarse hair while others show unmistakable Arab or Turk features.

Many expert horsemen and women prefer Thoroughbreds above all other breeds. Noted for courage, 'heart' and for being highly strung, its temperament is often unstable, but it will give its all when handled and ridden by people whom it trusts and who can coax the best from it.

Like its ancestor the Arab, the Thoroughbred has been used to improve many breeds, not only riding breeds, but also high-quality carriage horses.

Its use today goes much farther than racing for which, however, it is still principally bred. It races on the flat and over hurdles and steeplechase obstacles, but also participates in show jumping, three day eventing, dressage and the hunting field. Many polo ponies are Thoroughbred and the smaller representatives of the breed are also used to breed children's show ponies, as is its relative, the Arab.

THOROUGHBRED

EARS
The ears are of medium to long length, finely moulded and very mobile, displaying an alert attitude. When racing, they are often pressed flat back.

EYES
The eyes are large, usually with a 'questing' look to them.

NOSTRILS
The nostrils are capable of opening wide ('flaring') to permit maximum air flow. This is essential for a horse bred for maximum physical effort at speed.

HEAD
The head is straight, lean and elegant.

WITHERS AND SHOULDERS
The withers tend to be high and the shoulder big and muscular.

RIBCAGE
The ribcage should be deep and rounded for lung and heart room.

HOOVES
The hooves should be well conformed and tough, but many individuals have poor horn, low heels and flat soles.

Height 16 hands.

Colour solid colours.

Physique varies from close-coupled sprinters with large, powerful hindquarters to big framed, longer backed, big-boned chasers. Must have an elegant head, long neck, sloping shoulder, prominent wither and silky coat.

Features fast and active.

Temperament bold, brave and spirited.

Use racing, riding and improving other breeds.

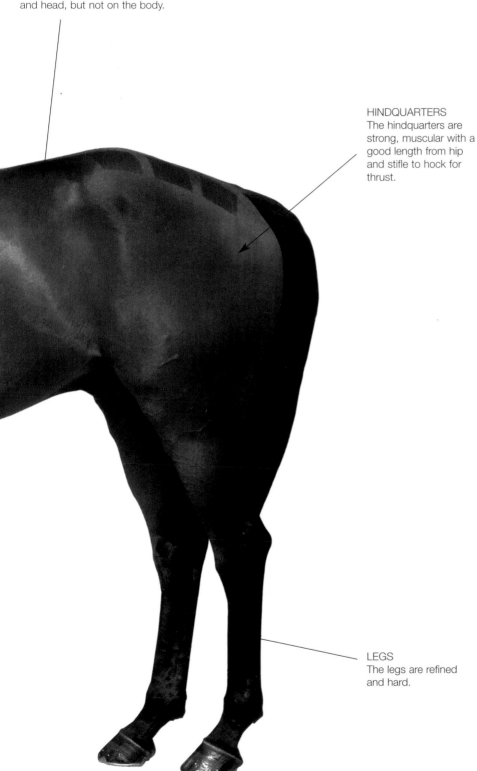

COLOUR
Solid colours; brown, bay, chestnut, grey and sometimes black. White markings on legs and head, but not on the body.

HINDQUARTERS
The hindquarters are strong, muscular with a good length from hip and stifle to hock for thrust.

LEGS
The legs are refined and hard.

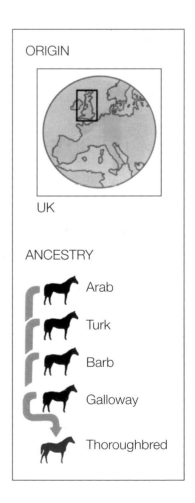

ORIGIN

UK

ANCESTRY

Arab

Turk

Barb

Galloway

Thoroughbred

WELSH PONY (Pony)

SECTION A

Height not over 12 hands.
Colour any colour except piebald or skewbald.
Physique small head, concave face, crested neck, sloping shoulders, short back, tail set high, short legs and neat feet.
Features great endurance.
Temperament intelligent, kind, brave, spirited.
Use riding, foundation stock for riding ponies.

ORIGIN

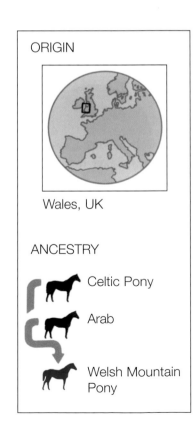

Wales, UK

ANCESTRY

Celtic Pony

Arab

Welsh Mountain Pony

THE WELSH NATIVE PONIES are considered by many to be the prettiest of the British pony breeds. The Welsh Pony stud book is divided into four sections: A, B, C and D.

The Welsh Mountain Pony (section A) is the original, and smallest, of the Welsh breeds, and is probably descended from the Celtic pony. There are references to wild mountain ponies going as far back as Roman times, and Julius Caesar established a stud at Lake Bala, Merionethshire. Within the last 200 – 300 years, two Arab stallions have been allowed to roam the Welsh Mountains to improve the native stock, and this probably accounts for the breed's Arab looks. Because it has lived on the mountains for over 1,000 years, this breed has become tough, resilient, sure-footed and quick. In addition, it combines all the best pony qualities – courage, endurance, intelligence and gentleness. It also has natural jumping ability. As a result, it makes an excellent children's pony, and many children's riding ponies today have some Welsh blood in them. In addition, it has a good trot and goes well in harness.

The Welsh Mountain Pony has always bred out in the mountains, ensuring the continuance of the breed's natural qualities, and breeders from around the world import fresh stock from Wales to replenish and improve their own breeding stock. The Welsh Mountain has been used as foundation stock for three other Welsh breeds.

WELSH PONY (Pony)

SECTION B

Height 12 – 13.2 hands.
Colour solid colours.
Physique larger version of section A.
Features good action.
Temperament intelligent, high-spirited, kind, good children's pony.
Use riding.

THE WELSH PONY (section B) has been bred as a quality children's riding pony. It was created by crossing Welsh Mountain mares with a small Thoroughbred stallion called Merlin, a direct descendant of the Darley Arabian, and these ponies are also known as Merlins. Arab and section C blood may also have been added. It is similar to the Welsh Mountain except that it is taller and more lightly built. It has retained all the pony characteristics

The Welsh Pony (section C) is a smaller version of the Welsh Cob (under 13.2 hands). It is energetic and brave, and very versatile. At one time it was used mainly in harness, although there is not much demand for it in that role now. However, it is ideally suited to the popular pastime of trekking as it can carry an adult comfortably. It is also a good hunting pony for a child.

The Welsh Cob (section D) is a larger version of the cob-type pony (14–15.1 hands). It is thought to have been created around the 12th century, by crossing Welsh Mountain ponies with Spanish horses. It may also be related to the now extinct Old Welsh Cart-horse. During medieval times it was used as a pack-horse and for riding. Welsh Cobs are good trotters, and the breed has been used to create and improve trotting breeds around the world.

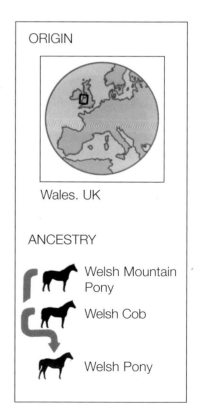

ORIGIN

Wales. UK

ANCESTRY

Welsh Mountain Pony

Welsh Cob

Welsh Pony

49

CLEVELAND BAY (Warmblood)

ORIGIN

Yorkshire, UK

ANCESTRY

Native Chapmen Horses

Thoroughbred

Cleveland Bay

THE CLEVELAND BAY is probably the oldest of the British horse breeds. Its origins are thought to go back to a type of horse brought to Britain by the Romans. Certainly by medieval times, a type of pack horse called the Chapman Horse was being used by travelling merchants, or 'chapmen', in the north of England. It is from this horse that the Cleveland is descended.

The breed was developed in north-east England, where it was used as an all-rounder, for agricultural and draught work, in harness, and for riding and hunting. However, it was as a pack animal that the Cleveland was most valued, its strength and endurance enabling it to carry very heavy loads.

During the 19th century, owing to its strength, good looks and tractable nature, it became popular as a carriage horse. At this time the breed received an injection of Thoroughbred blood, and the result was so popular that another breed with additional Thoroughbred blood, the Yorkshire Coach Horse, was created. This classy and fashionable carriage horse became extinct in the 1930s.

It is as a carriage horse that the Cleveland Bay excels today, and it is consistently successful in driving competitions. It also has natural jumping ability, and crossed with the Thoroughbred, produces international - class jumpers and dressage horses.

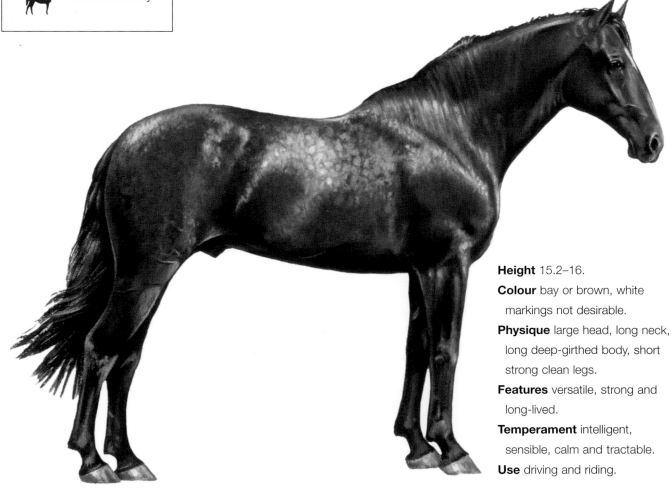

Height 15.2–16.

Colour bay or brown, white markings not desirable.

Physique large head, long neck, long deep-girthed body, short strong clean legs.

Features versatile, strong and long-lived.

Temperament intelligent, sensible, calm and tractable.

Use driving and riding.

ANGLO-ARAB (Warmblood)

Height 16 hands.

Colour most solid colours.

Physique delicate head, withers set well back, deep chest, short back, well-proportioned hindquarters, tail set high, long slender legs.

Features stamina and good movement.

Temperament brave, spirited, sweet-tempered and intelligent.

Use riding, competitions and racing.

ALTHOUGH THE ANGLO-ARAB, which is a cross between an Arab and a Thoroughbred, is found in many parts of the world, in France it has been developed as a distinct breed.

The French Anglo-Arab originated from English Thoroughbreds and pure-bred Arabs during the 1840s. In the beginning there were two strains, the southern part-bred and the pure-bred. The southern part-bred was developed in the Limousin area of south-west France by crossing Arabs or Thoroughbreds with native mares that were themselves of Arab or Oriental origins. The pure-bred Anglo-Arab was developed from direct crosses between Arab and Thoroughbred blood. Because the part-bred and pure-bred strains are now very similar in temperament and type, they have been combined in one stud book which is open to any horse resulting from a combination of English Thoroughbred, pure-bred Arab and Anglo-Arab as long as it has at least 25 per cent Arab blood.

The Anglo-Arab has excelled as a competition horse, and Anglo-Arab stallions have been used to up grade the quality of other breeds, particularly the Selle Française, or French Riding Horse. This term covers the breed previously known as the Anglo-Norman, created by crossing local Normandy mares with Thoroughbred blood, together with other French pedigreed riding horses.

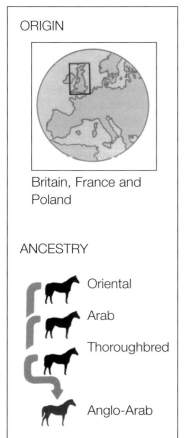

ORIGIN

Britain, France and Poland

ANCESTRY

Oriental

Arab

Thoroughbred

Anglo-Arab

IRISH DRAUGHT (Coldblood/Warmblood)

Height 16 hands.

Colour bay, brown or grey.

Physique straight face, short, muscular neck, longish back, strong, sloping hindquarters, good bone, little feather and large round feet.

Features good jumper.

Temperament quiet, sensible, willing and active.

Use multi-purpose, but mainly breeding riding horses.

THE IRISH DRAUGHT was created in the 18th century by crossing Thoroughbred stallions with native Irish mares, but its previous origins are unknown. This cross-breeding resulted in a fine, powerful and versatile horse. It was strong enough for heavy agricultural work and carriage-driving. At the same time, it was an active horse with powerful hindquarters, making it excellent for riding and hunting.

The Irish Draught flourished until the agricultural recession in 1879. After that its numbers declined sharply until the Irish Government stepped in, in 1907, to help promote the interests of the breed. It was found that when crossed with the Thoroughbred, it produced an excellent competition horse which became popular all over the world.

The Irish Draught Horse is an active, short-legged, powerful horse with substance and quality. Unexpectedly agile and enthusiastic for its type and weight, this breed is spirited and amenable, active and courageous. It is athletic and has a natural jumping ability and plenty of stamina.

Its use today is mainly as a medium- to heavyweight riding horse and hunter, and as breeding stock for hunter and competition horses. The crossing of the Irish Draught with the Thoroughbred has produced some superb show jumpers and eventers.

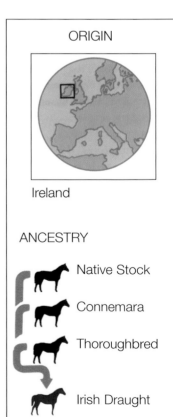

ORIGIN

Ireland

ANCESTRY

Native Stock

Connemara

Thoroughbred

Irish Draught

IRISH HALFBRED (Warmblood)

Height 16.1 hands.

Colour any solid colour.

Physique varies – classic hunting or show-jumping type.

Features strong and athletic.

Temperament intelligent, bold, sensible and enduring.

Use hunting, show jumping and eventing.

THE IRISH HALFBRED, or Irish Hunter, was until recently classed as a type, and the breed is still being developed. It is produced by crossing a Thoroughbred with an Irish Draught. This has produced top-class competitive horses that are outstanding as show jumpers and eventers.

Since the 1970s the Irish Horse Board has been overseeing the development of the breed. It still shows a variety of types, depending on the parentage, but the majority have good, alert heads and are strongly built.

ORIGIN

Ireland

ANCESTRY

Irish Draught

Thoroughbred

Connemara

Irish Halfbred

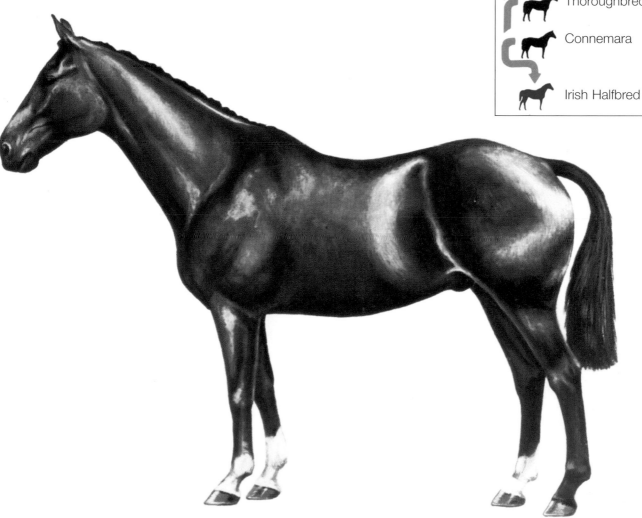

EUROPE

TARPAN

BRABANT

CAMARGUE

FRANCHES MONTAGNES

FRENCH TROTTER

PERCHERON

BRETON

NONIUS

NORIKER

ANDALUSIAN

ARDENNAIS (ARDENNES)

FRIESIAN

FURIOSO

GELDERLANDER

FJORD

AVELIGNESE

BAVARIAN

ALTER REAL

DANISH WARMBLOOD

BOSNIAN

DØLE

FINNISH

EAST FRIESIAN

HANOVERIAN

ICELANDIC

FREDERICKSBORG

HAFLINGER

ITALIAN HEAVY DRAUGHT

HOLSTEIN

SWEDISH HALFBRED

TRAKEHNER

OLDENBURG

SALERNO

LIPIZZANER

WIELKOPOLSKI

LUSITANO

KLADRUBER

KONIK

KNABSTRUP

MURAKOSI

MURGESE

SCHLESWIG HEAVY

DRAUGHT

SHAGYA ARAB

FRANCHES MONTAGNES (Warmblood)

Height 14.3–15.2 hands.

Colour most solid colours, blue roan or grey.

Physique conformation varies; small head, compact body, strong legs with a little feathering.

Features stamina and strength.

Temperament active, versatile and hard-working.

Use agricultural and army work.

THE FRANCHES MONTAGNES (also known as the Freiberger) is a light draught horse from the Jura Mountains of Switzerland. Its origins are a mixture of Norman, Anglo-Norman, Thoroughbred and draught breeds.

Having developed in the mountains, the Franches Montagnes is agile, strong, sure-footed and full of stamina. It has been an invaluable working horse for the Swiss farmers, who have used it for all types of agricultural work until quite recently, and still use it on the higher fields that are too steep for a tractor. Its value is also recognized by the Swiss Army, who depend on it for transporting men and equipment quickly through the mountains.

Because of its importance to Swiss agriculture and defence, and because it is also seen as a good source of alternative energy and transport by the Swiss, the government controls the breeding programme at the state-financed National Stud at Avenches. Because it is bred for character and ability rather than conformation, there is no fixed type.

The Franches Montagnes has also been used to develop a new breed, the Freiberger Saddle Horse, by crossing it with the Shagya Arab. The Freiberger is an elegant riding horse with an excellent temperament.

ORIGIN

Switzerland

ANCESTRY

Norman

Anglo-Norman

Thoroughbred

Draught Breeds

Franches Montagnes

FRENCH TROTTER (Warmblood)

THE FRENCH TROTTER was developed principally in Normandy during the middle part of the 19th century. The first trotting course to open in France was at Cherbourg in 1836, and others sprang up soon afterwards. As the sport grew in popularity, so did the demand for good horses.

The early horses were produced by crossing good English trotting blood, usually Norfolk Trotters, with the Anglo-Norman to produce a strain of Anglo-Norman specially suited to the sport.

Later in the century these Anglo-Normans were further improved by the importation of foreign stallions, notably the Standardbred from America, which by that time had been developed into a very fast harness-horse.

In 1922 a stud book was opened for Anglo-Normans that had proved themselves by trotting 1km (0.6 miles) in 1 minute 42 seconds in a race. These horses came to be known as French Trotters, and the new breed was established. In 1941 the stud book was closed to horses other than those with registered parents. In recent years, however, some selected American Standardbred blood has been used again to help maintain quality and further increase speed, although the French Trotter is accepted as being as good as any other trotting breed in the world, including the Standardbred.

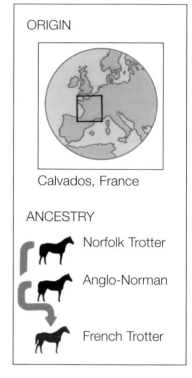

ORIGIN

Calvados, France

ANCESTRY

Norfolk Trotter

Anglo-Norman

French Trotter

Height 16.1 hands.

Colour chestnut, bay, brown most common.

Physique alert head, strong straight shoulders, short back, well-muscled powerful hindquarters, long hard legs with short cannon bone.

Features athletic and fast.

Temperament tough, willing and competitive.

Use trotting, riding and cross-breeding.

PERCHERON (Coldblood)

Height 16.1 hands.
Colour grey or black.
Physique Oriental-type head, strong, well-proportioned body, full mane and tail, clean, hard legs without feather.
Features good action and great presence.
Temperament energetic, intelligent and docile.
Use draught.

ORIGIN

France

ANCESTRY

Oriental

Heavy Draught Breeds

Norman

Percheron

THE PERCHERON is the most famous and most numerous of the French draught horses, both in France and around the world. Its intelligent and docile nature inspires great enthusiasm and loyalty in its admirers, and much attention is paid to the quality and purity of the breed.

The breed originated in north-west France, in the Paris-basin area of La Perche, probably through the mixing of local Norman horses with Arabs and other Oriental breeds left behind in western Europe by the Moors. This produced a heavy horse that was used at first by the medieval knights. Subsequently the breed was crossed with heavier draught breeds to produce a very strong working horse. It is still used for agricultural work today, and is also popular in the show ring.

An infusion of Arab blood in the 19th century contributed to the Percheron being active and lively. It also has great elegance for a heavy breed. There is a smaller type of Percheron, known as the Postier Percheron.

The Boulonnais, another heavy draught breed from northern France, is descended in part from the same Oriental stock, together with Andalusian blood, and is very similar to the Percheron.

BRETON (Coldblood)

Height 15–16 hands; Postier Breton not above 15 hands.
Colour grey, chestnut and bay.
Physique wide short head, strong neck, broad body, short muscular legs, a little
feathering; Postier Breton lighter and more elegant.
Features strong and active, although the Draught is less energetic.
Temperament sweet tempered, lively and willing.
Use agricultural work and light draught.

THERE ARE TWO types of Breton, the Draught and the Postier Breton, both of which were
developed in the Brittany area of north-west France.

The Draught Breton developed originally from the Roussin, a native of Brittany in the
Middle Ages. The Roussin was a riding horse known for its comfortable, ambling fourth
gait. When a heavier horse was needed for draught and agricultural work, the Roussin was
crossed with the Percheron, the Ardennes (an ancient, gentle and particularly tough breed
of draught horse from the Ardennes region of France and Belgium) and the Boulonnais (an
active and lively draught breed from northern France), giving rise to the Draught Breton.
During the 19th century the Draught Breton was crossed with the Norfolk Trotter and
Hackney blood, creating the Postier Breton, a lighter, more elegant horse with a smart
action that was used as a coach and light draught horse.

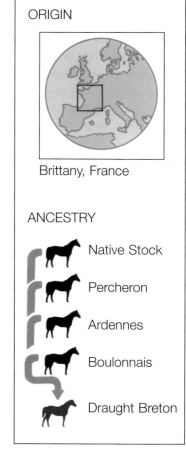

ORIGIN

Brittany, France

ANCESTRY

Native Stock

Percheron

Ardennes

Boulonnais

Draught Breton

NONIUS (Warmblood)

DUE TO THE prepotency of its founding stallion, the Nonius breed of Hungary can be said to resemble the American Morgan. Nonius Senior, the founding stallion, stamped his stock unmistakably with his own type, and to this day, all Nonius horses look very much alike.

In the late 19th century, a refining influence was felt necessary, so Thoroughbred and Arab blood was introduced. There are now two types of Nonius: the large type, derived from the Anglo-Norman, is an excellent carriage horse, but is also used for riding and farm work. The small Nonius, containing more Arab and Thoroughbred blood, is mainly a riding horse, but is also used for light draught work. Both types are calm, easy-to-handle and willing to please. They are late-maturing but generally long-lived.

The Nonius was formerly used extensively by the Hungarian army. Today both types of Nonius are versatile all-rounders.

Height Large Nonius, over 15.3 hands; small Nonius, under 15.3 hands.

Colour Black, dark brown or bay. A little white on head and lower legs may sometimes be seen.

Physique elegant head, long neck, strong back.

Features versatile, long-lived and active.

Temperament willing, consistant, calm and kind.

Use riding and agricultural work.

ORIGIN

Hungary

ANCESTRY

English Halfbred

Norman

Turk

Spanish

Lipizzaner

Holstein

Arab

Nonius

NORIKER (Coldblood)

THE NORIKER (or Pinzgauer, Oberlander, or South German Coldblood) is an ancient breed founded from various heavy horses introduced into its homeland some 2,000 years ago by the Romans, who had named the province Noricum. The province was made up of roughly the area occupied by today's Styria and Carinthia in Austria. In time a strong, sure-footed and hardy draught animal was developed, ideally suited to agricultural work in the harsh climate of the mountainous terrain.

In the 16th century, the breed was given more agility and presence by the introduction of Andalusian and Neapolitan blood. Later, in the 19th century, Norman, Cleveland Bay, Holstein, Hungarian, Clydesdale and Oldenburg blood was introduced into the South German strain of Noriker, which considerably lightened the local stock.

There are five recognizable strains of Noriker today, but all can be described as being smallish carthorses with an active movement, and are strong, calm and quiet, able to work the mountainous terrain of southern Europe, where they play an important agricultural role.

Height 16.1 hands.

Colour chestnut, bay, sometimes spotted.

Physique largish head, short, thick neck, straight shoulder, broad back and short legs with little feather.

Features sure-footed with good action.

Temperament reliable.

Use agricultural and mountain work.

ORIGIN

Austria and Germany

ANCESTRY

Ancient Stock

Noriker

ANDALUSIAN (Warmblood)

Height 15.2–16 hands.

Colour grey (predominantly), bay, an auburn-brown shade, some chestnuts and roans.

Physique broad forehead, large eyes, convex profile, long arched neck, deep short body, powerful rounded hindquarters, strong legs with short cannon bone, luxuriant mane and tail.

Features intelligent and athletic.

Temperament intelligent, docile, calm and easy to work with.

Use High School and general riding.

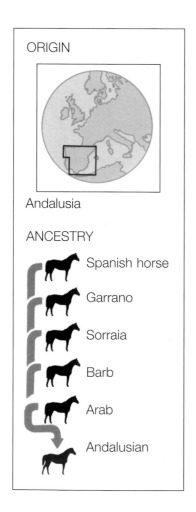

ORIGIN

Andalusia

ANCESTRY

Spanish horse

Garrano

Sorraia

Barb

Arab

Andalusian

BACK
Compact, well balanced, and sturdy with a straight, fairly short back.

LOIN AND QUARTERS
The loins and quarters are strong and muscular.

LEGS
The legs are elegant yet strong with short cannons.

MANE AND TAIL
The luxuriant, often wavy mane and tail are a feature of the breed, and much prized. In former times, manes and tails sweeping the ground were not unknown.

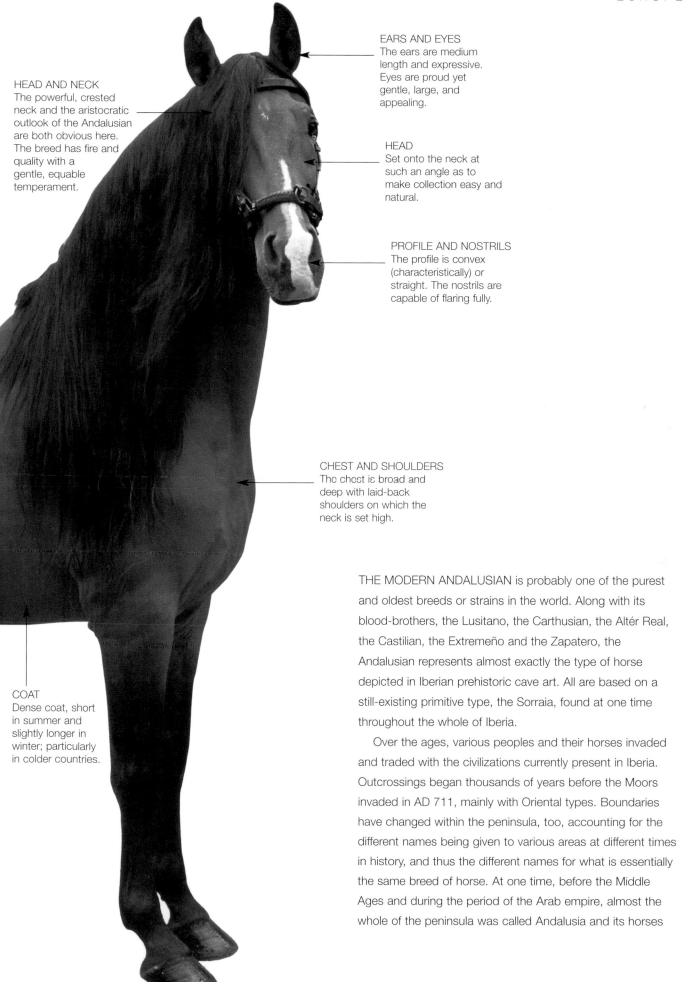

EARS AND EYES
The ears are medium length and expressive. Eyes are proud yet gentle, large, and appealing.

HEAD AND NECK
The powerful, crested neck and the aristocratic outlook of the Andalusian are both obvious here. The breed has fire and quality with a gentle, equable temperament.

HEAD
Set onto the neck at such an angle as to make collection easy and natural.

PROFILE AND NOSTRILS
The profile is convex (characteristically) or straight. The nostrils are capable of flaring fully.

CHEST AND SHOULDERS
The chest is broad and deep with laid-back shoulders on which the neck is set high.

COAT
Dense coat, short in summer and slightly longer in winter; particularly in colder countries.

THE MODERN ANDALUSIAN is probably one of the purest and oldest breeds or strains in the world. Along with its blood-brothers, the Lusitano, the Carthusian, the Altér Real, the Castilian, the Extremeño and the Zapatero, the Andalusian represents almost exactly the type of horse depicted in Iberian prehistoric cave art. All are based on a still-existing primitive type, the Sorraia, found at one time throughout the whole of Iberia.

Over the ages, various peoples and their horses invaded and traded with the civilizations currently present in Iberia. Outcrossings began thousands of years before the Moors invaded in AD 711, mainly with Oriental types. Boundaries have changed within the peninsula, too, accounting for the different names being given to various areas at different times in history, and thus the different names for what is essentially the same breed of horse. At one time, before the Middle Ages and during the period of the Arab empire, almost the whole of the peninsula was called Andalusia and its horses

Andalusians. Lusitania, for example, was the Roman name for roughly present-day Portugal.

Iberia was a noted horse-breeding area during its time as a Roman province, when Arab, Barb and other Oriental strains were brought there, and many thousands of years before that it contained horses of typical Spanish or Iberian type – high-headed, convex profile, compact, strong build, and high action, proud and gentle.

Today's Andalusian is a major world breed which has influenced many others and is very highly prized in Spain, especially in Andalucia in the heart of old Spain – Jerez de la Frontera, Seville and Cordoba. It was taken to the Americas by the *conquistadores*, and has influenced American breeds, and many of Europe's.

As a warhorse, it had all the qualities of conformation needed to perform the battlefield manoeuvres necessary of a knight's mount (Babieca, the mount of Spain's hero, El Cid, was an Andalusian) and also possessed endurance with a pleasant temperament. The height of its systematic breeding stretched from the 15th to the 18th centuries. In order to introduce height and more weight to the breed, heavier stallions were used, which almost decimated the breed's highly prized qualities of fire and pride with docility and tractability, and contaminated its compact conformation and

proud action. During his Iberian campaigns, Napoleon and his officers took most of the best remaining strains, and the breed was in real danger of dying out. Mercifully, the Carthusian monks of Castello, Jerez and Seville, who had bred the best and purest Andalusians from the 15th century, salvaged the best of what remained and selectively bred them to maintain the continuity of the breed. Most of today's best horses can be traced back to the Carthusian monks' lines.

The Andalusian today

The Andalusian is mainly used for display purposes and for bullfighting. The agility and power of the breed ideally suit it to the intricate movements needed of a bullfighting horse, from which some *Haute École* airs derive.

It is difficult to import the best examples of a breed which is jealously guarded in its homeland, but the breed is gradually spreading, and there are a limited number of Andalusians in Britain, more in the United States. Andalusians have the conformation and power to make good jumpers. They are athletic, energetic horses with ideal gaits for advanced dressage, but apart from being superb general riding and carriage horses, they are used in showing classes, both in hand and under saddle.

FURIOSO (Warmblood)

ORIGIN

Hungary

ANCESTRY

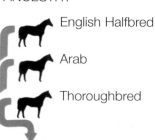

English Halfbred

Arab

Thoroughbred

Furioso

Height 16 hands.
Colour dark colours, often has white markings.
Physique long strong neck, powerful shoulders, long strong back, powerful hindquarters, low-set tail.
Features robust.
Temperament active, intelligent, tractable.
Use riding, competitions, driving and steeplechasing.

THE FURIOSO, or Furioso North Star, may have a slightly strange name, but, like other Hungarian breeds, it takes its name from the stallion (or in this case, stallions) who founded it. Nowadays the breed is simply known as the Furioso. The Furioso is only about 150 years old but it is firmly established as a great favourite in Hungary and Eastern Europe.

The Furioso is a substantial middle-weight plus Thoroughbred type. The Hungarians like quality, responsive and intelligent horses, and the Furioso shows all these qualities.

One of Hungary's most famous studs, the Mezöhegyes Stud, founded by the Hapsburg Emperor Joseph II in 1785, first developed the Nonius and later the Furioso and North Star breeds, following the importation of those stallions in 1840 and 1843 respectively. Furioso was an English Thoroughbred and North Star an English Norfolk Roadster. These two stallions were mated with Nonius and Arab mares to produce two distinct breeds, but by 1885 the offspring started to be interbred and are now blended into the one breed, with the Furioso being the dominant type.

GELDERLANDER (Warmblood)

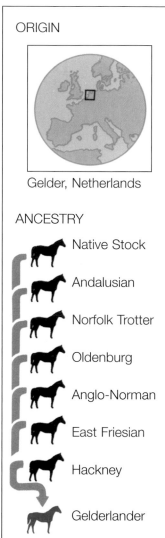

ORIGIN

Gelder, Netherlands

ANCESTRY

Native Stock

Andalusian

Norfolk Trotter

Oldenburg

Anglo-Norman

East Friesian

Hackney

Gelderlander

Height 15.2–16 hands.

Colour solid colours with chestnut or grey most common.

Physique plain head with convex profile, strong arched neck, deep shoulder, compact body, powerful hindquarters, high-set tail and short legs.

Features extravagant action and great presence.

Temperament quiet, good-natured and active.

Use carriage work, light agricultural work, driving and riding.

THE DUTCH GELDERLANDER was created by farmers who wanted horses not only for their own use but as produce to sell. During the 19th century, perceiving a gap in the market at that time for a quality carriage and riding horse, the farmers of the Dutch province of Gelder set about crossing native heavy mares with quality stallions imported from various European countries, each stallion fulfiling the farmers' criteria of quality, temperament, action and conformation. Iberian,

Neapolitan, early Norman, Norfolk Roadster and Arab blood were used extensively to obtain initial improvement, resulting in an all-round horse which could be used for farm work, carriage use and riding.

The Gelder breeders sought to further improve their horse, and used Oldenburg, East Friesian, Thoroughbred, Holstein, Hackney and Anglo-Norman infusions to create a horse of style, elegance and quality, fulfilling what the breeders had originally intended – a recognizable, marketable light carriage and substantial saddle horse. As a top-class carriage horse, the Gelderlander has been used by several royal houses of Europe on ceremonial occasions. The 20th century has seen the Gelderlander's refinement as an ideal carriage-driving horse and as a base for the modern competition Dutch Warmblood.

FJORD (Pony)

ORIGIN

Norway

ANCESTRY

Asiatic Wild Horse

Norwegian Fjord Pony

Height 13–14.2 hands.

Colour yellow or mouse dun with pronounced dorsal stripe, silver and black mane and tail.

Physique concave profile, coarse upright mane, short neck merging into shoulder with no definition, powerful body, short legs with some feathering.

Features sure-footed, very hardy.

Temperament tireless and tractable.

Use mountain work, agriculture, transport, riding and driving.

IF EVER A BREED of pony was instantly recognizable, it must be the Norwegian Fjord pony. Its colour, markings and the still-followed ancient method of trimming the mane are unique in the equine world.

The Fjord has been known in Norway for thousands of years. The Vikings made full use of it for battle, as shown by the many carvings on Viking runestones, and they used the bloodthirsty practice of horse-fighting to select the best stallions for use and breeding.

Other northern European breeds of pony have Fjord blood in them, notably Britain's Highland Pony and the Icelandic Pony. They have also been exported to many European countries, particularly those with no good native ponies of their own. The Fjord, or Vestland, as it is sometimes known, is very common throughout Scandinavia and appears in several similar varieties.

The Fjord is an ancient type of pony resembling Przewalski's Horse, which may well have been its ancestor. Its colouring and markings are primitive, and it is a true representative of the Celtic Pony group. It has a kind and willing nature, but some are said to be stubborn. It is very strong and tough, and has great stamina.

AVELIGNESE (Pony)

Height 14.3 hands.

Colour chestnut with flaxen mane and tail.

Physique medium-sized head with pointed muzzle, strong neck, deep girth, long broad back, well-muscled hindquarters, short legs.

Features sure-footed and long-lived.

Temperament good tempered, gentle, easy-to-train and tough.

Use pack work in the mountains and light agricultural work.

THE AVELIGNESE originates in the mountainous areas of northern, central and southern Italy. The Avelignese is a bigger Italian version of the Haflinger. The Avelignese has much the same background as the Haflinger with a common ancestor of the Arabian, 'El Bedavi'. The Avelignese is a mountain pony standing on average 14.3hh and used for both draught and pack work on farms where larger animals have difficulty working. These ponies are bred mostly in Bolzano and around Tuscany and Venetia. This mountainous environment creates horses that are sure-footed and hardy, ensuring the breeds ease to working on the steep mountain slopes.

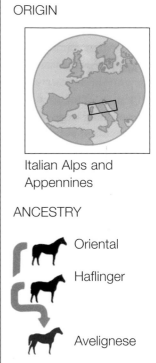

ORIGIN

Italian Alps and Appennines

ANCESTRY

Oriental

Haflinger

Avelignese

BAVARIAN (Warmblood)

ANCESTRY

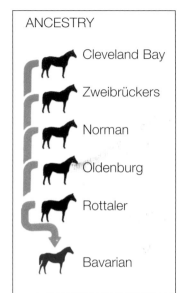

Cleveland Bay

Zweibrückers

Norman

Oldenburg

Rottaler

Bavarian

Height 16 hands.

Colour all solid colours.

Physique medium-sized frame, deep girth and broad chest.

Features derived from Rottaler war horse.

Temperament sensible, docile and willing.

Use riding.

ORIGIN

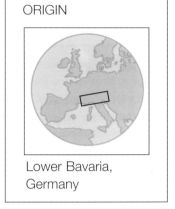

Lower Bavaria, Germany

THE BAVARIAN WARMBLOOD, previously called the Rottaler until the 1960s, originated in the fertile valley of Rott in Bavaria in Germany. In the beginning, these heavy draught horses were crossed with Andalusians and Barbs to produce a lighter type of working horse, which was refined still further during the 19th century by crossing with Cleveland Bays, Thoroughbreds, Anglo-Normans and Hanoverians. At this time, the breed was used as a high-class coach horse. It was also used for agricultural work and by the military. After World War I, it was no longer needed by the army, but continued to be in demand as a farm horse and coach horse until World War II. When it was no longer needed as a working horse, breeders began to cross it with Thoroughbred and Trakehner blood, in order to refine and lighten the breed to make it suitable for all-round riding. The modern Bavarian Warmblood is a beautiful horse which is best suited for dressage and jumping competitions.

ALTER REAL (Warmblood)

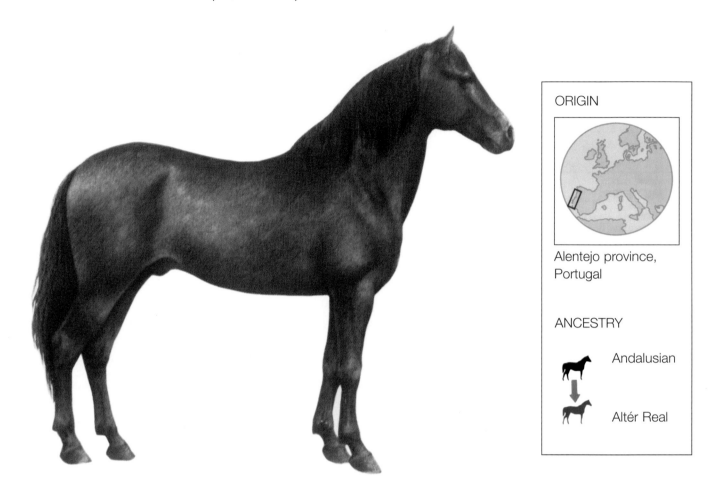

ORIGIN

Alentejo province, Portugal

ANCESTRY

Andalusian

Altér Real

Height 15–16 hands.

Colour bay, brown or grey, but usually bay.

Physique medium-sized head, convex profile, strong shoulders, deep broad chest, short body, powerful hindquarters, hard legs and flexible hocks.

Features spirited.

Temperament intelligent, quick to learn and responsive. Fiery to some extent, very self-aware and spirited. It is tough and hardy.

Use riding.

THE ALTÉR REAL is the national horse of Portugal. It was founded from the Andalusian, which it resembles quite closely.

During the 18th century, demonstrations of High School (*Haute École*) equitation were popular amongst the courts of Europe, and in 1747 the Portuguese Royal Stud was founded in the Alentego Province to breed suitable horses. About 300 Andalusian mares were imported from Spain to provide foundation stock. The intelligent, athletic horses that were bred there were well suited to the demands of High School.

At the beginning of the 19th century, during the reign of Napoleon, the breed's numbers were drastically reduced. High School had by this time gone out of fashion, and for several decades Altérs were crossed with Thoroughbred, Arab, Norman and Hanoverian blood, with the result that the breed's quality declined quite drastically.

By the early 20th century, however, the Altér's qualities were beginning to be appreciated again. and measures were taken to re-establish it bv crossing pure Altérs with Andalusians.

DANISH WARMBLOOD (Warmblood)

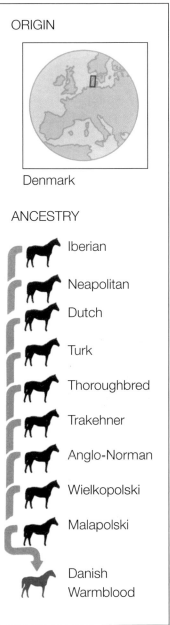

ORIGIN

Denmark

ANCESTRY

Iberian

Neapolitan

Dutch

Turk

Thoroughbred

Trakehner

Anglo-Norman

Wielkopolski

Malapolski

Danish Warmblood

Height 16.1–16.2 hands.

Colour All solid colours, bay being most common. Some white is permitted on the head and legs.

Physique the legs are virtually perfect, well-muscled in the upper parts, substantial, yet refined, with big, clean joints and excellent, well-made feet. Ears are long and fine, with expressive and generous eyes.

Features excellent general riding and competition horse.

Temperament equable and willing, with spirit, courage and individuality.

Use riding and competition.

THE DANISH WARMBLOOD, along with the Swedish, Hanoverian and the Dutch, is one of the world's premier warmbloods. Holstein, now again in Germany, was Danish land until seized by Prussia in 1864, and this gave Denmark access to German breeds. Monasteries often seem to have taken particular interest in breeding horses, and the Cistercian monks, in what is now Holstein, bred horses from the early 14th century, putting mares of large German breeds to high-quality old Iberian stallions.

Danish Warmblood horses are hugely successful at the highest level of equestrian competition, in dressage and show jumping in particular. Their temperament is almost always equable and willing, and yet they still possess spirit and courage and retain their individuality. Their action is particularly supple, elastic and flowing.

BOSNIAN (Pony)

ORIGIN

Bosnia, Herzegovina

ANCESTRY

Tarpan

Arab

Bosnian

Height 12.2–15 hands.
Colour dun, brown, chestnut, grey and black.
Physique compact mountain pony, thick mane and tail.
Features endurance.
Temperament intelligent, enduring, tough and affectionate.
Use pack work, farm work and general riding.

THE BOSNIAN is a native of the mountain areas of Bosnia and Herzegovina, although today it is bred in large numbers all over the Balkans. It is of ancient lineage, being descended from the wild Tarpan pony, and has been improved by crossing with Arab blood.

It shows all the characteristics of good mountain pony breeds. It is intelligent, hardy, surefooted, strong and has great powers of endurance. The government recognizes its value for farm work and pack work in Serbia and Montenegro (former Yugoslavia), and it is selectively bred in state studs. Only stallions that have passed an endurance test, consisting of carrying a heavy load for 16km (10 miles), are allowed to breed. It is currently being bred to increase the size.

There is still great demand for the Bosnian. In addition to being a good working pony, it is also used for riding.

DØLE (Warmblood)

Height 14.2–15.2 hands.

Colour solid colours, usually black, brown or bay.

Physique varies from draught type to lighter pony type; small head, crested neck, strong shoulders, deep girth, powerful hindquarters, short legs, moderate feathering.

Features tough and versatile.

Temperament tough, adaptable and active.

Use draught, riding and harness.

THE DØLE is an ancient breed that originates from the Gudbransdal Valley between Oslo and the North Sea cost in Norway. It is the most widespread of the Norwegian breeds, accounting for about two thirds of its total equine population.

It is similar in type and appearance to the Friesian horse and the Dale and Fell ponies. This might be due to their being descended from the same prehistoric stock. However, it is more likely that the cross-breeding between indigenous breeds occurred when Friesian merchants took their horses to both Norway and England during the 5th to 9th centuries. However, there are no records to verify this.

The Døle varies in size due to the fact that some have been crossed with heavy draught breeds to produce a heavy working horse, while others have been crossed with Thoroughbreds to produce a lighter type. This variety of type means that døles can be found for heavy draught, lumber and agricultural work, general harness work and for riding.

An offshoot of the Døle, the Døle Trotter, was created in the 19th century by crossing the Døle with Thoroughbred blood to produce a fast, active harness horse which is now used for racing.

ORIGIN

Norway

ANCESTRY

Danish Coldblood

Thoroughbred

Trotter

Døle

FINNISH (Coldblood)

ORIGIN

Finland

ANCESTRY

Indigenous Forest Pony

Finnish Draught

Finnish

Height 15.2 hands.

Colour chestnut, bay, brown and black.

Physique medium-sized head, short neck, upright shoulder, deep chest, long back, strong hindquarters, strong legs with light feathering.

Features tough, long-lived and fast.

Temperament quiet, docile, tractable, lively and intelligent.

Use farm-work, riding and trotting races.

THE FINNISH horse is the only native breed of horse in Finland. It is a descendant of the northern European domestic horse with both warmblood and heavier draught influences. This breed is also known as Finnish Universal because it is able to fulfil all the needs for horses in Finland. Not only is it the fastest cold-blooded trotter in the world, capable of pulling heavier loads than many larger draught horse breeds, it is also a versatile riding horse.

In 1924 it was ordered that breeding of the Finnish horse be divided into two branches. Breeding of the heavy type for agricultural and forestry work continued, with increased attention to developing a lighter type suitable for riding and racing. Today, the heavy Finnish horse is still used for forestry work, as a horse is less damaging to a young forest than heavy equipment. However, it is not used as frequently in agriculture since mechanization.

Today, Finnish horses participate in dressage, show jumping, eventing and long-distance riding competitions, as well as driving classes and trotting races. Trotting is a very popular sport in Finland and about 40 per cent of the horses racing there are Finnish horses. In addition they are popular family horses and riding school mounts.

EAST FRIESIAN (Warmblood)

Height 15.2–16.2 hands.

Colour any solid colour.

Physique similar to the Oldeburg but lighter, and with a more elegant head.

Features quality saddle and carriage horse.

Temperament bold, spirited and good-natured.

Use general riding and driving.

ORIGIN

East Germany

ANCESTRY

Arab

Hanoverian

Oldenburg

East Friesian

THE EAST FRIESIAN is a blood brother of the Oldenburg, and both were regarded as one breed for about 300 years, until World War II split Germany in two. The East Friesian stems from stock left in eastern Germany, which was identical to that from which the Oldenburg was developed farther to the west.

Historically, Eastern European horse breeders have usually been excellent, tending to favour a lighter and more Oriental type of blood horse. Therefore, when the East Friesian stock was being further refined, its breeders turned to the Arab, to add quality, spirit and a lighter frame to the existing breed.

Arabs from the Babolna Stud in Hungary, one of the best and oldest in Europe, were used, and the stallion Gazal had a particular influence on the breed. Horses from Poland were also used. The East Friesian is a good example of how a breed can change and be changed until it bears virtually no resemblance to its original stock.

This horse is a quality all-rounder, being spirited, courageous, good-natured and energetic. It is strong and has excellent stamina, but, like similar breeds, it needs reasonable shelter, feeding and health maintenance.

HANOVERIAN (Warmblood)

ORIGIN

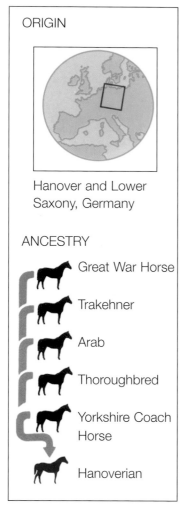

Hanover and Lower Saxony, Germany

ANCESTRY

Great War Horse

Trakehner

Arab

Thoroughbred

Yorkshire Coach Horse

Hanoverian

Height 15.3–17 hands.
Colour all solid colours.
Physique varies; compact, powerful body, short strong legs.
Features athletic.
Temperament intelligent, courageous, sensible and willing.
Principal uses competition and general riding.

MANY OF THE GERMAN breeds are defined according to the area that they come from, and the Hanoverian originates from Hanover in north-western Germany. Since it was created in the early 18th century, it has been altered quite considerably in order to adapt it for different uses at different times.

The breed was founded in 1735 by Royal decree at the Celle state stud. Holstein stallions were used to lighten the native mares descended from the Great War-Horse of the Middle Ages, to produce horses that were good for agricultural and coaching work. This process was continued by crossing with Thoroughbreds and Cleveland Bays imported from England and, towards the end of the 18th century, other imported breeds such as Andalusians.

In 1867 a breed society was formed with the aim of producing a horse equally suited to coach and military work and remarkable results were achieved. However, after World War I, horses were no longer needed in the same numbers by the military, and the breed society re-stated its aims: to produce a bold horse good for general farm, coach and riding work. From that time all stallions have been tested for speed, strength and endurance before being allowed to breed.

ICELANDIC (Pony)

Height 12–13 hands.

Colour most colours, but particularly grey and dun.

Physique large head, short strong neck, deep compact body, strong clean legs, large feet and thick mane and tail.

Features tough and able to amble.

Temperament docile and friendly, but also independent.

Use draught, transport, farm work and riding.

THE ICELANDIC PONY is based on stock taken to Iceland by the Vikings when they colonised it between AD 870 and AD 930, and probably included the Fjord pony and a group of ponies from the Lotofen islands. Later, settlers from Scotland, the Orkneys and Shetland brought their own ponies. These have blended into one breed, but various types and sizes can still be seen Many centuries of isolated breeding by natural selection in harsh and rugged conditions has produced ponies that are tough, agile, strong, sure-footed and full of stamina.

The Icelandic has always been invaluable to the Icelanders, and is still bred in large numbers. It is used as a pack-horse, for transport, communications, agricultural work and riding, as well as for meat. A useful feature of the breed is that on a one-way trip it can always be relied upon to find its own way home. Another distinctive feature is that in addition to the walk, trot and canter, most ponies have two very easy and comfortable riding gaits, the amble and the tølt. The amble is a running walk; the tølt is a very rapid version of the amble which can increase to the speed of a canter. The tølt is particularly valuable for travelling fast across steep, icy terrain, and ponies with this gait are much in demand.

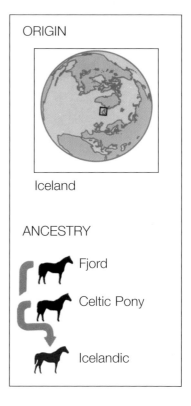

ORIGIN

Iceland

ANCESTRY

Fjord

Celtic Pony

Icelandic

FREDERICKSBORG (Warmblood)

THE FREDERICKSBORG is the oldest, and was for a long time the most important, horse breed in Denmark. It was established at the Royal Fredericksborg Stud founded in 1562 by King Frederick II, and was named after him.

Andalusians and Neapolitans were used as foundation stock. The resulting breed was considered to be the best of all at the High School equitation which was so popular in the courts of Europe from the 16th to the 18th century. In addition, it was good in harness.

The Stud supplied Fredericksborgs to all the courts of Europe, and it was also popular for improving other breeds – including even the Lipizzaner. The breed was so much in demand that by the early 19th century its quality had declined, and by 1839 there were so few Fredericksborgs left there that the Fredericksborg Stud was closed. The remaining stock was used to keep the breed going, but it has had to be built up using imported blood. In 1923 Fredericksborgs began to be registered again, but even today its numbers are not great.

The pure-bred Fredericksborg is a very strong horse that is good in harness and for light draught work. Attempts have been made to lighten it to make it more suitable for general riding. Although the Fredericksborg is somewhat plain in appearance, it is strong and agile with an equable disposition.

ORIGIN

Denmark

ANCESTRY

Andalusian

Neapolitan

Fredericksborg

Height 15.1–16.1 hands.

Colour almost always chestnut.

Physique large plain head, strong neck, powerful shoulders, deep chest, long strong body, straight coup and strong legs.

Features active.

Temperament good-tempered, active and tractable.

Use light draught, harness and riding.

HAFLINGER (Pony)

Height 14 hands.

Colour chestnut with flaxen mane and tail.

Physique medium-sized head with pointed muzzle, strong neck, deep girth, long broad back, well-muscled hindquarters and short legs.

Features frugal, tough, sure-footed and long-lived.

Temperament docile, good tempered, adaptable and hard working.

Use mountain pony, riding, driving and pack work.

THE HAFLINGER is the native pony of the Austrian Tyrol. Small Arab horses taken there from Italy are thought to have bred with the native mountain ponies to create the foundation stock for the breed. The first record of the breed was made in 1868 when an Arab stallion called El Bedavi XXII was used to upgrade the local stock. All members of the breed today can be traced back to him. His son, 249 Folie, who had the typical colouring of the breed, became the foundation sire.

The Haflinger was ideal for pack and transport work in the mountains, and developed into a robust and sure-footed animal. It is still used by the Austrian farmers for transporting hay. In addition it makes a good riding and harness pony.

The Austrian state monitors the breeding of Haflingers, and its numbers are on the increase. It is still reared in the mountains, and animals are allowed to mature until the age of four before being broken in. It is also remarkably long-lived; some Haflingers are said to have worked until at least 40 years of age.

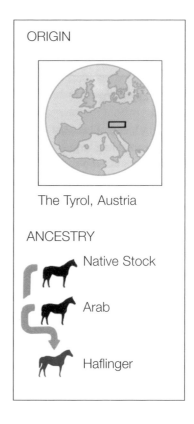

ORIGIN

The Tyrol, Austria

ANCESTRY

Native Stock

Arab

Haflinger

ITALIAN HEAVY DRAUGHT (Coldblood)

ORIGIN

Italy

ANCESTRY

Breton

Italian Heavy
Draught

Height 15–16 hands.

Colour liver chestnut with flaxen mane and
tail. Red roan and bay also occur.

Physique fine long head, short crested
neck, powerful shoulders, deep broad
chest, robust body with broad flat back,
round hindquarters, muscular legs and
some feathering.

Features fast and strong.

Temperament active, willing, kind and
docile.

Use meat and agricultural work.

THE ITALIANS HAVE never had much
inclination to breed massive, phlegmatic
horses, so even when they produced their
own heavy draught type, they went for a
smaller animal with a lively action and bright
temperament.

The Italian Heavy Draught is a relatively new
breed, having only been developed in 1860
when the state stud at Ferrara began
crossing stallions from the Po Delta region
with native mares, and also introducing Arab,
English Thoroughbred and the Hackney
blood into the breed.

At the beginning of the 20th century, greater
size and strength were required, and so more
massive breeds were introduced into the Italian
Heavy Draught – the Belgian Brabant was tried,
as were the French Boulonnais, Ardennais, and
Percheron. Results did not please, however,
and it was not until the lighter, more active
Postier-Breton was tried that a type evolved
which everyone was happy with.

Although some are still used in
agriculture, the breed's main use today is as
a meat animal.

HOLSTEIN (Warmblood)

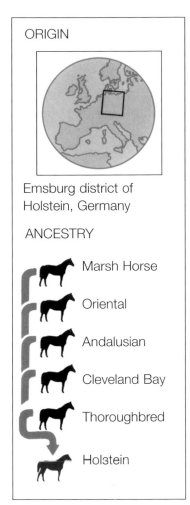

ORIGIN

Emsburg district of
Holstein, Germany

ANCESTRY

Marsh Horse

Oriental

Andalusian

Cleveland Bay

Thoroughbred

Holstein

Height 16 17 hands.

Colour black, bay or brown.

Physique elegant head, strong neck, powerful shoulders, deep
girth, compact body, strong hindquarters and short legs.

Features good action.

Temperament intelligent, willing, bold, versatile and good-
natured.

Use general riding and competition.

THE HOLSTEIN is probably the oldest of the German horse
breeds. It comes from the marshlands of Schleswig-Holstein
in northern Germany, and is known to have been bred there
since the 14th century. In the beginning, Andalusians and
Neapolitans were crossed with the local Marsh Horse (one of
the Great Horse types) to produce a large, powerful horse
that was popular all over Europe.

During the 19th century, the Holstein was crossed with
Cleveland Bays and Thoroughbreds to refine the breed and
produce a powerful carriage horse with a high-stepping
action and great stamina. The Cleveland Bay and
Thoroughbred blood also contributed to the breed's jumping
ability and talent for dressage.

The breed's numbers had dwindled by the end of
World War II, and since that time great success has been
achieved in building up and further refining the breed
using Thoroughbred blood to produce a top-quality
competition horse.

Today the Holstein is successful in all areas of competitive
riding at the highest level.

The Holstein is one of several breeds that have contributed
to the Swiss Halfbred. This outstanding horse is powerful and
athletic, and has a good temperament.

SWEDISH HALFBRED (Warmblood)

THE EARLIEST traces of horses having existed in Sweden date back to 2300 BC. However, there is not enough evidence to indicate what type of horse they were. The Swedish Halfbred (also known as the Swedish Warmblood) was first developed some 300 years ago, to provide a good cavalry horse. Imported Oriental (i.e. Barb and Arab), Andalusian and Friesian stallions were crossed with local native mares. The breed was built up using Hanoverian Thoroughbred and Trakehner stallions.

In 1894 the Halfbred stud book was opened. All stallions were, and still are, put through rigorous tests for conformation, character and performance before being allowed to breed. They are also tested for their ability at show-jumping, cross-country, dressage and harness work.

This strict selection procedure has led to the development of one of the very best breeds of sports horse in the world today. It is a powerful, athletic horse, with good conformation and a straight, extravagant action. It excels in show jumping, eventing and dressage. It has been so successful that only Halfbred horses are used in the Swedish Olympic team, and it has won medals in all three competition disciplines. It is now in demand all over the world.

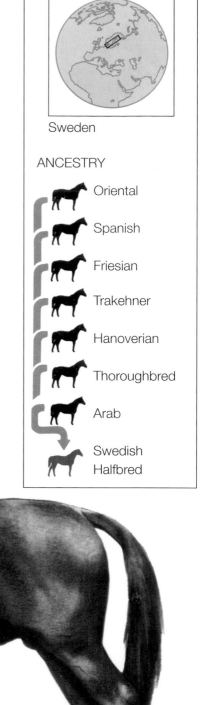

ORIGIN

Sweden

ANCESTRY

Oriental

Spanish

Friesian

Trakehner

Hanoverian

Thoroughbred

Arab

Swedish Halfbred

Height 16.1 hands.

Colour any solid colours.

Physique smallish, intelligent head, large bold eye, longish neck, deep girth and straightish back.

Features extravagant, straight action.

Temperament intelligent, bold, sensible and obedient.

Use general riding and competitions.

TRAKEHNER (Warmblood)

Height 16.1 hands.
Colour dark colours.
Physique elegant head, long neck, prominent withers, deep chest, strong medium length back, flattish hindquarters, slender legs and good feet.
Features extravagant action.
Temperament intelligent, active, good-tempered and loyal.
Use competitions and riding.

ORIGIN

Poland

ANCESTRY

Oriental

Schweiken

Thoroughbred

Trakehner

THE TRAKEHNER originally came from the area once known as East Prussia, now part of Poland. The breed was originally developed at the Trakehnen stud which was established in 1732. The local Schweiken horses were used as foundation stock, and crossed with Thoroughbred and Arab blood to produce an elegant coach and cavalry horse.

The breed was badly depleted during World War II, and in the winter of 1945 about 700 Trakehner mares and a few stallions travelled west with refugees fleeing from the Russians. These horses were used to re-establish the breed in West Germany. It has been carefully nurtured since that time, and today is one of the most elegant of horses. It also breeds very true to type.

The Trakehner's good looks, free, extravagant action and versatility has made it popular as a show and dressage horse as well as for general riding.

The Trakehners that were left behind in Poland have been used to create the Wiekopolski breed. It was one of several breeds used to create the Wurttemburg, a good heavyweight riding and light draught horse. It has also been used to refine other breeds, such as the Hanoverian.

OLDENBURG (Warmblood)

THE OLDENBURG has flourished in the north-west region of Germany since the 17th century.

The breed was based on the Friesian horses of the Netherlands. In the beginning these heavy draught horses were crossed with Andalusians and Barbs to produce a lighter type of working horse which was refined still further during the 19th century by crossing with Cleveland Bays, Thoroughbreds, Anglo-Normans and Hanoverians.

At this time, the breed was used as a high-class coach horse. It was also used for agricultural work and by the military. After World War I, it was no longer needed by the army, but continued to be in demand as a farm horse and coach horse until World War II. When it was no longer needed as a working horse, breeders began to cross it with Thoroughbred and Trakehner blood, in order to refine and lighten the breed to make it suitable for all-round riding.

The Oldenburg, together with the Thoroughbred, Cleveland Bay and Norman, has been used to modify the old Rotteler draught breed to produce a riding horse that is now known as the Bavarian Warmblood.

ORIGIN

NW Germany

ANCESTRY

Andalusian

Barb

Hanoverian

Cleveland Bay

Thoroughbred

Anglo-Norman

Oldenburg

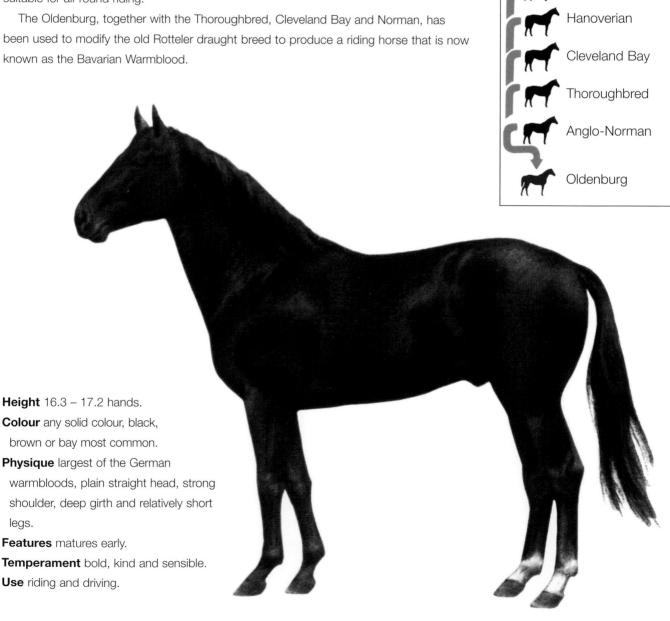

Height 16.3 – 17.2 hands.
Colour any solid colour, black, brown or bay most common.
Physique largest of the German warmbloods, plain straight head, strong shoulder, deep girth and relatively short legs.
Features matures early.
Temperament bold, kind and sensible.
Use riding and driving.

SALERNO (Warmblood)

ITALY WAS ONE of the first areas in the world where horses were bred; the Etruscans are known to have bred horses there 2,500 years ago. Ever since, horse-breeding has played an important part in the life of the country, and in the Salerno they produced a top-class riding horse.

The Salerno was developed during the 16th century in the Salerno area near Naples. It evolved from cross-breeding between Andalusians and Neapolitans (a cross between Barb, Arab and Spanish stock, and now extinct).

The Salerno was popular with the Italian army, and it is now used as a general riding horse. Although its numbers are on the decline it is playing an important part in the creation of the new Italian Saddle-Horse. The Italian Saddle-Horse is being developed by crossing and upgrading the regional Italian saddle-horse breeds to produce a good general riding and competition horse.

Height 16 hands.
Colour solid colours.
Physique large, refined head and good conformation.
Features aristocratic, quality saddle horse.
Temperament intelligent, responsive and gentle.
Use riding, especially army.

ORIGIN

Meremma and
Salerno, Italy

ANCESTRY

Neapolitan

Salerno

LIPIZZANER (Warmblood)

Height 15-16 hands.

Colour grey: born dark and lighten as they mature.

Physique largish head, small ears, straight profile, crested neck, compact body, powerful rounded hindquarters, strong clean legs.

Features athletic, late to mature.

Temperament intelligent, obedient and willing.

Use High School dressage and driving.

COLOUR
A peculiarity of the breed is that they are nearly all grey. Foals are born black, but whiten with age. Traditionally, a bay Lipizzaner is always kept at the Spanish Riding School to indicate the breed's links with the past, when bay, brown, black and roan horses were also common.

WITHERS AND BACK
The withers are usually low and broad, the back rather long but shapely and strong, though occasionally a little hollow.

LOINS
The loins are strong and broad.

QUARTERS AND TAIL
The quarters are strong, rounded, and very muscular with a well-carried tail.

LEGS AND FEET
The legs are sturdy, and the feet tend to be rather small but strong.

ORIGIN

Austria

ANCESTRY

 Arab

Barb

Andalusian

Danish

German

 Italian

 Lipizzaner

PROFILE
The Barb/Iberian influence is seen in this aristocratic convex profile.

NOSTRILS
The nostrils are open and mobile.

HEAD
The head is noble and longish. The ears are of medium length, alert and pointed, the eyes large and expressive.

NECK AND SHOULDERS
The neck is strong, arched, and well set onto imposing, sloped shoulders.

AFTER THE ARAB and the Thoroughbred, the Lipizzaner is probably the most famous breed of horse in the world, and that is due almost entirely to its prominence as an *Haute École* riding horse at the Spanish Riding School of Vienna in Austria. The Spanish Riding School was so titled not because it originated in Spain (it did not), nor because it promoted Spanish style riding principles, but because of the ancestry of the breed and type of horse used there in the past.

Like most European breeds, the Lipizzaner is heavily indebted to the old Spanish (Iberian) horse, the Andalusian, and the Lusitano, for many of its desirable qualities. Without all this Spanish blood, the Lipizzaner as a recognizable and highly regarded breed would simply not have evolved.

The name of the Lipizzaner breed itself comes from the stud at Lipizza or Lipica, formerly in Italy but now in the Karst region of north-western Slovenia. It is true to say that most breeds are named after the geographical area from which they originate, yet the origins of the Lipizzaner go back even

LIPIZZANER

farther to the Moorish occupation of Spain from AD 711, when the invaders brought with them to the Iberian peninsula Arab and Barb (Berber) horses, crossing them with native heavy horses and the old Spanish type. The result of the Moors' horse-breeding activities was the Andalusian, which is the main progenitor of the Lipizzaner.

When the Hapsburg Archduke Charles II of Austria, son of the Holy Roman Emperor Ferdinand I, inherited the Austro-Hungarian-Spanish empire in 1564, his new possessions included Lipizza. Classical manège riding was very much in fashion in the 16th century, and Archduke Charles wanted to have the best horses in the world capable of carrying out the demanding airs or movements. He waited until 1580 before founding his stud, and in July of that year began importing the best Andalusian stallions and mares Spain had to offer. He wanted to stock his own stables with his own Spanish horses so as to be able to breed them and not be dependent on imports.

Very soon the stud in Lipizza was stocked with horses of fine Spanish blood. This is significant because, no matter what the subsequent name of the breed, it is the Spanish genes it contained which influenced subsequent produce, and the Lipizzaner breed contained all the qualities found in the Spanish horses – nobility, pride, sensitivity, affectionate temperament, agility and courage. Furthermore, the lofty, naturally cadenced action of the Spanish types had not been bred out by the significant infusions of Oriental blood, and this action was one of the main requirements of the classical manège, the other being the very strong haunches that are demanded in the *Haute École* movements.

The Lipizzaner was, however, expected to produce not only riding horses but also quality carriage horses which, because of the different strains in its foundation stock and the differing types evident in the breed, it was well able to do.

The Spanish Riding School was set up in 1572 for the purpose of instructing noblemen in the art of classical riding. Initially the lessons took place in a wooden structure, but the beautiful building which is still standing today was commissioned in 1735 by Emperor Charles VI. Charles VI was extremely interested not only in the riding skills taught at the school but also in the scientific and practical aspects of breeding, and greatly fostered these pursuits with his considerable resources of land, money and horses.

German, Italian (including Neapolitan), Danish and Kladruber breeds were crossed with the Lipizza stock down the centuries. By the 19th century, some Arab blood was also being used.

With the fall of the Austro-Hungarian empire, the stud at Lipizza was moved to Piber in Austria, but during World War II, the breed was evacuated farther west, mainly to Germany, to avoid capture by the Russian army. Today, Lipizzaners are again bred at Piber and also at Lipizza and Babolna (where the Hungarians breed their favoured bigger, freer-moving strain), as well as in Italy, Romania, the former Czech Republic, and Slovakia. The breed is very popular in the US, but has a limited number of representatives in Britain.

A gentle but proud temperament is the hallmark of the Lipizzaner. The horse is willing, intelligent, and possesses stamina as well as strength, agility and natural balance.

The Lipizzaner today is almost exclusively used as a *Haute École* horse at the Spanish Riding School in Vienna, where its training sessions and displays are always sold out. The Lipizzaner has also always been popular, along with its relatives, the Andalusians and Lusitanos, in circuses around the world. The breed makes an excellent carriage horse and is used as such in Hungary. It is also sometimes used in general draught work.

The Lipizzaner is a late-maturing breed and serious work requiring strength and mature physique cannot be asked of the horse usually until it is seven or eight years of age. It takes seven years to train a Lipizzaner fully in *HAUTE ÉCOLE* equitation, but they are a long-lived breed, and stallions can give top-level performances even when well into their 20s.

WIELKOPOLSKI (Warmblood)

THE WIELKOPOLSKI of Poland has been created by amalgamating the old Masuren and Poznan breeds.

The Masuren was a continuation of the Trakehner breed. It was bred from horses left behind at the Trakehnen stud (formerly in East Prussia) at the end of World War II. It was bred there with great care, following the principles laid down for the Trakehner breed. The Poznan was another breed based on Trakehner stock. These two breeds were extensively cross-bred, and they have now been combined into one stud book under the new breed name of Wielkopolski.

Poland has a total of 42 major studs, and the Wielkopolski is bred at 13 of them. All stallions must pass both conformation checks and performance tests. They also continue to work either under saddle or in harness. This careful programme of selective breeding is resulting in an increase in the size and quality of the Wielkopolski.

The Wielkopolski makes a good all-rounder. It is used for light draught work on some farms, and also makes a good general riding horse. It is also proving itself as a competition horse, and this aspect of the breed is being specifically developed.

Height 16 hands.
Colour chestnut or bay.
Physique a compact, well-proportioned horse.
Features formed by amalgamating the Masuren and Posnan.
Temperament exellent, courageous and hard-working.
Use competitions, riding and light draught.

ORIGIN

Poland

ANCESTRY

Trakehner

Hanoverian

Thoroughbred

Kronik

Poznan

Wielkopolski

Masuren

East Prussian

LUSITANO (Warmblood)

Height 15-16 hands.

Colour usually grey; can be any solid colour.

Physique small head, straight profile, small ears, muscular neck, compact body, powerful hindquarters, long fine legs, abundant mane and tail.

Features Frugal, hardy.

Temperament intelligent, responsive and very brave.

Use riding and bull fighting.

THE LUSITANO, like the Andalusian, is descended from the old Iberian saddle horse. Named after its country of origin, Lusitania being the Roman name for Portugal, this name only came into use as a description of Portugal's Iberian horses in the early 20th century, and was officially adopted in 1966.

The Lusitano is bred mainly in the agricultural heartland of Portugal, and the fertile south and west around the River Tagus, for participation in the *corrida* or bullfight. In Portugal the bull is not killed, the whole fight takes place on horseback, and it is a major disgrace if the horse is injured. The horses are highly prized, painstakingly schooled, and are the epitome of agility, courage and grace. Their temperament is spirited, willing and co-operative.

In addition, the stallions are normally schooled to the highest standards of *Haute École* before being sent out to stud. The Lusitano is a late-maturing but long-lived breed, and is generally not broken in until at least three and a half years of age. Fighting horses are retained entire, since it is generally considered that geldings lack the courage, sensitivity, interest and spark needed to face up to the bull.

The Lusitano is a proud, gentle, nimble and extremely well-balanced horse. It is most courageous and willing and obedient by nature.

The Lusitano is mainly bred for bullfighting and the associated schooling in *Haute École*, and is used for general farm work.

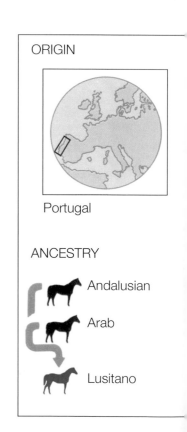

ORIGIN

Portugal

ANCESTRY

Andalusian

Arab

Lusitano

KLADRUBER (Warmblood)

ORIGIN

Czech Republic

ANCESTRY

Andalusian

Anglo-Norman

Hanoverian

Oldenburg

Kladruber

THE KLADRUBY STUD in the former Czechoslovakia is the oldest operational stud in the world. It was founded by Emperor Maximilian II in 1597, and is the home of the Kladruber breed. The Kladruber is closely related to the Lipizzaner, both being directly descended from the Andalusian, but is a taller and heavier horse.

Maximilian imported Andalusians from Spain and created a new breed that had great purity of line, the only other blood being Lipizzaner from the Lipizza stud, and possibly Barb and Neapolitan.

The Kladruber was bred specifically as a ceremonial coach horse, particularly for use at the Imperial Court in Vienna.

The Kladruber's numbers had become seriously depleted by the end of World War II, and Anglo-Norman, Hanoverian and Oldenburg blood have been used to rebuild the breed. Today grey Kladrubers are still bred at the Kladruby stud, while black Kladrubers are bred at the nearby Slatinany stud.

Although the Kladruber is used for riding, it has the perfect temperament for a coach horse, being obedient, good-natured, proud and intelligent, and it is in this area that it excels. It is seen in marathon driving competitions, and demonstrations of Kladrubers driven 16-in-hand are popular features at international shows.

Height 16–17 hands.

Colour grey, sometimes black

Physique Andalusian type but larger: convex profile, strong arched neck, long body, rounded hindquarters.

Features superb carriage horse

Temperament proud, intelligent, obedient, good-natured.

Use agriculture, driving and riding.

KONIK (Pony)

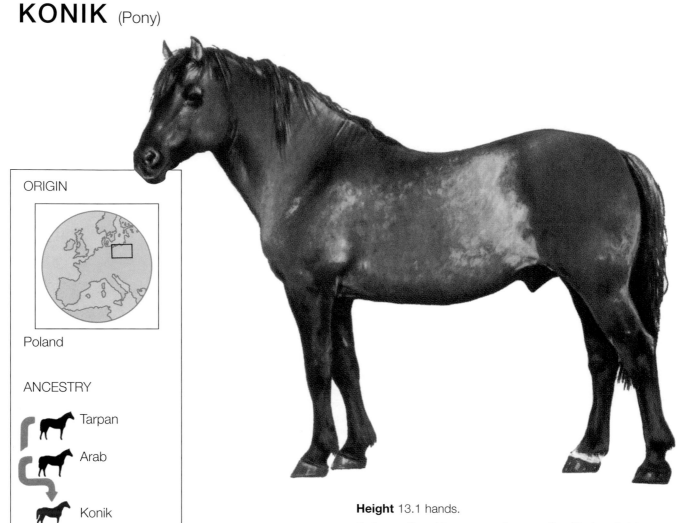

ORIGIN

Poland

ANCESTRY

Tarpan

Arab

Konik

Height 13.1 hands.

Colour yellow, blue or grey dun, usually with dorsal stripe.

Physique large head, well-proportioned body, tendency to cow hocks.

Features long-lived, frugal and hardy.

Temperament good natured, tough and willing.

Use farm work and riding.

THE POLISH KONIK PONY is much closer to its ancestors than other ponies. The word 'konik' means 'little horse' in Polish; it does not denote a specific breed, and there are various strains (about five) of Konik. The type normally referred to as the formal Konik breed is believed to have descended from the original wild Tarpan of Eastern Europe, which was an Oriental type of small horse, with a fine head and the primitive markings of a dorsal stripe and zebra markings on the legs.

The wild Tarpan was hunted to extinction late in the 19th century, but efforts were later made to gather together the Konik ponies descended from it, in order to collect as many Tarpan genes as possible. The ancient wood of Bialowieza was made into a national reserve, and the Konik ponies were turned free there. Today, the descendants of the Konik ponies

(referred to as reconstituted Tarpans) still roam in Bialowieza, and possess the Tarpan colouring and many of its characteristics. Koniks are used on Polish farms mainly to the east of the River San.

Late-maturing but very long-lived, the Konik survives on little keep and can live out all year round. Although most are easy to handle, some retain the wild streak of the Tarpan and may be independent and difficult. Today they are mostly used for farm work, though the more amenable ones are used as children's ponies. The Konik has been used in the formation of many Eastern European and Russian breeds.

KNABSTRUP (Warmblood)

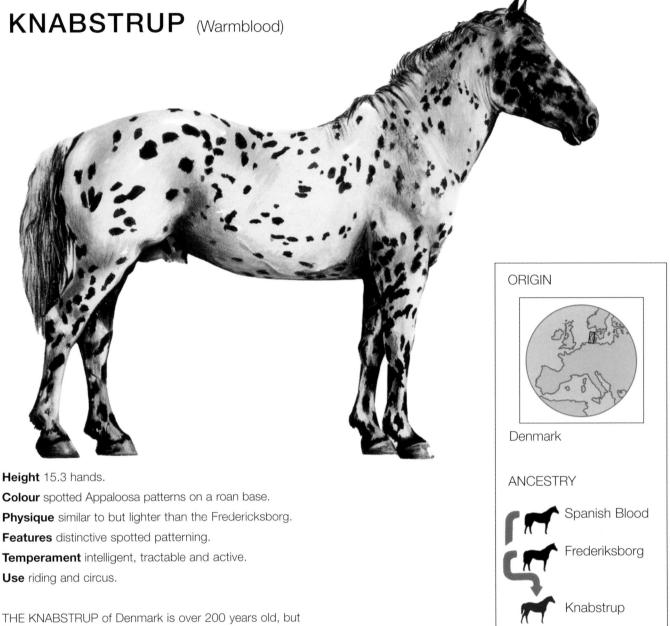

Height 15.3 hands.

Colour spotted Appaloosa patterns on a roan base.

Physique similar to but lighter than the Fredericksborg.

Features distinctive spotted patterning.

Temperament intelligent, tractable and active.

Use riding and circus.

ORIGIN

Denmark

ANCESTRY

Spanish Blood

Frederiksborg

Knabstrup

THE KNABSTRUP of Denmark is over 200 years old, but having gone from great popularity to near obscurity, it is now swinging back into favour. A particular characteristic of the Knabstrup is its spotted coat. The horse's early ancestors were forest-dwellers, and spotted horses appear in prehistoric cave paintings.

In the 16th and 17th centuries, spotted horses were fashionable in European courts. One spotted Iberian mare was sold by her Spanish owner to a Danish butcher called Flaebe. Of great stamina and speed, she was sold to Major Villars Lunn, a noted breeder of riding horses, and, at his Knabstrup estate, was mated with a palomino Frederiksborg stallion. In 1813 Flaebehoppen foaled a multicoloured spotted colt with a metallic sheen to his coat. Named Flaebehingsten,

he founded the Knabstrup breed.

As often happens when a horse is bred for colour, the Knabstrup had, by the 19th century, deteriorated, becoming coarse, disproportionate, and with differing types developing within the one breed. The breed eventually developed into a strong, plain harness type. Recently, the addition of Thoroughbred blood has resulted in a much improved animal.

The Knabstrup is a quality riding horse and is intelligent, perceptive, tractable, and easy to handle. Today it is used for general riding and showing in breed classes and because of its spotted coat it is in demand for circus work.

MURAKOSI (Coldblood)

THE MURAKOSI is Hungary's draught horse, and comes from the area around the River Mura in the south of the country. It was developed during the late 19th and early 20th centuries, when there was great demand for a strong, fast draught horse.

It was created by crossing native Hungarian mares, known as Mur-Insulan, with Percherons, Ardennes, Norikers and Hungarian half-breds (which contained Thoroughbred and Arab blood). This produced a very strong and active draught horse that was ideal for heavy farm work. It was also used by the army.

The Murakosi was so popular that after World War I, one in every five horses in Hungary was a member of the breed. However, many were killed in World War II, and now that it is no longer much in demand for farm work, its numbers are not likely to increase again.

Height 16 hands.

Colour chestnut with flaxen mane and tail.

Physique strong frame, little wither, dip in back round hindquarters and little feather.

Features strong and active.

Temperament docile and willing.

Use general draught and agricultural work.

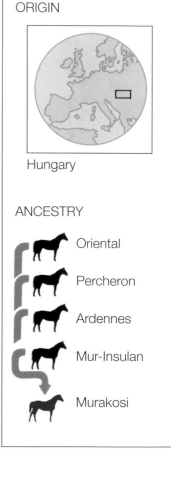

ORIGIN

Hungary

ANCESTRY

Oriental

Percheron

Ardennes

Mur-Insulan

Murakosi

MURGESE (Warmblood)

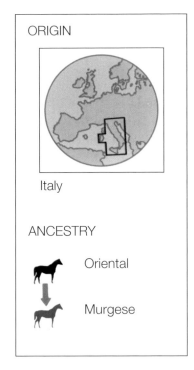

Italy

ANCESTRY

Oriental

Murgese

THE MURGESE is a light draught and riding horse similar to the Friesian. Found in the area of Murege, Apulia, in Italy, the breed is rare. Usually black, but also seen in grey, they originated from Oriental horses crossed with the local horses. The herdbook for this breed was established in 1926.

A ride-and-drive horse, also used for farm work and mule breeding, the Murgese is a surprisingly good jumper and quite a popular riding horse.

Height 15.2 hands.
Colour Usually black, but can be found in grey.
Physique Oriental features but heavier frame.
Features versatile.
Temperament high quality, good tempered.
Use dual-purpose horse for agricultural work and riding.

SCHLESWIG HEAVY DRAUGHT (Coldblood)

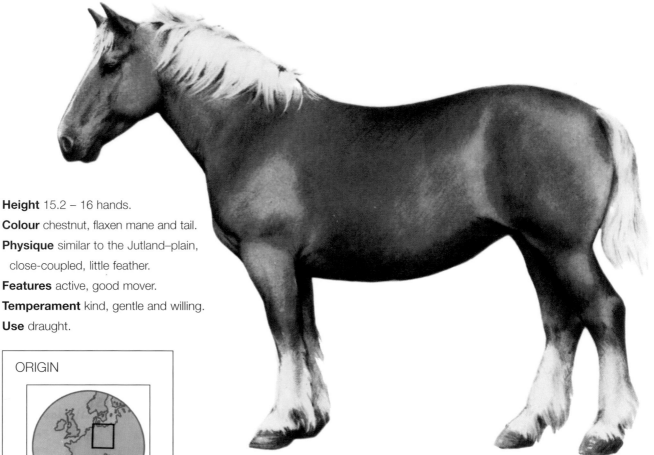

Height 15.2 – 16 hands.

Colour chestnut, flaxen mane and tail.

Physique similar to the Jutland–plain, close-coupled, little feather.

Features active, good mover.

Temperament kind, gentle and willing.

Use draught.

ORIGIN

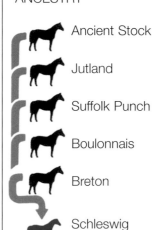

Germany

ANCESTRY

Ancient Stock

Jutland

Suffolk Punch

Boulonnais

Breton

Schleswig

A SMALLISH heavy-type horse, the Schleswig Heavy Draught has been the subject of some controversy as to whether or not it should be called a true heavy horse, because of its lack of height and cob-like character. Although originally based on native heavy stock, the breed as it is now known was only developed during the 19th century. The present breed was created to meet the demands for strong, fast draught power and, along with many other heavy draught breeds, it was carefully bred for military and general heavy draught work.

The Schleswig's immediate neighbour from Denmark, the Jutland, had a lasting influence on the breed, a situation greatly facilitated by the fact that the province of Schleswig-Holstein in northern Germany, where the Schleswig Heavy Draught comes from, was once owned by Denmark. Both the Jutland and the Schleswig were influenced by the stallion Oppenheim LXII, who was brought to Schleswig-Holstein in 1860 and was almost certainly a Suffolk Punch.

Toward the end of the 19th century, considerable Thoroughbred blood was introduced to lighten the breed. In this century, however, faults such as an over-long, rather weak back and soft feet were causing concern, so further crosses, this time of Breton and Boulonnais, were added to eliminate these defects. More recently, Jutland blood has again been introduced.

SHAGYA ARAB (Warmblood)

ONE OF THE HIGHEST quality yet most underrated horse breeds is the Hungarian Shagya Arab. Though strongly Arab in appearance and character, it is a part-bred, with a strong preponderance of Arab blood.

Mezöhegyes, the oldest stud in Hungary, was founded in 1785; the Babolna Stud was founded four years later, and this stud is the home of the superb Shagya Arab. In 1816 a military edict was passed to the effect that the broodmares at Babolna must be mated with Oriental stallions to provide light cavalry and harness horses. Stallions of mixed Oriental blood were used as well as Old Spanish crosses.

The results following the 1816 edict were so satisfactory that a generation later it was decided that Babolna should concentrate on producing horses of exclusively Arab blood, and these became the forerunners of today's Shagya, descending from an Arab stallion of that name who was imported to Babolna from Syria in 1836 as a six year old. At 15.25hh, Shagya was big for an Arab. He was of the Seglawy or Siglavi strain, which embodied the most 'traditional' Arab appearance, with a delicate, dished head; a crested, arched neck; and a high-set banner-like tail.

ORIGIN

Hungary

ANCESTRY

Syrian Arab

Shagya Arab

Height 15 hands.

Colour grey.

Physique Arab features, small head.

Features hardy, frugal and active.

Temperament versatile, alert and intelligent.

Use cavalry, general riding and driving.

THE AMERICAS

APPALOOSA

FALABELLA

CRIOLLO

MORGAN

GALICENO

CANADIAN CUTTING HORSE

LLANERO

AMBLER (PERUVIAN STEPPING HORSE)

MANGALARGA

PALOMINO

QUARTER-HORSE

PASO FINO

SADDLEBRED

PINTO

STANDARDBRED

TENNESSEE WALKING HORSE

APPALOOSA (Warmblood)

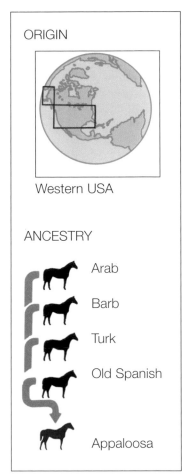

ORIGIN

Western USA

ANCESTRY

Arab

Barb

Turk

Old Spanish

Appaloosa

Height 15 hands.

Colour six basic patterns of spots usually on roan or white, white sclera around the eye.

Physique short-coupled thin mane and tail, hard feet which are often striped.

Features striking appearance.

Temperament tractable, hardy with great endurance and easy to care for.

Use as a cow pony, a pleasure and parade horse and also in the circus.

THE APPALOOSA can truly be said to be the horse of the Americas because it was bred by the native American tribe, the Nez Percé from the north-west of the United States, from stock brought by the *conquistadores*.

The horse's ancestors were forest-dwelling animals that would have had mottling and possibly striping on their coats which camouflaged them in the dappled shade of trees, protecting them against predators. Their modern-day

Appaloosa descendants have inherited the genes for patterned coats.

There are many variations of mottling and spotting in the breed, but for ease of classification there are six main coat patterns. The *leopard* pattern has chestnut, brown or black spots all over the body on a white coat, the *snowflake* has white spots on a chestnut, brown or black coat; the *blanket* pattern has a large white area over the horse's loins, croup, and thighs and is of two types – spotted with chestnut, brown or black, or unmarked with no spots or mottles. The *frosted* pattern is a dark coat bearing a few white spots on the hips and loins, and the *marble* variation is a dark coat in the foal changing through speckling and splashing to almost white in the older horse, apart from the retention of dark markings on the head and legs.

The variations to the main patterns include roan coats (chestnut or grey mixed in with white hairs) and light (not white) spots.

Appaloosas are of compact, well-muscled build, the Quarter Horse-type conformation being generally favoured. Emphasis is laid on the strong, correct legs and feet, because most of the breed work as stock or pleasure horses, or compete in various events, especially Western-style ones. This picture shows the markings of a blanket pattern.

FALABELLA (Pony)

ORIGIN

Argentina

ANCESTRY

Shetland

Thoroughbred

Arab

Falabella

THE FALABELLA is claimed to be the smallest horse in the world which was created by the Falabella family on their Recrio de Roca Ranch near Buenos Aires in Argentina.

The original progenitors were said to be a very small Thoroughbred stallion and a Shetland mare. Over the years, other small Thoroughbreds, Shetlands and also small Arabs have been used to produce this tiny miniature horse. Continual breeding for smaller size, sadly, has resulted in inherited and congenital physical weaknesses in the animals, which breeders are now having to try to overcome. As it is, even the best-conformed Falabellas are not at all strong in relation to their size.

The Falabella is a perfectly proportioned miniature horse, resembling the Thoroughbred or Arab, of around 76cm (30in). The Falabella has a sleek-coated, slim frame but unfortunately this breed is not strong enough even for the smallest child to ride. However, they make ideal pets and are capable of pulling small vehicles.

Due to increasing interest in the delightful breed, showing is becoming more commonplace, with specially allocated classes.

The temperament of the Fallabella is usually quiet, friendly and very obedient. Constitutionally they are not very strong, having lost vigour due to inbreeding. They need the type of care normally given to a full-size Thoroughbred horse.

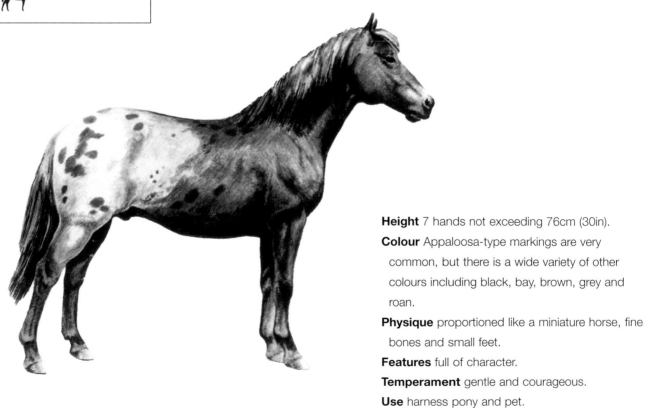

Height 7 hands not exceeding 76cm (30in).
Colour Appaloosa-type markings are very common, but there is a wide variety of other colours including black, bay, brown, grey and roan.
Physique proportioned like a miniature horse, fine bones and small feet.
Features full of character.
Temperament gentle and courageous.
Use harness pony and pet.

CRIOLLO (Warmblood)

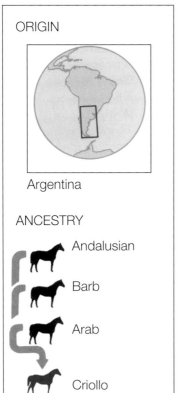

ORIGIN

Argentina

ANCESTRY

Andalusian

Barb

Arab

Criollo

Height 14–14.2 hands.

Colour dun with dark points an dorsal tripe, sometimes roan, chestnut or bay.

Physique short, broad head, muscular neck, strong shoulders and broad chest, deep body, fine strong legs and small feet.

Features tough and manoeuvrable.

Temperament tough, willing, great endurance.

Use riding and stock work.

WHEN THE SPANISH explorers Cortés, Pizarro and their successors brought their Iberian and Oriental horses to the Americas in the 16th century, they had no idea of what the long-term result of their actions would be. From the point of view of the horses, landing on that huge continent meant a completely new way of life for them. It was also the start of the development, by nature and man, of many new breeds and types of horse. Nature and man both create what suits them best out of the available material, and one of the most remarkable breeds in which both man and nature have had a hand is the Criollo of South America.

The breed's ancestors were the Iberian Barb, and Arab horses which arrived with the *conquistadores*. These horses lived wild on the pampas for around 300 years, where their genes eventually blended together, forming the distinctive Criollo breed with its hardy constitution, tailor-made to bear the great extremes of temperature and climate found in South America.

MORGAN (Warmblood)

ORIGIN

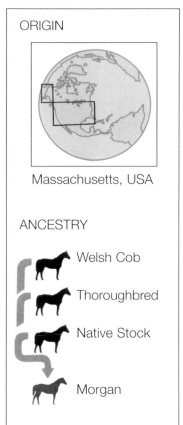

Massachusetts, USA

ANCESTRY

Welsh Cob

Thoroughbred

Native Stock

Morgan

THE MORGAN is an old-established American breed. It was founded from a single stallion called Figure, foaled in Massachusetts in 1793, which eventually came to be known after one of its owners, Justin Morgan of Vermont. The origins of this stallion are unknown, but it is thought to be a combination of Welsh Cob, Thoroughbred and native stock of Arab and Barb descent. The horse excelled at both saddle and harness racing, and at pulling heavy weights, as well as being a good riding and ranch horse, and it was in great demand as a sire. It stamped its size, conformation and character on its offspring with such consistency that by the time of its death in 1821 a new breed had been created.

During the 19th century the Morgan was itself used in the foundation of other great American breeds, including the Standardbred, the Saddlebred and the Tennessee Walking Horse. In the past the Morgan was used mainly for ranch and harness work, and proved its strength by doing heavy

Height 15 hands.
Colour bay, brown, black or chestnut.
Physique short broad head, thick neck, strong shoulders, back and hindquarters, good bone and full mane and tail.
Features versatile, tough and high action.
Temperament kind, independent, active and hard working.
Use riding and driving.

draught work. Even today, the Morgan is the only breed that has to be shown as a harness, show and draught horse.

With its strength and stamina, elegant high-stepping action and good nature, the Morgan is still popular today. It makes an ideal family horse as it takes easily to any form of equestrian activity, be it pleasure riding, endurance riding, or showing in harness.

GALICENO (Pony)

Height 12–13.2 hands.
Colour bay, black, dun, sorrel and grey.
Physique intelligent head, straight shoulders, narrow chest, short back, fine legs and small feet.
Features versatile, natural running walk.
Temperament alert, kind and intelligent.
Use ranch work, transportation and riding.

THE GALICENO is probably the least-known breed to be taken across to the Americas by the Spanish *conquistadores*. It is descended from the Spanish pony the Garrano, from Galicia in north-western Spain, and also from the north Portuguese Minho. It does not have the old Iberian conformation, but is light and narrow in type, probably as a result of the Arab genes in the Garrano.

The original ponies that travelled across the Atlantic landed in Mexico and, although used by man, were allowed to breed indiscriminately among themselves, and so the present type evolved as a result of natural selection rather than artificial selection by man.

It was not until 1959 that Galicenos were brought to North America, where they have turned out to be a very, popular in-between type of pony for older children. The breed has adapted to showing and competing with enthusiasm and is also good at jumping. It has great stamina and has a natural fast running walk which means riders can be carried comfortably and speedily over long distances.

The Galiceno seems to have inherited many Arab characteristics; it is a tough and hardy quality pony, intelligent, courageous, and a quick learner with a lovely temperament. It is also fast and enduring.

In Mexico today, the Galiceno is used for ranch work and light harness work. It is ridden by small adults and children, and in North America excels as a competition pony.

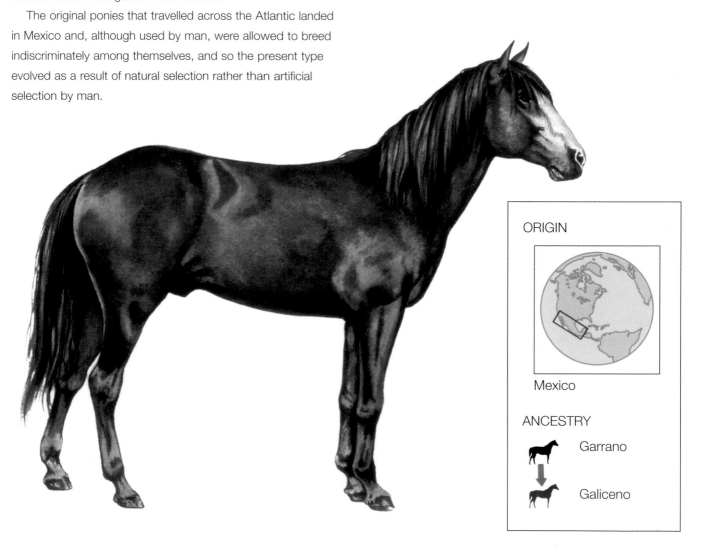

ORIGIN

Mexico

ANCESTRY

Garrano

Galiceno

CANADIAN CUTTING HORSE (Warmblood)

Height 15.2–16 hands.

Colour any colour.

Physique like the American Quarter Horse; long body, short legs, powerful hindquarters.

Features intelligent, fast and agile.

Temperament intelligent and easy to break.

Use ranch work and competition.

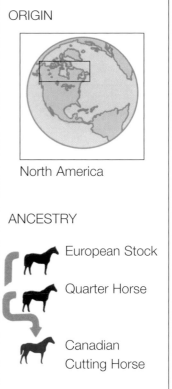

ORIGIN

North America

ANCESTRY

European Stock

Quarter Horse

Canadian Cutting Horse

CANADA HAS NO native horse breeds (although it does have a native pony, the Sable Island Pony). However, horse breeding has been carried out from imported stock since the first settlers arrived. One product of this breeding is the Canadian Cutting Horse, which has been developed along the lines of the Quarter Horse. It is exceptionally strong, fast and agile, and like the Quarter Horse, is ideally suited to working with cattle. The Canadian Cutting Horse is not yet recognized as a breed, only as a type.

Cutting has been around since the early 1800s. The need to 'cut' cattle to isolate them from the rest of the herd was a requirement in order to treat any medical conditions they might have had, or for branding purposes. It was discovered that by using a specially trained horse this task could be accomplished very efficiently, thus introducing the 'cutting horse' and the art of cutting.

LLANERO (Warmblood)

VENEZUELA, like most South American countries, has its own Criollo type, derived from adapting imported Spanish and Portuguese stock to the hot, rough local conditions. This is known as the Llanero. The horse's name can vary from one country to another – Criollo in Argentina, Crioulo in Brazil, Costeño or Morochuco in Peru, Corralero in Chile and Llanero in Venezuela.

Height 14 hands.

Colour dun, yellow with dark mane and tail, white and yellow/cream or pinto.

Physique lighter frame than the Criollo; head similar to Barb.

Features Resistant to diseases, capable of long distances, medium speed and tough.

Temperament courageous and enduring.

Use ranch work and transport.

ORIGIN

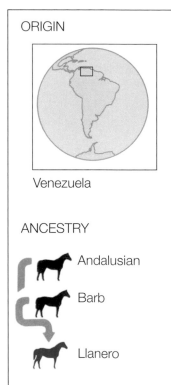

Venezuela

ANCESTRY

Andalusian

Barb

Llanero

AMBLER, PERUVIAN STEPPING HORSE (Warmblood)

Height 14.2–15.2 hands.

Colour bay, chestnut, brown, black and grey.

Physique long crested neck, deep broad chest and body, strong fine legs, full mane and tail and high head carriage.

Features endurance and a special extended gait, similar to an amble.

Temperament tough and hardy, the Peruvian Stepping Horse is calm, energetic, strong, enduring and a willing worker.

Use riding and stock work.

THE PERUVIAN STEPPING HORSE, or Ambler, is the blood brother of the Paso Fino, both having exactly the same foundation of Barb and Iberian blood brought to the Americas by the Spanish *conquistadores*, but each breed has subsequently evolved different characteristics to accommodate the climates of their now-native lands. The horse of Peru was developed to carry a rider comfortably for long distances over rough and treacherous mountainous terrain, and over narrow, rocky tracks at high altitude.

This horse has developed an exceptionally large, strong heart and lungs which enable it to perform athletically in an atmosphere with a very low oxygen level. The horse also possesses 'mountain sense' or the instinct to pick its way without fear or panic over rocky ground, sliding shale, deep water and steep inclines.

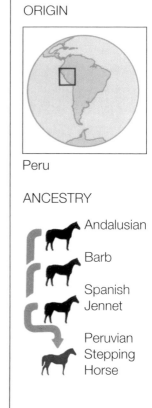

ORIGIN

Peru

ANCESTRY

Andalusian

Barb

Spanish Jennet

Peruvian Stepping Horse

MANGALARGA (Warmblood)

Height 15 hands.

Colour bay, chestnut, roan and grey.

Physique longish head, short back, powerful hindquarters, low-set tail, long legs.

Features hardy; gait called *marcha* between a canter and a trot.

Temperament intelligent, enduring, good riding horse.

Use riding and ranch work.

ORIGIN

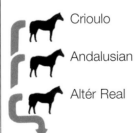

Brazil

ANCESTRY

Crioulo

Andalusian

Altér Real

Mangalarga

THE MANGALARGA breed of Brazil is founded on a single Altér Real stallion imported into the country in the middle of the 19th century by Emperor Peter II. To create the Mangalarga breed, the original stallion was later assisted in his duties by Andalusian and other Altér Real stallions, which were mated with South American Criollo mares.

The Mangalarga today seems to have reverted back to the original Barb type, from which the Altér Real is descended. The horse is a finely-built, nice quality riding horse with a good temperament.

Like many horses of Iberian origin, the Mangalarga is not content to simply walk, trot, canter and gallop. It has a characteristic fifth gait called the *marcha* or *marchador*; which are gaucho terms. The *marcha* is a fast, rolling gait halfway between a trot and a canter which can be maintained for long distances, so it is very useful for stock work in open pampas.

The Mangalarga is essentially a working horse. It is sure-footed, tough and cooperative. It is also wiry and has phenomenal stamina. Used primarily as working horses, few Mangalargas find their way into displays, parades or the show ring. They are used extensively for stock work on the vast ranches of Brazil.

PALOMINO (Warmblood)

Height 14 hands.

Colour golden with no markings other than white on the face or below the knee, mane and tail white, silver or ivory, dark eyes.

Physique varies; should be riding/horse or pony type.

Features distinctive colouration.

Temperament intelligent.

Use riding, driving and stock work.

THE DISTINCTIVE and beautiful colour of the Palomino has made it popular all over the world. It is defined by its colour rather than its conformation, and as it does not breed true to type, it is not recognized as a breed except in the United States. Elsewhere it is registered as a type, and Palomino societies and stud books exist.

The Palomino's origins are believed to go back to ancient China, where the early emperors are reputed to have ridden golden horses. However, they reached America from Spain along with the early Spanish settlers. When the Spanish were defeated and their horses escaped, the Palominos gradually joined up with the herds of wild mustangs roaming North America. Later, they were picked out from these herds of wild horses, and became a popular mount of the cowboys.

The colour of the Palomino should be that of a newly-minted gold coin, although in the United States slightly lighter and darker shades are also allowed. The mane should be white. In North America the Palomino has been bred as a quality riding horse, and is used extensively for trail riding, stock work and rodeos. In Britain Palomino ponies are popular mounts for children.

The Albino is another colour type that is recognized in the United States, where it has been bred since the early 20th century. It is probably descended from an Arab-Morgan stallion, and has bred true to type over several generations.

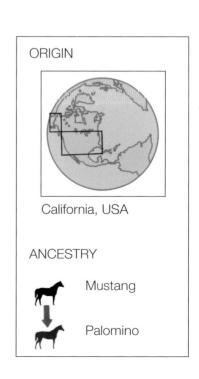

ORIGIN

California, USA

ANCESTRY

Mustang

Palomino

QUARTER-HORSE (Warmblood)

Height 15.3 hands.

Colour solid colours, usually chestnut.

Physique short head, powerful, short-coupled body, large round hindquarters and fine legs.

Features fast and versatile.

Temperament intelligent, sensible, active and nimble.

Use riding, racing, ranching and rodeos.

THE QUARTER-HORSE is the oldest surviving American horse breed, although it was not officially recognized as a breed until 1941.

In the 17th century, on Sundays and holidays, the settlers of Virginia and the Carolinas used to enjoy racing their horses down the main street of the local town – usually a distance of about 0.4 km (a quarter of a mile). Horses that had been bred by crossing local Chicasaw Indian ponies (mustangs of Arab, Barb and Turk origins) with Thoroughbreds imported from England proved extremely fast over this distance, and were soon in demand as breeding stock. Among these a stallion called Janus, imported from England in 1756, is recognized as the foundation stallion of the breed. Janus had raced over 6.4km (4 miles) in England; however, his offspring were very successful over a quarter-mile.

Soon the Quarter-Horse was being carefully bred to produce a very fast horse with great powers of acceleration for sprint racing. With the development of Thoroughbred racing, quarter-mile racing also became more organized and more popular.

The breed quickly came to be valued for other qualities as well as its speed. It is a tremendously strong horse with very powerful shoulders and hindquarters, and it was able to carry heavy men and packs for long distances. It is able to make quick starts and tight turns, which make it the perfect horse for roping and cutting work with cattle. In addition it seemed to have a good instinct for cattle work. It was taken west with the pioneers, and proved to be the ideal horse for working on the big ranches that were springing up across the country.

The modern Quarter-Horse combines strength, speed and agility with intelligence, and is also easily broken and handled, making it extremely popular. There are different types of Quarter-Horse depending on what type of work they have been bred for, but they all share the same Quarter-Horse qualities. The heavier type is produced for stock work, and a lighter type for racing. To see a cutting horse at work, springing into a gallop from a standing start, skidding to a halt and turning on a sixpence, is an exhilarating spectacle. Working cattle, it moves fast and low, anticipating every move that the calf makes.

The versatility of the Quarter-Horse is illustrated by the many types of class in which it is shown, such as working classes, jumping, hunting and polo classes. It is also successful in open classes against other breeds.

The Quarter-Horse is the most numerous breed in the United States today, with two million registered there. Its popularity has led to its being exported all over the world, and a further 800,000 are registered worldwide. It is now bred in Canada, South America, Australia, England and South Africa.

The Quarter-Horse, named after the distance over which it excels, is still bred for racing, and the richest horse race in the world is the All American Futurity for three-year-old Quarter-Horses.

Despite the challenge provided by the Thoroughbred, the Quarter-Horse is still the fastest horse in the world over 0.4 km (0.25 of a mile), the current record being around 20 seconds.

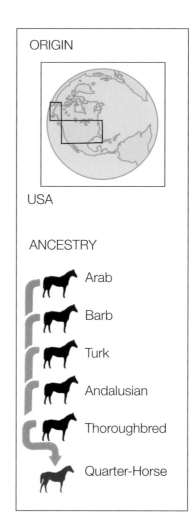

ORIGIN

USA

ANCESTRY

Arab

Barb

Turk

Andalusian

Thoroughbred

Quarter-Horse

EARS
The ears are moderately long and well pricked, their mobility indicating an interested temperament.

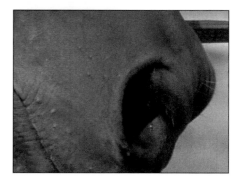

MUZZLE AND NOSTRILS
The muzzle tends to be small and 'tight' with large, mobile nostrils to facilitate rapid air exchange.

PASO FINO (Warmblood)

Height 14.3 hands.

Colour most colours.

Physique Arab-like head, strong back, loins and quarters and hard legs which are light of bone.

Features spirited; extra four-beat gaits.

Temperament alert, tractable and willing.

Use riding.

THE PASO FINO is one of the three main types of South American gaited horse which come from the same genetic stock, but which have all developed some minor changes due to having evolved separately in different environments.

The Paso Fino is probably the most famous and comes from Puerto Rico, the others coming from Peru and Colombia. The intended purpose of the Paso Fino was for display and transportation. The Puerto Rican horse has obviously not developed the ability to work in high altitudes, but its gaits are, if anything, even more refined. It performs the *paso corto*, the *paso fino*, and the *paso largo* with breathtaking beauty and skill.

Two other variants of the basic gaits at which the Paso Fino excels are the *sobre paso* and the *andadura*. In the *sobre paso* the horse is relaxed and natural on a loose rein; this gait is not used in the show ring. In the *andadura* the horse performs a fast lateral pacing gait which is not comfortable and is used only for shortish distances when speed is of the essence.

The Paso Fino has an exceptionally gentle temperament. It is probably the best-looking example of the existing Paso types, having an Arab-type head and an Andalusian body. The horse is intelligent and easy to handle. The Paso Fino is much in demand for leisure riding, showing, parade and display work, and also for general transportation around the coffee plantations of Puerto Rico.

ORIGIN

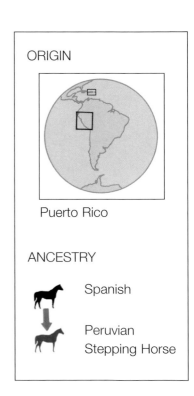

Puerto Rico

ANCESTRY

Spanish

Peruvian Stepping Horse

SADDLEBRED (Warmblood)

Height 15.2 hands.

Colour black, brown, bay, grey or chestnut.

Physique small head with straight profile, strong body and hindquarters, tail carried artificially high.

Features five-gaited action, three normal gaits plus a four-beat rack, at which it can reach 48kph (30 mph).

Temperament great presence, gentle and sweet temper.

Use showing, riding and driving.

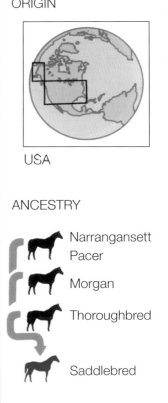

ORIGIN

USA

ANCESTRY

Narrangansett Pacer

Morgan

Thoroughbred

Saddlebred

THE SADDLEBRED was developed in Kentucky during the 19th century by plantation owners, who were looking for a horse that provided a comfortable ride for plantation work combined with a stylish, eye-catching action in harness. By crossing the best of their original stock of Thoroughbreds, Morgans and Narragansett Pacers, they produced a horse that was intelligent and responsive and which also had speed and stamina. With its high head carriage and high-stepping action it is extremely elegant.

Intensive breeding has enhanced the Saddlebred's conformation and action, and it is now a very popular and successful show horse. The breed is divided into three divisions for showing. The Three-Gaited horse is shown in the three natural gaits. The Five-Gaited horse is shown in the three natural gaits and two man-made gaits, the slow gait and the rack. The slow gait is a very slow, smooth, four-beat movement. The legs, especially in front, are lifted very high. The rack is a fast version of the slow gait requiring a very snappy knee and hock action. The Fine Harness horse is shown with a four-wheel vehicle and is judged in two gaits, an animated walk and an airy part-trot.

Although it is best known as a show horse, the Saddlebred also makes a good general riding and driving horse.

PINTO (Warmblood)

Height Varies.

Colour black with white or white with any colour but black.

Physique varies.

Features colour breed traditionally associated with the Native American tribes.

Temperament intelligent and enduring.

Use showing, ranch work and riding.

THE TERMS 'pinto', 'paint' or, less commonly, 'calico', are US terms for horses with large patches of white and another colour on their bodies. In some other English-speaking countries, they are called piebalds (black and white), skewbalds (any other colour or colours plus white) or 'coloured' or 'odd-coloured' horses. None of these terms is used to describe horses with mainly spotted markings such as Appaloosas or Knabstrups. Only in the US is the Pinto regarded as a true breed, although various other countries do have registries for coloured horses.

In the US, Canada and Australia and, to a lesser extent, New Zealand, coloured horses are admired and sought for their uniqueness, no two Pintos being quite the same. They were popular generations ago for trade deliveries because they were eye-catching, and a good advertisement for business. Romany people have liked them for their bright and showy appearance, and they will probably always be popular in circuses for the same reason.

Pinto-type colouration has been known for thousands of years, and many of the quality breeds now appearing only in solid colours had part-coloured ancestors. The colouring may or may not be primitive, and, despite what has been said about its being eye-catching, it does in fact provide excellent camouflage. The Native American tribes loved pinto types of horses for their showy appearance, but also because their broken outline provided a partial disguise on forays and raids.

The Pinto Horse Association of America has been breeding Pintos for colour, good conformation and action since 1956, and the Pinto was recognized as a breed in 1963.

Four types are now recognized in the US: Stock Horses (Quarter Horse type), Hunters (Thoroughbred type), Pleasure type (a good riding horse of Arab/Morgan type) and Saddle type (of Saddlebred type). Height is variable as Pintos can be ponies or horses.

There are two recognized Pinto coat patterns: the Tobiano, with large, well-defined patches of white and coloured coat and normally with a coloured head and dark eyes, and the Overo, with smaller patches, with the white always appearing to originate from the belly, the back, mane and tail usually coloured and the face white with blue eyes.

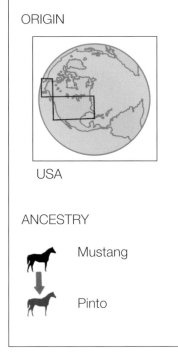

ORIGIN

USA

ANCESTRY

Mustang

Pinto

STANDARDBRED (Warmblood)

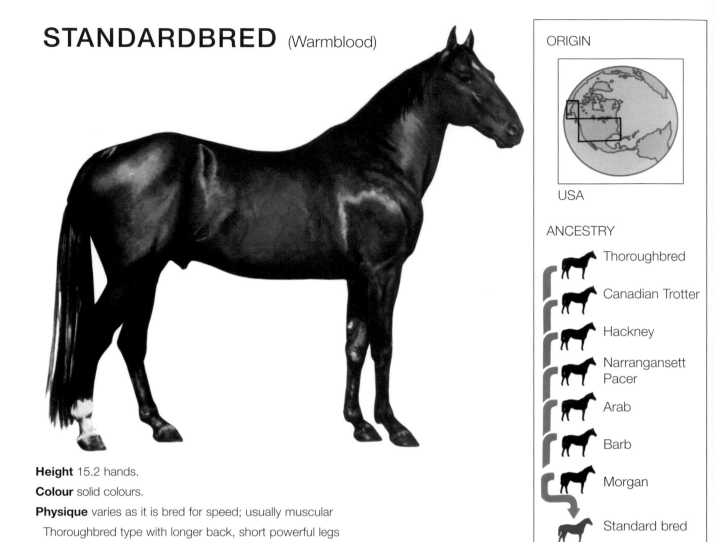

ORIGIN

USA

ANCESTRY

Thoroughbred

Canadian Trotter

Hackney

Narrangansett Pacer

Arab

Barb

Morgan

Standard bred

Height 15.2 hands.

Colour solid colours.

Physique varies as it is bred for speed; usually muscular Thoroughbred type with longer back, short powerful legs and shoulders.

Features stamina and speed.

Temperament bold, active, brave and enduring.

Use driving and racing.

IN THE MIDDLE of the 19th century cross-breeding produced one of America's greatest breeds, the Standardbred, which today is the fastest harness racing horse in the world.

The breed can be traced back to a Thoroughbred stallion called Messenger which was imported to the United States in 1788. Harness racing was popular at that time, but it was an amateur affair, and no thought had been given to founding a breed of trotters. However, when Messenger was crossed with the fastest of the local harness racers, horses resulted that had exceptional trotting speed. He sired four sons to which almost all Standardbreds can be traced. As harness racing became more popular during the 19th century, selective breeding was practised to produce faster trotters.

Thoroughbreds were crossed with more robust strains that had a talent for trotting, such as Canadian Trotters, Hackneys, Narrangansett Pacers, horses of Arab and Barb origins and Morgans.

The most famous and successful of Messenger's descendants, his great-grandson Hambletonian 10, born in 1849, sired over 1,300 offspring. He is regarded as the father of the modern Standardbred.

In 1871 the American Trotting Register was founded, and in 1879 a standard was laid down for inclusion in it. Over a distance of 1.6km (1 mile) trotters had to attain a time of 2 minutes 30 seconds, and pacers a time of 2 minutes 25 seconds. It is from this standard that the breed takes its name.

TENNESSEE WALKING HORSE (Warmblood)

Height 15 – 16 hands.
Colour chestnut, black, bay roan; white markings common.
Physique straight profile, long powerful neck, sloping shoulders and broad chest, short back, strong sloping hindquarters, legs fine, profuse tail carried high.
Features running walk with the forefeet raised high and the hind legs moving with long strides.
Temperament docile, kind willing and alert.
Use showing and riding.

ORIGIN

Tennessee, USA

ANCESTRY

Narrangansett Pacer

Standardbred

Canadian Pacer

Saddlebred

Morgan

 Tennessee Walking Horse

THE TENNESSEE WALKING HORSE (the Walker for short) was developed from the Thoroughbreds, Morgans, Standardbreds, Saddlebreds and Narragansett Pacers owned by the Tennessee settlers in the 18th century. Crosses of these led to the foundation stock of the modern breed.

In the beginning the Walker was intended as a general-purpose working horse, but its extreme comfort as a riding horse made it very popular with the owners of the vast southern plantations.

The Walker's conformation is unique. It has a compact and powerful frame. Its forelegs are set slightly apart, and its hindlegs are set with the hocks well away from its body. Its gaits – the flatfoot walk, running walk and canter – have been developed specifically to produce a very smooth ride, and cannot be taught to any other breed. The flatfoot walk consists of a smooth, gliding action as the horse floats over the ground, its hind feet overstriding the front by 30–50cm (12–20in). The running walk is a faster version of this gait, in which the horse achieves great elevation, and can sustain a speed of up to 24kph (15mph). In the canter it elevates its forehand with a rolling motion while its hindquarters remain almost level. The running walk is now inbred; foals are seen performing it just by copying their dams.

AUSTRALIA, ASIA AND AFRICA

AUSTRALIAN STOCK HORSE
BARB
YONAGUNI
MANIPUR
MONGOLIAN WILD HORSE
ARAB
JAVA
CASPIAN
BURMA
DON
AKHAL TEKE
BASUTO
PERSIAN ARAB
SUMBA

AUSTRALIAN STOCK HORSE (Warmblood)

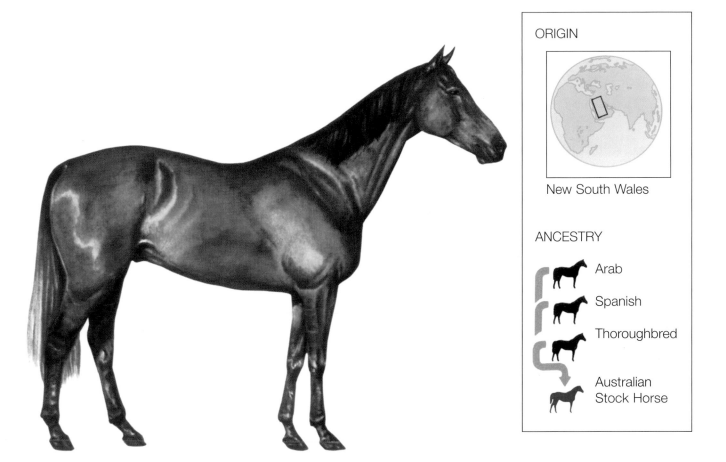

ORIGIN

New South Wales

ANCESTRY

Arab

Spanish

Thoroughbred

Australian
Stock Horse

Height 16 hands.

Colour bay is common, although all solid colours are permitted. White is allowed on the head and legs.

Physique varies, usually alert head, deep girth and a strong back.

Features hardy, with a strong constitution.

Temperament reliable, hard working and versatile.

Use general riding, stock work, rodeos and as a competition horse.

IN 1971 THE NAME The Australian Stock Horse was given to Australia's oldest horse breed, the Waler.

The Waler was originally developed from stock brought over from South Africa by the early settlers at the end of the 18th century. These horses were of Spanish, Arab, Barb and Dutch origins, and could have been Cape Horses. They were crossed extensively with Thoroughbred blood from England over the next hundred years to produce a hardy, agile horse that was full of stamina. It was good for stock work on the big cattle stations, for harness work and for riding. It was also popular with the British army in India as a cavalry horse.

During the 20th century, more Thoroughbred blood has been added, along with a little Percheron and American Quarter-Horse. The stud book was opened at the time that the breed's name was changed to Australian Stock Horse. Owing to the many influences on the breed conformation varies, and it does not yet breed true to type, although progress is being made towards achieving a Uniform breed type. It is a robust Thoroughbred type of horse. It is still used for cattle work and rodeos, and it also makes a world-class competition horse, particularly, in the areas of jumping, eventing and endurance riding.

BARB (Warmblood)

ORIGIN

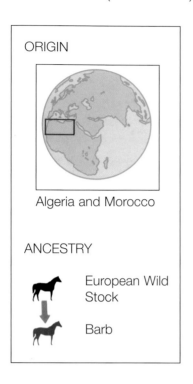

Algeria and Morocco

ANCESTRY

European Wild Stock

Barb

Height 14.2 hands.

Colour bay, brown, chestnut, black and grey.

Physique long head, straight profile, sloping quarters, low-set tail and long, strong legs.

Features frugal and tough.

Temperament good, docile and patient.

Use improving other breeds, riding and transport.

THE BARB IS THE traditional mount of the Bedouin tribes of the north African deserts. It takes it name from its native land, the Barbary Coast – now Morocco, Algeria and Libya – where it has lived since prehistoric times. In gallop, the Barb can evenly compete in speed and distance with the Arabian horse in the Sahara desert terrain. The African Bedouins knew well the quality of their desert horses and tried to protect them from mixing with the Arabian and the English Thoroughbred. It was only on the coastlines of North Africa that the Barb was crossbred with the Arabian to be more refined.

The Barb is thought to be derived from the wild ancient horse type of northern Europe, unlike the Arab which is derived from the Asiatic type. It is distinguished from the Arab by its ram-like head and broad, straight face and muzzle, its lower-set tail and wilder temperament.

The Barb has played an important part in founding and improving many other breeds. It was taken to Spain in large numbers by the Moors in the 8th century, and was crossed with local mares to produce the Andalusian. While the Turks occupied the eastern Mediterranean and the north coast of Africa, traders from all parts of Europe and Asia acquired Barbs and took them home to be crossed with the local horses. Charles II imported many to improve the speed and stamina of England's early racehorses, and it contributed to the founding of the Thoroughbred.

There are not many pure-bred Barbs left; crossing with the gentler Arab makes them easier to train as riding horses. The Barb has been crossed with the Arab to produce the Libyan Barb, a common breed in North Africa. It is predominantly a working horse, and is not selectively bred.

YONAGUNI (Pony)

Yonaguni Uma Preservation Meeting was established and devoted its energies to the breeding of the Yonaguni. As a result, there are now around 120 horses in existence today.

Height around 14.2 hands.

Colour usually chestnut.

Physique short, thick neck and large head.

Features At one time each island household would have owned one of these extremely tractable, strong little horses for general transport and fieldwork. Notable is the high set of the tail, which suggests that there is a heritage from the same bloodlines as the Arabian. These horses are now listed as rare and have become a cultural asset.

Temperament gentle, very strong and enduring.

Use riding and work.

THE YONAGUNI is a small native pony of the south-west islands of Japan. In 1996 there were about 75 living Yonaguni ponies on East and North Ranches on Yonaguni Island, located on the west side of the Yaeyama Islands.

Little is known about the origin of the Yonaguni. Horses in Japan can generally be divided into two groups, larger specimens from Hokkaido and smaller individuals from Yonaguni. Many people believe that the small horses were introduced from the southern islands during the Jyomon Period, about 2,000 years ago.

The Yonaguni are usually chestnut. The head is large with well-placed eyes and relatively small ears; the neck is short and thick; the shoulders tend to be straight; the back is long; the croup is often quite level with a high tail-set; the quarters are slight; the legs often tend to be splayed; the hooves are vertically long and very hard. This pony is gentle in nature and very strong and enduring.

The numbers of Yonaguni dramatically decreased to 59 horses in 1975. In the same year, the

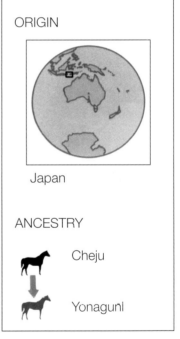

ORIGIN

Japan

ANCESTRY

Cheju

Yonaguni

MANIPUR (Pony)

Height 12 hands.

Colour most colours.

Physique long head with broad muzzle, thick set with high-set tail and clean hard legs.

Features quick and manoeuvrable.

Temperament adaptable and lively.

Use riding and polo.

THE MANIPUR PONY has been bred in the state of Manipur, India, for many centuries. It is derived from the Mongolian Wild Horse, and has been crossed with Arab blood to improve its conformation and give it more speed. The Manipur became famous in the 19th century as the original polo pony. Polo had been played in Asia for 2,000 years. Although the game died out in most of India, it continued to be popular in Assam and the Himalayan states. A 7th-century manuscript records polo being played in Manipur on Manipur ponies. In the 1850s, British tea-planters in Assam discovered the game being played on these fast, manoeuvrable ponies and took it up themselves, spreading its popularity throughout the world.

The Manipur is still used for polo in its homeland, but has been superseded elsewhere by larger, faster horses. It was also reputed to be a good cavalry horse. Being very tough, sturdy and sure-footed, and able to carry heavy loads for long distances, it has always been an invaluable working pony.

ORIGIN

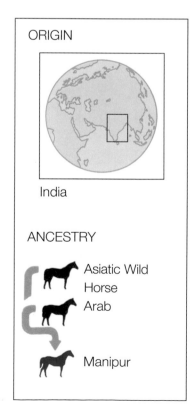

India

ANCESTRY

Asiatic Wild Horse

Arab

Manipur

MONGOLIAN WILD HORSE (Pony)

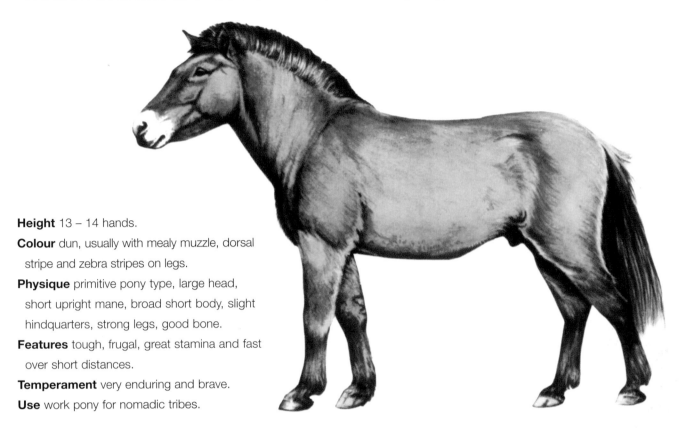

Height 13 – 14 hands.

Colour dun, usually with mealy muzzle, dorsal stripe and zebra stripes on legs.

Physique primitive pony type, large head, short upright mane, broad short body, slight hindquarters, strong legs, good bone.

Features tough, frugal, great stamina and fast over short distances.

Temperament very enduring and brave.

Use work pony for nomadic tribes.

ORIGIN

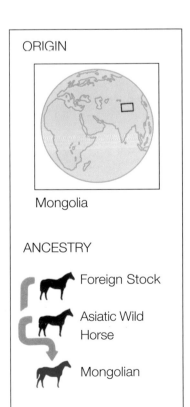

Mongolia

ANCESTRY

Foreign Stock

Asiatic Wild Horse

Mongolian

THE MONGOLIAN WILD HORSE *(Equus przewalski poliakov)* is the only surviving truly wild horse, as opposed to those that have escaped from domestication. At one time it was thought to be the basic breed from which all domesticated breeds evolved. Recent evidence suggests, however, that there were four basic groups, and that the Mongolian Wild Horse belonged to the Northern group known as the Primeval Pony.

The Mongolian Wild Horse was discovered in 1881 by Colonel Przewalski roaming the steppes of the Tachin Schara Nuru Mountains (the Mountains of the Yellow Horses), on the western edge of the Gobi desert in Mongolia. The breed is also known as Przewalski's Horse after its discoverer. It has changed little since the Ice Age, due partly to its isolation, and partly to the ferocious temperament of the stallions. Intruders would be seen off long before they got near a herd of mares.

The Mongolian Wild Horse has always been hunted for meat, and it is now nearly extinct, although measures are being taken by the Russian and Chinese governments to preserve it. Specimens are kept in zoos around the world. It has provided the foundation stock for many domesticated breeds, including the Burma pony, the Manipur of India, and the Mongolian pony. The Mongolian pony is one of the oldest domesticated breeds in the world, and was the work pony of the nomadic tribes of Mongolia.

ARAB (Thoroughbred)

Height 14.3 hands.

Colour bay, chestnut and grey.

Physique small, tapering head, concave face, broad forehead, large, dark eyes, small ears, arched neck, long sloping shoulder, short straight back, straight croup, high-set tail, fine legs but very hard bone.

Features fast free-floating action, stamina and toughness.

Temperament spirited, enduring, intelligent and bold.

Use improving other breeds, long distance and general riding.

THE HORSE WE now call the Arab or Arabian has probably influenced more other breeds of horse and pony than any other in the world. This breed suffers from a good deal of romanticism, probably because most individuals are very beautiful horses with spirited temperaments, intelligence, and an affectionate attitude toward humans. In practice, it would do the breed a better service if it were respected more for its toughness, individuality and stamina.

The modern breed is called 'Arab' because during the last century and, to a lesser extent, the preceding century, breeding stock was imported to Britain from the Arabian peninsula, but the breed's distant ancestors almost certainly evolved from the small, wiry, Oriental-type ('hot blooded') wild horses living in Eastern Europe and the Near and Middle East. Although the breed is claimed to be the oldest and purest, it includes different strains which physically resemble earlier types from which the modern breed developed, and these different physical types can still be seen in the breed today. Whatever its sources, the Arab is a riding horse without equal and is regarded as priceless by those who understand the breed and are willing to treat it as a partner rather than a servant.

Character and care

Arabs are intelligent horses, perceptive, sensitive and thoughtful, not only in the sense of being considerate and gentle towards people and other animals, but also in thinking out situations for themselves. They do have a reputation for being difficult among those who have tried to force them to do something against their will, but they are extremely courageous and will try their best for someone they trust.

The Arab or Arabian horse originates from the desert lands of Asia and the most famous are the horses of the Bedouin Arabs, known as the Original or Elite Arab. Through selective breeding the Bedouins developed an Arab horse which was tough and yet beautiful. It was these Arab horses that were used as cavalry horses by the Moslems and taken to North Africa and into Spain and France. Many Arab horses were left behind when the Moslems went and they started to breed with local horses creating such breeds as the Andalusian horse. The UK imported Arab horses in the late 19th and early 20th centuries from Arabia.

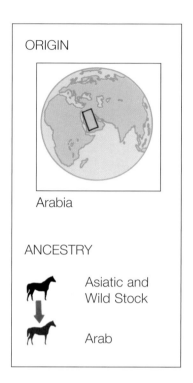

ORIGIN

Arabia

ANCESTRY

Asiatic and Wild Stock

Arab

As they originated in hot climates, they are fine-skinned and have all the physical characteristics facilitating easy heat-loss from the body, but tend not to be so sensitive to cold weather as the Thoroughbred. They can usually be handled by novices and children, provided those concerned have a regard for their nature and a sensitivity towards them.

The Arab today

Arabs make excellent all-round riding, and very light harness horses. They are also good family horses because of their affectionate disposition, and their average height which makes them suitable for both adults and older children.

In competition, Arabs should be judged as good riding horses first, with their unmistakable type and breed-conformation points second.

In-hand showing classes are extremely popular with many Arab enthusiasts, and they are divided into the normal age and sex groups with overall championships to be won in the different categories.

Increasingly, the Arab is being seen as a saddle horse not only in showing classes, but in competitive disciplines involving dressage, jumping and endurance riding. They are now also raced. In all categories of competition, Arabs compete internationally under the auspices of the World Arabian Horse Organization.

Arabs are sometimes said to be the jacks of all trades and masters of one – endurance riding. Their legendary stamina makes them superb long-distance riding horses in any sphere, working or showing, and Arabs can be found working cattle on a ranch as well as taking most of the prizes in competitive endurance riding.

A common misconception is that Arabs can't jump. Arabs certainly can and will jump, but do not have the scope for high-level eventing or show jumping.

The high-set tall and flattish quarter/croup region indicates natural speed which has resulted in the revival of Arab racing. All in all, they are excellent all-rounders and family horses, and have an inimitable panache in harness.

JAVA (Pony)

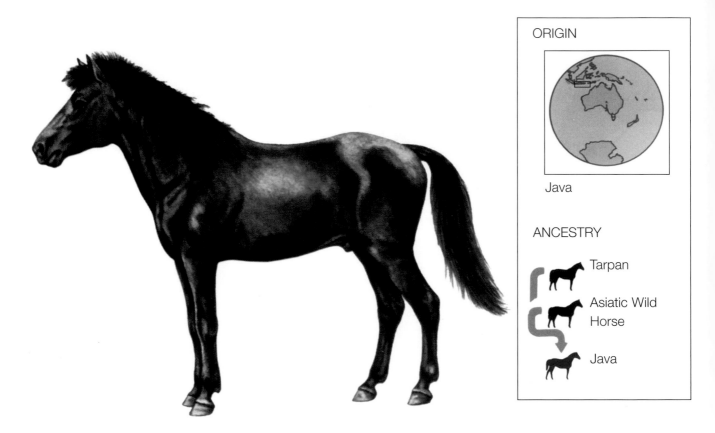

ORIGIN

Java

ANCESTRY

Tarpan

Asiatic Wild Horse

Java

Height 12.2 hands.

Colour most colours.

Physique strong frame.

Features ugly but strong and tireless.

Temperament willing and good worker.

Use pulling *sados* (two-wheeled taxis), all-round work.

INDONESIA'S PONIES are vital to the transport, communications and agriculture of the country, and many of the islands have their own breed. The breeding of many of these ponies is supported by the state. These ponies are generally of primitive type, and over the centuries they have adapted to working in the tropical heat.

The Java is a native of the island of Java and is descended from the Mongolian Wild Horse (*right*). As well as being used for general work, it pulls the *sados*, or two-wheeled taxis, that are used on the island. It is a strong and tireless pony, and willingly pulls a full load all day.

Other island breeds include the Timor, a small, finely-built and very wise pony; the Bali, a very primitive type of pony used for packwork; the Batak from Sumatra, which has been refined and improved by crossing with Arab blood; the Gayoc, also from Sumatra; the Sumbawa, which is very similar to the Sumba; and the Sandalwood, from the islands of Sumba and Sumbawa, a fast, finely-built pony.

CASPIAN (Pony)

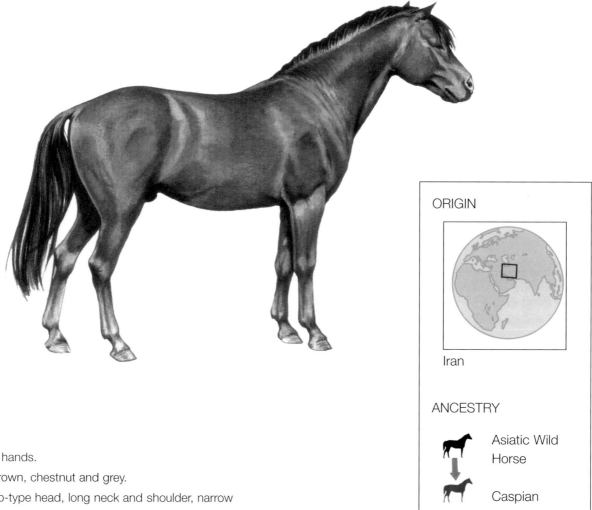

ORIGIN

Iran

ANCESTRY

Asiatic Wild Horse

Caspian

Height 10–12 hands.

Colour bay, brown, chestnut and grey.

Physique Arab-type head, long neck and shoulder, narrow body with short back, tail set high, fine legs.

Features sure-footed.

Temperament gentle, tractable, intelligent, quick-witted and ideal for children.

Use riding and driving.

THE CASPIAN should be regarded as a small horse rather than a pony because it does have horse rather than pony character. Remarkably, despite having been domesticated, it seems to have descended in pure form from an Oriental prehistoric horse, the fossils of which have been found in Iran and match the Caspian's skeletal features. One of the best depictions of this ancient horse can be found on the seal of Darius the Great, ruler of Persia in 500 BC.

All theories pointed to the horse's extinction in around the 10th century, but in 1965, 40 Caspians were discovered in a remote area of the Elburz Mountains in Iran by Mrs. Louise Firouz, who shipped them to Britain. A breed society was set up to promote and foster the Caspian, and now there are studs in Britain, the United States, Australia, New Zealand and Iran.

It is claimed that the Caspian is the oldest pure breed in the world. It is also claimed to be the progenitor of the Arab.

The Caspian is a miniature Oriental type, with a free, floating action and an alert yet equable and affectionate temperament, and is sensitive without being too highly strung. The Caspian makes a superb riding pony for children, being narrow, responsive, intelligent, gentle and cooperative. It also makes a very good driving pony.

BURMA (SHAN) (Pony)

ORIGIN

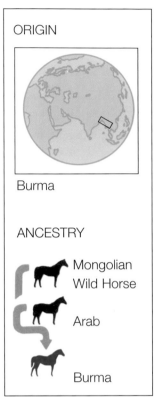

Burma

ANCESTRY

Mongolian Wild Horse

Arab

Burma

Height 13 hands.

Colour all colours.

Physique thickset with high-set tail, larger version of the Manipur.

Features strong hill pony.

Temperament active, but can be slow in response.

Use all-round working pony and polo.

THE BURMA (also known as the Shan) has been bred for a long time by the Shan hill-tribes of eastern Burma. It is closely related to the Manipur, being descended from the Mongolian Wild Horse, but has more Arab blood added, making it larger.

It is very strong and has always been used as a working pony. At one time it was also used by the British for playing polo, but it is too slow and unresponsive to be successful in this field.

DON (Warmblood)

Height 15.2–16.2 hands.

Colour chestnut, bay, grey most common.

Physique medium-sized head with wide-set eyes, long neck, long broad back, strong hindquarters, long hard legs.

Features versatile, frugal, with great stamina.

Temperament energetic, calm and reliable.

Use the original Cossack horse, now used for driving, riding and long distance riding.

THE DON was the horse of the famous Russian Cossacks and comes from the area around the River Don on the Russian steppes. Originally the Don was a tough, wiry, light-framed, active, Oriental type based on local stock. It more than proved its worth against Napoleon's retreating army in the winter of 1812. While the French horses died of starvation and exhaustion, the Cossacks mounted on their Dons and came back again and again until they had driven the French out of Russia.

During the 19th century the breed was upgraded by crossing with Turkoman, Karabakh and Karabir stallions that were allowed to run free with the Dons. It was further refined by crossing with Thoroughbred and Orlov Trotter blood. As a result the Don became a larger, better-looking horse.

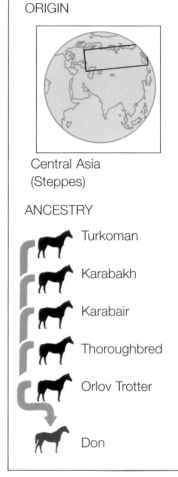

ORIGIN

Central Asia
(Steppes)

ANCESTRY

Turkoman

Karabakh

Karabair

Thoroughbred

Orlov Trotter

Don

AKHAL TEKE (Warmblood)

ORIGIN

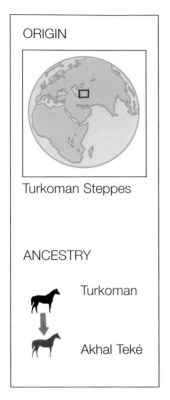

Turkoman Steppes

ANCESTRY

Turkoman

Akhal Teké

Height 14.2–15.2 hands.

Colour bay, grey, chestnut and black occur, but the mostly highly prized colour is the honey-golden dun with black points. The coat has a peculiar and strong metallic sheen.

Physique small elegant head, long thin neck, high sloping shoulder, long back, shallow body, low-set tail, long legs, sparse mane and tail.

Features hardy, temperamental, fast and versatile.

Temperament they are noted for being stubborn, rebellious, somewhat wild, independent, even bad-tempered, and inclined to be vicious.

Use riding.

THE AKHAL-TEKÉ from Turkmenistan is the living descendant of the now-extinct old type of Turkmene horse, and is very highly regarded in its home country. It is known to have existed in very much its present type around 3,000 years ago, when it was used as a fast warhorse. Evolved and reared in varying climates from searing heat to freezing cold, the breed is one of the hardiest and most enduring in the world.

Historically, the Akhal Teké is a true desert horse, coming from an arid region with vast expanses of steppe and desert. Although they did (and still do) run in herds under the management of a mounted herdsman, today many are still traditionally tethered and hand-fed barley, eggs, alfalfa, mutton fat, and a heavy fried type of bread when they are needed for work. Heavy covers were used to protect these fine-skinned horses, from both the bitter nights and daytime desert sun. In the past, foals were traditionally weaned at two months, and yearlings were raced hard.

BASUTO (Pony)

Height 14.2 hands.

Colour chestnut, bay, brown and grey.

Physique quality head, longish neck and back, strong, straightish shoulder, short legs and hard hooves.

Features sure-footed and tough, with great stamina.

Temperament fearless and self-reliant.

Use racing, polo and general riding.

ORIGIN

South Africa

ANCESTRY

Arab

Barb

Thoroughbred

Persian

Basuto

THE BASUTO PONY comes from Basutoland, South Africa, but is derived from the Cape Horse of the Cape Province.

Traders first imported horses, mostly Arabs and Barbs, into the Cape Province during the 17th century. Further imports of Persian Arabs and Thoroughbreds during the 18th and 19th centuries were crossed with those to produce a tough native horse, the Cape Horse, that was sold in large numbers to the British army in India as cavalry remounts. Around the 1830s, Cape Horses were used in border raids on neighbouring Basutoland, and when these were over some were left behind to fend for themselves. As a result of in-breeding, harsh terrain and climate and poor feed, the Cape Horse deteriorated into the Basuto pony. However, the harsh new conditions also made it tough, brave and enduring. It is said to be able to carry a full-grown man up to 96 to 129km (60 to 80) miles a day.

The Basuto was used in large numbers by the British Army during the Boer Wars. It has been used for polo and racing. It is now in demand all over South Africa as a riding pony, and particularly for trekking.

PERSIAN ARAB (Thoroughbred)

Height 15 hands.

Colour grey or bay.

Physique elegant compact body, otherwise as Arab.

Features possibly older than the desert Arab.

Temperament spirited and intelligent.

Use riding and improving other breeds.

ORIGIN

Iran

ANCESTRY

Asiatic Wild Horse

Persian Arab

DIFFERENT STRAINS OF Arab have developed which vary slightly from each other in type and size according to climate, pasture, and national preferences. The Persian Arab, raised in a temperate area, is larger and softer than its desert-bred cousins, and does not have the typical 'dished' face.

The bones of a horse excavated in western Iran prove that the Arab existed there long before domestication. They also show that the Arab has changed very little since prehistoric times, man having had little influence over its build or appearance. The Iranians have always claimed that they were the first to domesticate the Arab, and the Persian Arab is one of the oldest pure Arab lines in the world. It has been very carefully maintained through selective breeding and attention to purity of line.

Other strains of Arab in Iran have now been grouped together under the breed name of Plateau Persian. The Plateau Persian was crossed with the Thoroughbred to create a new breed, the Pahlavan.

SUMBA (Pony)

ORIGIN

Indonesia

ANCESTRY

Mongolian

Sumba

THE SUMBA PONY is a primitive type from the islands of Sumba and Sumbawa. It bears a close resemblance to the Mongolian and Chinese ponies descended from a mixture of the Mongolian Wild Horse and the Tarpan. This pony has a heavy head with almond eyes, an upright shoulder, straight back and sloping croup. The Sumba is most commonly primitive dun with an eel stripe and dark points, and stands at about 12hh. It is this breed that is used for equestrian 'dancing' competitions throughout Indonesia in which the horses wear bells on their knees and perform dance steps to a tom-tom rhythm while carrying young boys. Its performance is judged on elegance and lightness.

Height 12.2 hands.

Colour dun with dorsal stripe, dark mane and tail.

Physique primitive type.

Features special use as a dancing pony

Temperament tough, willing and intelligent.

Use dancing and general work.

RUSSIA AND THE BALTIC STATES

BASHKIR (BASHKIRSKY)
BUDYONNY
ORLOV TROTTER
KARABAKH
TERSKY

BASHKIR (BASHKIRSKY) (Pony)

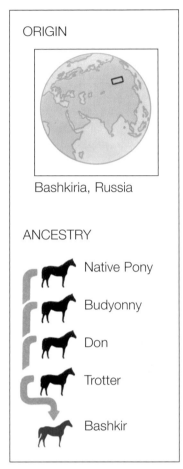

ORIGIN

Bashkiria, Russia

ANCESTRY

Native Pony

Budyonny

Don

Trotter

Bashkir

Height 13.2 hands.

Colour bay, dun or chestnut.

Physique thickset, prominent wither, longish back, low-set
  tail and short legs.

Features tough.

Temperament good, docile and patient.

Use riding and pulling sleighs; mares are milked for kumiss,
  a medicinal and alcoholic drink.

THE BASHKIR, OR BASHKIRSKY, is one of the most unusual
breeds in the world. It has been bred on the southern slopes
of the Ural Mountains in Russia by the Bashkiri people for
many centuries. They use it for pulling sleighs and troikas, and
for making *kumiss*, an alcoholic liqueur, from the mares' milk.

Its home climate is one of the coldest on Earth. It has the
features of a true cold-climate horse – stocky body, biggish
head with small nostrils, short legs, and a tail held close to its
hindquarters. It also develops a thick layer of insulating fat
under its skin in winter. Bashkirs have very small, soft
chestnuts on the legs. Their blood is also of a different
composition and their heart and respiratory rates are higher
than in other breeds.

The most remarkable feature is, however, its long, thick,
wavy winter coat: a common variant is tight curls, like Persian
lamb, and the most startling of all are tight ringlets up to
about 15cm (6in) in length. The summer coat is short and
straight.

There are about 1,200 Bashkir 'Curlies' (as they are called)
in the United States, where they clean the horse in winter by
vacuuming it! The Bashkiri people use the body, mane and
tail hair for spinning textiles and making clothing.

In their home country, they are still used today for
transportation, meat, milk and clothing. The Mountain type is
small and light; the Steppe type is heavier and better in
harness. In the United States the 'Curly' is used for
endurance riding and showing.

BUDYONNY (Warmblood)

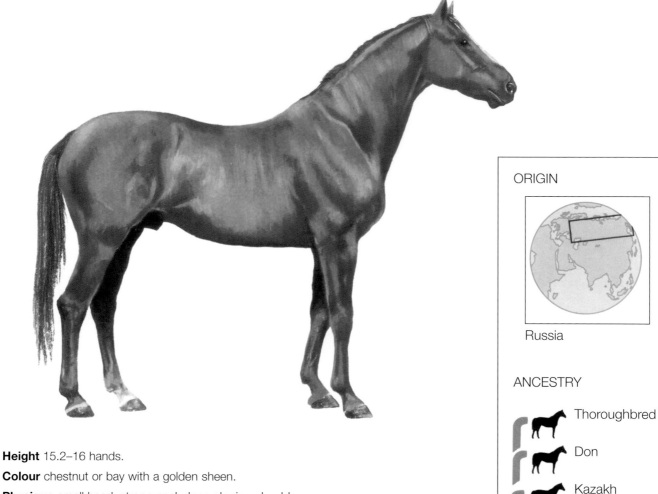

Height 15.2–16 hands.

Colour chestnut or bay with a golden sheen.

Physique small head, strong neck, long sloping shoulders, strong compact body, croup long and rounded, low-set tail, fine hard legs.

Features fast and enduring.

Temperament calm, intelligent, good-natured.

Use riding, steeplechasing and competitions.

ORIGIN

Russia

ANCESTRY

Thoroughbred

Don

Kazakh

Budyonny

THE BUDYONNY is a relatively recent Russian breed, having been created in the early 20th century at the army stud at Rostov by a famous cavalry officer, Marshal Budyonny. His intention was to produce a good cavalry horse.

The breed was created by crossing Dons and Thoroughbreds – Thoroughbred stallions on Don mares achieving much better results than the other way round. Kazakh blood was also added. A highly selective breed programme was followed, with all animals being tested for speed, fitness and endurance. As early as 1948 the breed

had been fixed and was breeding to type. It was used for cavalry, harness and draught work. It has since been used to improve other Russian regional breeds.

When the Budyonny was no longer in demand as a cavalry horse, it was re-crossed with Thoroughbred blood to produce a top-quality riding horse. It has good jumping ability, and excels in all areas of equestrian sports. It is also a successful steeplechaser due to its Thoroughbred blood.

The Budyonny is a kind-natured, patient, intelligent horse, but it has, nevertheless, spirit, courage and enthusiasm as well as speed, stamina and an ability to jump well.

ORLOV TROTTER (Warmblood)

Height 16 hands.

Colour usually grey or black.

Physique small head, long neck, upright shoulder, broad chest, deep girth long straight back, muscular hindquarters, fine hard legs with some feathering.

Features active and fast.

Temperament bold and courageous.

Use trotting races, harness and riding.

ORIGIN

Russia

ANCESTRY

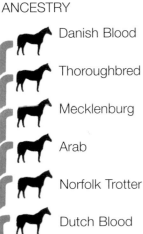

Danish Blood

Thoroughbred

Mecklenburg

Arab

Norfolk Trotter

Dutch Blood

Orlov Trotter

THE ORLOV TROTTER is probably the best known of the Russian horse breeds. It was developed during the 18th century at a time when trotting races were very popular in Russia.

The breed was the creation of Count Alexius Grigorievich Orlov who in 1777 crossed an Arab stallion, Smetanka, with a mare of Danish origins (probably Fredericksborg). This produced a colt, Polkan, who inherited the bad as well as the good features of his father. In particular his forehand action was poor. However, when crossed with a black Dutch mare, Polkan sired a stallion, Bars 1, who was to become the foundation sire of the breed.

Further crossing with Arab, Thoroughbred, Norfolk Trotter and Mecklenburg blood, together with in-breeding to Polkan, established the breed type, and careful selective breeding further improved it.

During the 19th century, the Orlov Trotter was the best trotting horse in the world. However, it has now been superseded by the American Standardbred. More recently, the Orlov has been crossed with the Standardbred to produce the Russian Trotter.

The Orlov Trotter was also used as the basis for the German Trotter, a breed that has since been improved by crossing with the Standardbred and the French Trotter to produce a small horse with a very long-striding action.

KARABAKH (Warmblood)

ORIGIN

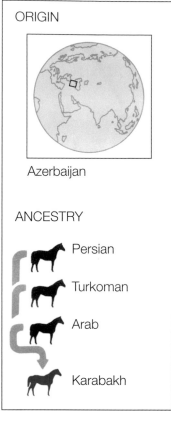

Azerbaijan

ANCESTRY

Persian

Turkoman

Arab

Karabakh

THE KARABAKH horse, although of pony size, comes from the Karabakh Mountains of Azerbaijan. Karabakhs look like Arabs, which isn't surprising as both horses come from the same genetic type.

The Karabakh's existence was documented as far back as the 4th century AD, and it has remained popular ever since as a riding mount. In the 18th century, it was suddenly very much in demand and was exported to many other Asian and European countries.

Today, it is said that no pure Karabakhs are left because in the past the breed was diluted by Persian, Turkmene and Arab blood.

The Karabakh is a spirited and refined hot-blooded horse. It is beautiful, calm and gentle, but also has energy and stamina. Like all true mountain breeds, it is sensible and very sure-footed with an innate sense of direction.

The Karabakh today is used largely for racing; it also makes an excellent small riding and pack horse. It is also popular for mounted ball games.

Height 14.1 hands.

Colour dun, bay or chestnut with a metallic sheen.

Physique small fine head, strong neck, prominent withers, strong compact body, strong hindquarters, low-set tail, fine legs and good feet.

Features ancient breed, energetic and tough.

Temperament energetic, calm, robust.

Use riding, equestrian games and racing.

TERSKY (Warmblood)

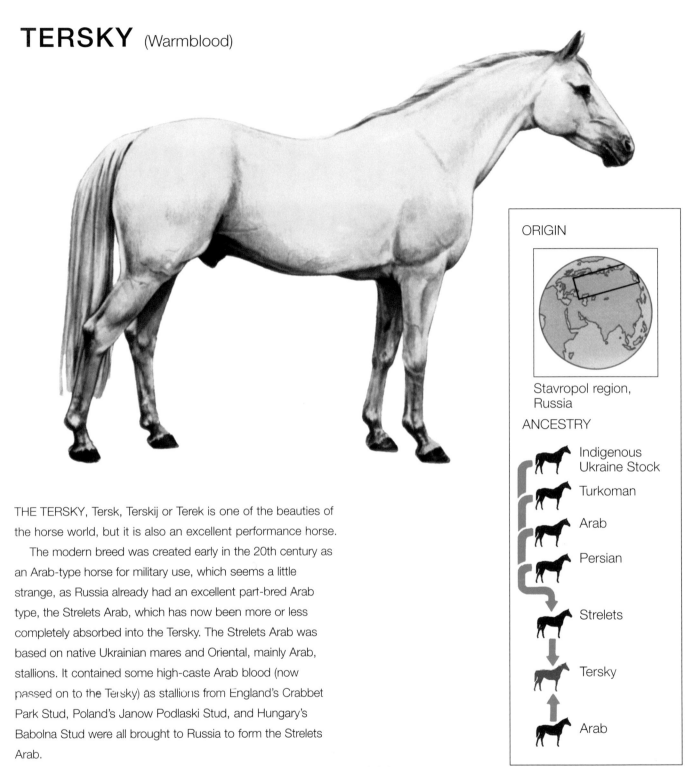

ORIGIN

Stavropol region, Russia

ANCESTRY

Indigenous Ukraine Stock

Turkoman

Arab

Persian

Strelets

Tersky

Arab

THE TERSKY, Tersk, Terskij or Terek is one of the beauties of the horse world, but it is also an excellent performance horse.

The modern breed was created early in the 20th century as an Arab-type horse for military use, which seems a little strange, as Russia already had an excellent part-bred Arab type, the Strelets Arab, which has now been more or less completely absorbed into the Tersky. The Strelets Arab was based on native Ukrainian mares and Oriental, mainly Arab, stallions. It contained some high-caste Arab blood (now passed on to the Tersky) as stallions from England's Crabbet Park Stud, Poland's Janow Podlaski Stud, and Hungary's Babolna Stud were all brought to Russia to form the Strelets Arab.

The old-type Tersky horse was used by the Cossacks because it was tough and enduring, but in the 20th century Marshal Budyonny refined the breed by adding more Kabardin, Don, Arab and Thoroughbred blood.

There are three types of horse within the breed: a light, fine, Arab-looking type; a more substantial intermediate type; and a thicker-set type with sturdier legs and a longer body.

Height 15 hands.

Colour grey with a metallic silver sheen.

Physique Arab-looking in appearance, showing all typically Arab characteristics.

Features three types; light, medium and thick-set.

Temperament kind, intelligent and enduring.

Use racing, competitions and the circus.

143

THE COMPLETE
GUIDE TO KEEPING
A HORSE

BUYING A HORSE

For even an experienced rider, buying a horse can be an operation fraught with hazards. For example, the horse can turn out to be unsound, 'nappy', a rearer or a runaway, traffic-shy, bad in the stable, or difficult in company with other horses or when left alone. It may, on the other hand, be a paragon of virtue, but simply not what you are looking for. Buying a horse is as highly personalized a procedure as choosing a car or a partner.

There are many methods of buying a horse – riding magazines, for example, list horses for sale. But generally, if you are buying a horse for the first time, the soundest course of action is to find a reputable dealer and rely on his or her judgement. This is far preferable to purchasing a horse at a sale. Sales are sometimes used to unload undesirable horses – the chronically sick, for instance, which have to be kept going on drugs, or those which have serious vices. Of course, if a horse is warranted sound when it is sold and then turns out not to be, the purchaser can return the horse and get the money back. But it is simpler and safer not to get into this situation in the first place.

Few reputable dealers will take advantage of someone who confesses their ignorance. The beginner should therefore admit his lack of experience and trust in the dealer's judgement, though an experienced friend is by far the greatest asset.

Points to watch for

There is a saying that a good horse should 'fit into a box'. This means that a classically conformed horse should, excluding its head and neck, be capable of fitting into a rectangle. A horse of this type is most likely to be, and remain, sound.

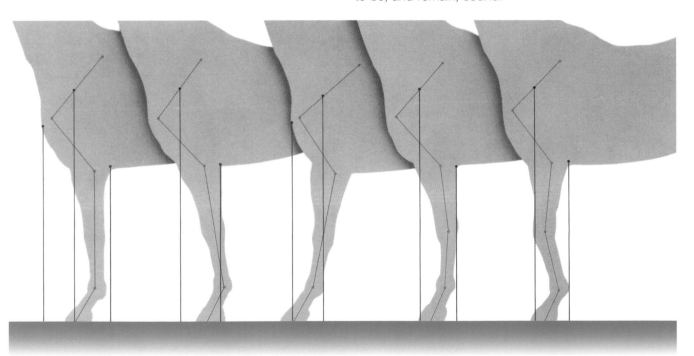

Good conformation. Hoof is centred between shoulder and elbow points.

Horse is under itself in front. This makes for less stability.

Horse is cramped in front, a common fault that causes tendon strain.

Hollow-kneed stance. This throws strain on the ligaments behind the knee.

Knee-sprung stance. Horse liable to stumble or fall on its knees.

Good limbs are, of course, essential. The foreleg should give the overall impression of being 'over', rather than 'back' of the knee. Pay attention, too, to the horse's centre of gravity – the part of the creature on which the greatest strain devolves. Points before or behind the centre are also liable to strain, but a well-conformed horse is far less at risk.

To assess the horse's personality, look it squarely in the eye; the character and intentions of a horse are fairly easy to read and interpret with a little experience. A bold but kind eye, generously proportioned, indicates a reliable, sympathetic temperament. Piggy little eyes, especially if the skull is convex between them and runs down to a Roman nose, are sure signs of an untrustworthy beast.

The role of the vet

Before any purchase is made, always have the horse examined by a veterinary surgeon, who should be first told what the horse is required for. A general hack, for instance, will not make an event horse. The examination should begin with the horse being 'run up in hand', in order to check that the horse moves straight, and that it is sound. A sound horse can be heard to be going level and evenly, as well as seen to be. An unsound horse will favour the lame leg, keeping it on the ground for as little time as possible. If very lame, it will nod its head as it drops its weight on to the sound leg.

The feet and limbs are then examined, the vet being on the watch for any heat or swelling, exostoses (bony enlargements such as spavins, sidebones or ringbones), and signs of muscular unsoundness, such as curbs, thorough-pins or thickened tendons.

If all appears satisfactory, the horse's eyes are examined for cataract; it is then mounted and galloped to check its wind. This is to ensure that there are no latent troubles with breathing or lungs – defects that are betrayed by a 'roar' or a 'whistle'.

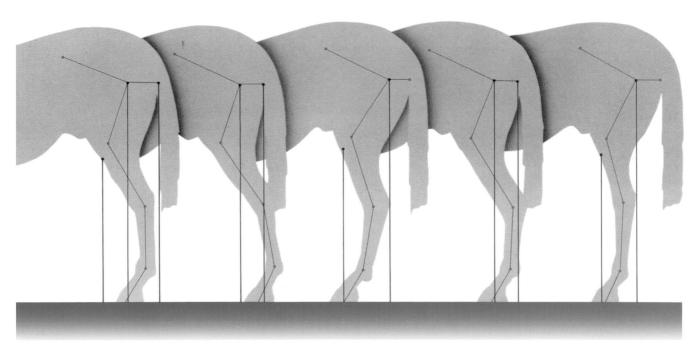

Good conformation. Hoof is centred between stifle and buttock point.

The horse is cramped behind (leg too far back). This can cause sway.

Horse is under itself behind, a fault that can lead to forging.

Back at the knee, a fault that strains the tendons of the fetlock.

Straight hocks may give speed, but also tend to limit movement.

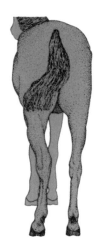

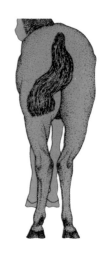

Good conformation. Point of buttock is in line with hock and hoof.

A cow-hocked stance looks awkward, but is no problem.

Bow-legged conformation puts strain on hock bones and ligaments..

Good conformation. Point of shoulder is in line with knee and hoof.

Pigeon-toed stance puts strain on the knees. The horse may tend to stumble.

Horse is closed in front. Has little heart room, may tend to brush.

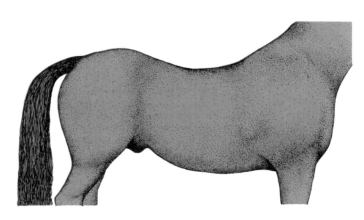

Above *A hollow back lacks strength and flexibility. It can be a sign of age.*

Above *A straight croup means little flexibllity and less power in jumping.*

Above *Acutely sloping croup means lack of power in hindquarters.*

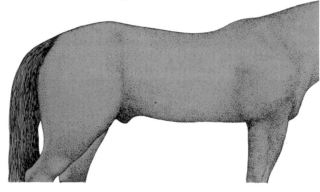

Below *A shallow-bodied horse has little stamina as it lacks lung capacity.*

Below *A straight back restricts movement. The horse will lack power.*

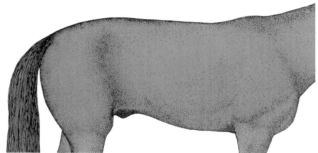

147

Horses with wind afflictions may also have cardiac problems, for the effort of breathing in such cases naturally imposes an added strain on the heart. For this reason, after the gallop, the heart is tested with a stethoscope.

The general condition of the horse is also examined and checks made for worms or other parasites. Finally, the vet submits a report of his findings.

Trial before buying

It is sometimes possible to have a horse on trial for a limited period to see if horse and rider are compatible, though usually only if the dealer has a personal knowledge of the buyer. Horses are prone to all kinds of ailments and afflictions, and no dealer should be expected to entrust a horse to an inexperienced prospective purchaser.

A trial period is exceptionally valuable when buying a pony for a child. Here, the normal problems can be further compounded by the child's lack of strength, as well as, possibly, of experience. The safety of the child must be the first priority. Children have been killed when their ponies take fright and bolt – a particular hazard when riding on or near

roads. It is therefore of the utmost importance only to buy from people with impeccable credentials. The outgrown family pony is ideal, but often hard to find, as these animals are often passed on to the owner's friends and relations. Ponies are also sold by their breeders, and breed societies will supply the names of studs.

For a first horse, do not make the mistake of buying too young an animal. A well-trained horse that knows its job and is a willing and co-operative ride is a much better buy than a young, inexperienced one. Two novices together is a bad combination; the horse is very likely to dominate its inexperienced rider.

Thus, a horse of four, five or six years of age is not a beginner's ride. At eight years, it is mature, and, providing it is sound and healthy, it should be useful and active until aged well over 20. The more nervous the rider, the more docile the horse should be.

It is possible that as a rider becomes more proficient, he or she will look for a horse with more quality. This is a natural and correct progression, but resist the temptation of buying a horse with too much 'fire in its belly'. This may well pull your arms nearly out of their sockets when, say, in company with other

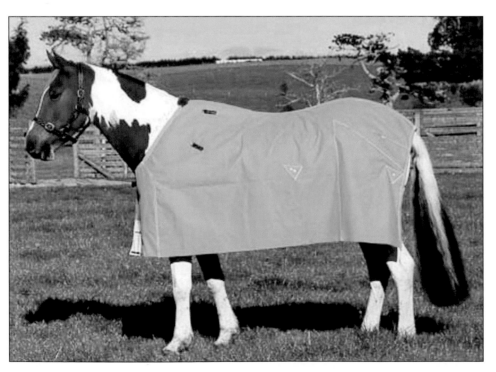

horses. Remember, too, that well-bred horses are far more expensive to keep than, say, a cob, for they usually have to be stabled in winter. A cob, on the other hand, can winter out in a New Zealand rug (*left*) quite happily, as long as it has access to a shelter and is given hay and one or two feeds a day.

BREEDING A HORSE

Breeding and raising a foal is one of the most satisfying things involved with horses, but it is a complex business, and should never be undertaken without careful consideration of all the problems involved. For instance, a foal cannot be produced simply for the amount of the stud fee; the additional expenses of veterinary fees, upkeep, and of transporting the mare to and from the stud all have to be taken into account. The vet must be consulted, both to check for hereditary defects and also to ensure that the animal is free from disease – the usual method is to take a cervical and clitoral swab. Most studs require a veterinary certificate to this effect. So, unless the facilities are right and time and money are of no object, think twice about becoming a horse-breeder.

The role of the mare

Mares come into season at regular intervals of between 18 and 21 days, and it is at this time that they can be 'served' (inseminated) by a stallion.

However, it is possible for a mare to apparently 'hold' to a service and then to 'return' (come into season again) six weeks later. To make doubly sure, a vet should test a specimen of the mare's blood or urine after 45/100 days and 120 days respectively.

It is best not to ride the mare for a few weeks, until it is certain that she has held to the service. Usually, most studs prefer to keep mares for six weeks in any case, and do not send them back before then unless quite certain that they are in foal. The cost of their keep, of course, raises the price still further.

The mare will not need any special care when she returns from the stud, apart from a more nourishing diet. If she is fed nuts or cubes, buy the stud variety instead

Sexual organs of the mare

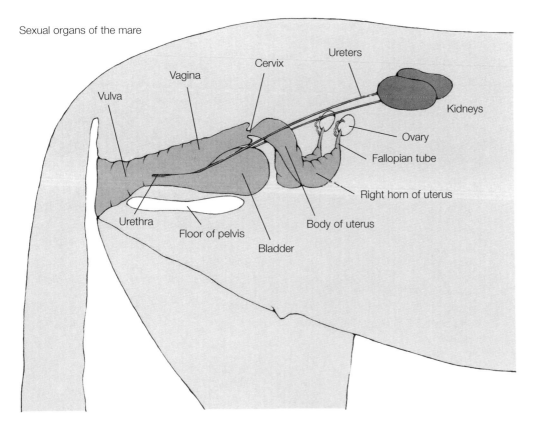

Left A mare's sexual organs consist of ovaries, Fallopian tubes, uterus, cervix, vagina and vulva. At birth, the ovaries contain thousands of eggs; some of these are released into the Fallopian tubes during the sexual cycle to allow fertilization to occur.

149

Sexual organs of the stallion

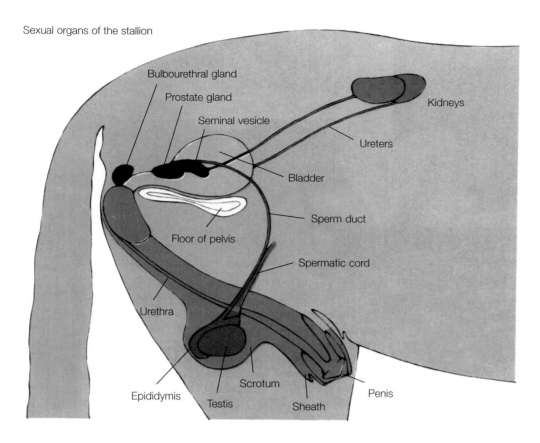

Bulbourethral gland

Prostate gland

Seminal vesicle

Kidneys

Ureters

Bladder

Sperm duct

Floor of pelvis

Spermatic cord

Urethra

Epididymis

Scrotum

Testis

Sheath

Penis

Left A stallion's sexual organs consist of two testes in the scrotum, collecting ducts, linked to the urethra through the spennatic cord, prostate, bulbourethral and vesicular seminal glands, and the penis, in the prepuce. Spermatoza are produced in the testes.

of the ordinary horse and pony ones. If she is not, introduce a suitable vitamin preparation and some cod liver oil, which has been especially enriched for animal feeding, into the diet.

Unless it is unavoidable, it is wise not to turn a pregnant mare out with geldings. These may tease or worry her and cause her to 'slip' (lose) her foal.

Choosing a stallion

The choice of stallion depends on the type of horse that you are hoping to breed. Bear in mind that a good quality big horse may be expected to grow into money, while a small one is unlikely to.

Breeding is an uncertain venture at the best of times, with all kinds of risks of hereditary unsoundness. Therefore, choose a stallion that has been certified by a recognized, official body – most countries have regulations covering this. In the UK, for instance, the Hunter's Improvement and National Light Horse Hunter

Breeding Society have awarded premiums to sixty Thoroughbred stallions. Each of these has undergone a stringent examination by a panel of vets and they are the only stallions in the country warranted to be sound and free from hereditary disease.

Stallions are generally advertised for breeding purposes in the spring. At one time they used to travel the roads and railways in the company of a stallion man, staying for the night at various points along the route where the owners of mares in season would bring them to be served. Nowadays, in most countries, stallions remain on their base farms throughout the spring and early summer, and the mares are brought to them to be served there.

Many novice breeders make the mistake of choosing a stallion purely on the strength of geographical convenience. Nothing could be more short-sighted, for it is essential to select a stallion that will be likely to offset any conformational defects in the mare.

The stallion and the stud

Although it is important to keep a stallion under control, and to demand respect from him, he should never be treated as a dangerous wild animal. Knowledgeable stallion men lead or ride their horses out for daily exercise and their horses are contented and relaxed. Some owners ride them around the farm and along quiet country roads, while others turn them out to grass with the mares.

At many studs, a horse called a 'teaser' is kept for trying mares, that is, to ascertain whether they are ready for service. Teasers are used to safeguard the stallions that are actually doing the serving, for all horses used at stud are liable to be kicked by an irritable mare at some time during their careers. Some studs insist on hobbling all mares before they are served; in any case, a mare should never be sent to a stud unless its hind shoes have first been removed.

When the attentions of the teaser have satisfied the stud groom that the mare is fully on and ready to accept the stallion – the usual signs are that the mare stands still, with the vulva damp with fluid and opening spasmodically – the stallion is brought out of his box, or from behind the trying gate or wall. The stallion serves the mare in hand, that is, they are both on lead reins and wearing bridles, as a safety precaution. Mating normally takes one or two minutes, during which the mare must be kept as still as possible, especially during ejaculation. The head should be kept as high as possible and, at the moment of mounting, the leg hobble – if used – should be released. To achieve extra control over the mare during mating, some studs put a twitch on her. This is a loop of rope on the end of a stick, which is twisted tightly around the upper lip.

An instantaneous mating may not immediately ensue, however; horses, like humans, have their foibles. Mares have been known to take immediate and strong exception to the partner selected for them, while stallions also have their likes and dislikes. The premium stallion Little Cloud, for example, son of the Derby winner Nimbus, always refused to serve grey mares unless they were covered by a rug.

Nevertheless, if the mare does not accept the stallion willingly, it may well be that she has some internal illness, such as a cystic ovary. She should be thoroughly examined by a vet, as a reluctance to mate is often an indication that the mare is unlikely to breed. Or the time is not right – either she has passed the fertile period of her season, when the ovum is ready for fertilization, or she has not yet reached it. Healthy mares are seldom a problem to cover or to get in foal, though excess weight is not an aid to procreation.

Mares generally carry foals for 11 months and a few days – on average, 334 days for colts, and 332.5 days for fillies – but there is a possible variation of some 9.5 days each way, and some mares may be as much as two weeks late. A pregnant mare may safely be ridden to an advanced stage in pregnancy for seven months – as long as she is never overexerted. Exercise is beneficial for all healthy pregnant animals.

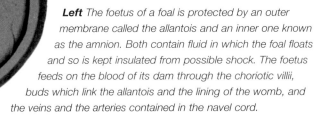

Left *The foetus of a foal is protected by an outer membrane called the allantois and an inner one known as the amnion. Both contain fluid in which the foal floats and so is kept insulated from possible shock. The foetus feeds on the blood of its dam through the choriotic villii, buds which link the allantois and the lining of the womb, and the veins and the arteries contained in the navel cord.*

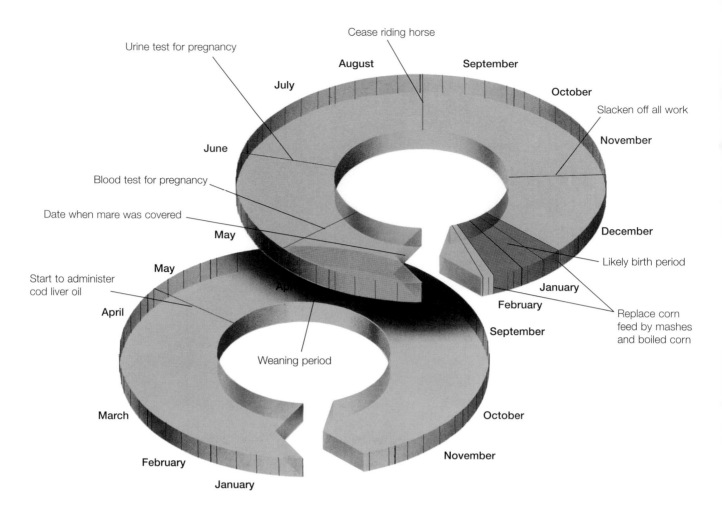

Urine test for pregnancy

Cease riding horse

August

September

July

October

Slacken off all work

June

November

Blood test for pregnancy

Date when mare was covered

December

May

Likely birth period

May

January

Start to administer
cod liver oil

April

February

September

April

Replace corn
feed by mashes
and boiled corn

March

Weaning period

October

February

November

January

*Above The cycle from conception to birth and (**below**) the first year of the foal's life. From the date of the last covering, the limits of the probable foaling date can be established. This also determines the times when pregnancy can be confirmed and feeding and the exercise are affected. In the bottom diagram, the crucial dates are those for weaning and starting to give cod liver oil.*

Foaling

Pony mares are usually best left out in a field to foal. They foal quickly and seem to have sufficient natural instinct to produce the foal, clean and dry it, as they would if part of a wild herd, when mare and foal would have to be prepared to move on with the rest of the band soon after birth. The more highly-bred the mare is, the more supervision she will require. Thoroughbred mares almost always foal in the stable, watched over by attendants. At all the major studs, closed-circuit television is employed. This gives the mare the illusion of being alone, while every move is being watched, and help is immediately at hand, if required.

Only a proper stud will have the facilities for sitting up all night for perhaps as long as two weeks – a task that is beyond most private owners. Therefore, it may be advisable to book the mare into a stud as early as possible. Make sure that the stud is reputable and responsible; a vet is a good person to consult.

Giving birth

The first sign of approaching birth is when the mare starts to pace around, showing signs of discomfort at regular intervals, glancing at her sides and swishing her tail. The wax formed on the udder drops off the teats and the muscles on either side of the croup drop inwards.

As the labour pains become strong, the mare lies down. Delivery is imminent when the membranes of the water bag, in which the foal is contained, break to release the mare's waters.

If, however, delivery is delayed and the mare seems to

be straining and visibly tiring, veterinary assistance must be obtained immediately, for the cause may well be a malpresentation. In a normal birth, the forefeet are delivered first, followed by the head and the rest of the body. Complications ensue if the presentation is incorrect – the most common examples being the frontal presentation, in which the foal's head is bent sideways; where the foal is on its chest, with its knees bent; when the head is bent backwards, and one knee half bent; the head bowed beneath the forelegs; and the dorsal presentation, in which the foal lies on its back, with the head and forelegs pointing backwards. Sometimes there may be a breech presentation (hind end foremost), in which the hindfeet come first, or some other abnormality, such as the twisting of the foetal membranes or the disintegration of the foetus. In many of these cases, the foal must be pushed back from the birth canal into the uterus, where there is room to turn the foal round, to straighten its legs, or reposition its head. To accomplish

Normal presentation

Breech presentation

this, professional veterinary help is essential.

Once the foal is born, most mares will instinctively start to wash it. Then, as it staggers to its feet, she gently pushes it towards her udder, where it begins to suckle. This early suck is all-important, for the first flow of milk is preceded by colostrum, a vitamin-rich substance that contains natural protection against several juvenile diseases and also stimulates the bowels of the newly-born foal into action.

The mare frees itself of the afterbirth. This should be retained for inspection by a vet to make sure that it is complete. If, for any reason, release of the afterbirth is unduly delayed, then the vet should be called to free it, or infection will follow.

When the foal is a day or two old – even a few hours old, if it is strong and healthy – a small headcollar, made of webbing or soft leather and known as a slip, may be put on it. This always involves a struggle, so it should be undertaken before the foal gets too strong. This will enable you to get it accustomed to being handled and led about, which is essential if it becomes necessary to administer medicines or injections. A good way to accustom the foal to human contact is to bring it into the stable with its mother at night. This also provides it with a dry bed to sleep on and minimizes the risk of chills. If the mare is fed dampened bran and crushed oats, night and morning from a bin on the ground, it will help her condition, and very soon the foal will be eating them too. If you have someone to help, the process of leading the foal in and out of the stall will be a valuable early lesson for the young horse, and may save time and trouble later during the breaking process.

Caring for the foal

Left A normal presentation contrasted with a breech presentation, in which the foal is presented hind-foremost. A normal breech presentation presents few difficulties, provided that skilled assistance can be obtained to manipulate the foal. The chief task is to make sure both hind legs are in the birth passage; the chief risk is that the umbilical cord may become trapped, so that the foal is in danger of suffocation. Speed is therefore essential as otherwise the foal will drown in the waters contained in the protective membrane.

With the approach of autumn, the foal must be weaned or it will become a heavy drain on the mother's strength. If she is in foal again, it will rob her of calcium, and the next foal may be born with deformed limbs. Weaning, however, vastly increases the owner's responsibilities. The mare, parted from her foal, bellows night and day, her cries evoking shrill replies from the foal. This lasts until she becomes resigned to the fact that the foal has passed from her care to that of their mutual owner.

The foal should remain in a loose box for at least two weeks; there, where it has become accustomed to eating hard feed together with its mother, it will give little trouble. It will welcome its feeds, which should be generous to compensate for the milk it now lacks. Milk pellets may be added to the feed if it seems to be losing condition.

It is when the two weeks are up, and the foal has to adapt to a new routine of loose box by night and outdoors by day, that the responsibilities mount.

First, you must find a companion for your foal to substitute for its mother. Ideally, another foal is the best companion.

It is as well, however, to keep the two foals in different boxes at night. If they are constantly together, one will dominate the other and take most of the food. They will also be so difficult to separate when they mature that you will have a performance almost akin to weaning all over again.

When the warm weather returns, they can stay out all night, and, as the summer days grow really hot, you may consider keeping them in by day and out by night, as a means of protecting them from flies. This should be the pattern of their lives for a couple of years or more, until the time comes for them to be broken. By the second winter, you may decide to let them remain in the field, which does, of course, save a lot of mucking out. Provided you give them some sort of shelter for cold,

Above Lifting a foal on to the scales to check its weight. Weighing should be carried out regularly to ensure all is well.

Above Leading should be done daily, using a halter to control direction and a hand for encouragement.

wet nights, they should not come to much harm. Throughout these early years, have the blacksmith check their feet – say, every six weeks, especially in long periods of dry weather.

If you live in an area of good grass, you can dispense with feeding from late spring to late summer. But as soon as the rains come, corn must be provided, together with as much hay as the young horses will eat.

Breaking and training

If you lack the knowledge or the time to break in a colt yourself, be very careful to whom you send it for training. Every area where horses are concentrated has at least one colt-breaker, and sometimes more. Ask the owner of your local riding school or the blacksmith, to find out which breaker has the best reputation. Make sure to send your colt to someone generally acknowledged to be expert. It takes a long time to 'make' a horse, but a very short time indeed to spoil it.

Owing to the colt's extreme youth, this will not in any case be a making operation, but rather just an erosion of the rough edges. Most breakers prefer to have a horse for a few weeks in the spring of its third year, when it is strong enough to undertake light work, but not powerful enough to put up too much of a fight. Battles may thus be avoided, rather than precipitated.

When to sell

It is always possible that when the foal has been bred and weaned, or even after it has been run on for a couple of years, you may decide to part with it. The horse may have an ungenerous temperament, or is unlikely to grow as tall, or stay as small, as you had hoped. Perhaps it has some conformational fault which you perhaps particularly dislike.

Young horses do not grow in even stages. A good foal, for instance, may go off as a yearling but be a brilliant two year old. On the other hand, a good yearling might become a plain two year old and then develop into a star long before its fourth birthday. However, it is a mistake to keep horses in the hope that they will improve, unless you have unlimited grass to keep them on, or a farm to provide plentiful supplies of corn free of charge. If you possess neither, it is impossible to keep colts without spending a great deal of money. There are also bound to be occasions when the vet must be called, and this is by no means cheap. For instance, if the foal is a male, he will have to be gelded as a yearling.

One way of avoiding disappointment is not to breed from your old mare that has become lame and incapable of work. Unsound stock produces youngsters with a tendency to unsoundness themselves, usually through bad conformation. Buy the soundest mare you can afford, send her to the most suitable stallion, and see, if possible, the stock that either have produced. A really bad horse is likely to be slaughtered when young as being too unsound to work. It is therefore vital that all breeding should be selective – there is no point in producing horses fit only for slaughter.

Remember, too, to decide what the horse will actually be used for well in advance of making the decision to breed. Sending a small mare to a small stallion, for instance, will inevitably produce a small foal.

BREAKING AND SCHOOLING

Since man domesticated the horse, its life style has adapted to meet its change in circumstances. Yet the natural instincts of its ancestors still remain firmly embedded in the horse's mind and character, from the most scientifically bred Thoroughbred to the humblest of ponies.

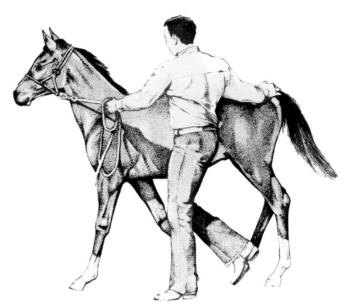

The first, and perhaps the most important, thing to remember is that the horse is an outdoor animal, and, in the wild, lived its life as part of a single community, the herd. In the herd, leadership came from the head horse, the stallion within the group with the most dominant and positive personality. The horse now looks to man for decisions and protection in the same way as once it did to the head horse, and a good trainer must understand and accept these responsibilities as an important part of his task. For instance, a horse with a strong personality should be treated with tact and firmness, while a nervous or less intelligent horse requires sympathy and patience.

Toughness is also a legacy from the horse's past, but so, too, are sensitivity and timidity. So another general principle to bear in mind when handling horses is not to surprise them with any sudden movement or noise. A frightened horse will often take weeks or even months to get over the experience. If a horse is frightened, then the handler must be calm and soothe it with a quiet voice. Do not make an issue of anything that may go wrong, for horses are very perceptive to the emotions of those around them. Such treatment will only confuse the horse; this is something that neither horses nor ponies like and it can often upset them so much that they become uncontrollable.

Thus, the mental approach of the trainer is the basic factor influencing the progress of the training programme. Bad horses are not born – they are made.

Observation is the key in establishing the right mental attitude. By watching the horse at liberty, at rest, feeding, by studying how the animal moves and how it reacts to situations around it, the trainer can determine and analyse just how the horse thinks and what he or she is going to do with it during the teaching process.

Handling – the first step

The training programme starts with handling the foal; early handling is just as important as backing and schooling, if not more so. But it must be remembered that, to give the horse time to mature physically, there should be a two to three year interval between early handling and concentrated training. In other words, we may be discussing the handling of a yearling, though it may not actually be backed until its third year.

A trainer should spend the early days with the foal just going out to it in the field, patting it, talking to it, feeling it, picking up its legs, and slipping a head collar on and off. The foal can also get used to being led; this should be established as part of the daily routine of bringing the foal in at night.

Through these processes, the foal becomes familiar

When lunging, the person (red) stands in one spot, and the horse moves in a circle (blue) around him. The person uses body language, voice, lunge line (yellow), and lunge whip (green) to direct the horse.

You can attach your lunge line to the horse's headcollar, to his bridle, or you can use headgear specifically designed for lunging, called a lunging cavesson.

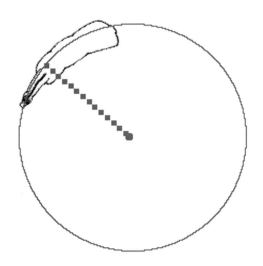

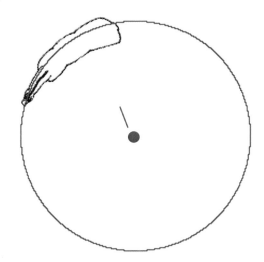

Visualize an imaginary line leading from the horse's shoulder to the centre of the circle. That's the dividing line. When you keep your body behind the line, that's 'behind'. Moving forwards will slow, then stop, then reverse the horse. It depends how far forwards you move and how quickly. You can also affect his movement by using your voice, of course; if he is trotting and you only want him to slow to a walk, then tell him 'waaaaaaalk' and move slightly forwards. If he is cantering and you want him to stop, tell him 'whoa' and step out 'in front' of his head.

with its trainer through physical contact, smell and mental 'feel'. The horse is gradually convinced that it has nothing to fear and comes to realize that the trainer will ask certain tasks of it which it will be able to comprehend and perform without harm to itself. Once the foal is used to being handled and led, the first foundation in its relationship with man has been laid. Next the trainer starts to get the youngster to obey some basic signals. This can be done by teaching it a few basic manners – to give its feet up so that they can be cleaned out, for example. Eventually, the horse will learn to give up each foot from just a touch of the hand.

Then, the horse is taught to move across the box. First, the trainer holds the horse's head still and then, by pointing with a short riding cane or stick, encourages the horse to move its hindquarters over to the left or right. The horse soon learns to move over in its box from the voice alone.

Thus, dressage, of a simple sort, has been started. In this, the whip or stick plays an important part, though it is only an aid to the trainer in communicating with the horse. It is a means of making commands and signals obvious and simple, not a means of punishment or of enforcing the trainer's own will upon the creature. The young horse should have complete confidence in the whip; it must not be afraid of it.

Leading in hand

Serious work with a young colt or filly starts with teaching it to be led in hand. This is the phase of training where many young horses can be spoilt for life. The basic aim of all training must be to encourage the horse to move willingly and quietly through all its paces, without loss of energy and balance, while carrying a rider. The handler should be level with the animal's shoulders and, above all, should not restrict its free forward movement.

The process can start quite early – even before the foal is weaned. Real control from the lead-rope, however, can be left to this later stage. The simplest exercise involved is teaching the young animal to come to the halt. This can be done in the stable yard, say, by walking the horse around, and every now and then standing still, while giving the command 'stand'. The trainer restricts the forward movement by standing still himself, but not by pulling backwards on the lead.

At first, the young horse will stop with the forehand, though the hindquarters may continue to move, describing a quarter circle. But the animal will quickly realize that this is a waste of energy; after a few lessons, it will teach itself to come completely to the halt, provided that the head has not been pulled about in the initial process.

These early lessons should only last about ten to fifteen minutes a day. Discipline between trainer and horse has now been established, but the essential key remains co-operation; the animal puts up no physical resistance and the trainer avoids the use of force, which is totally counter productive.

Lungeing

Lungeing starts when the trainer is certain that the horse is physically fit enough to undergo a more extensive work programme. Boots, bandages and knee pads should be worn. The lunge cavesson now takes the place of the head collar, with the lunge rein fitted to the central 'D' ring. A helper, lightly holding the cavesson, walks the horse around in a circle at the end of the lunge rein, with the trainer standing in the centre forming a triangle between him or herself, the lunge rein, the lunge whip and the horse. The same routine of stopping and starting is followed as that already established in the yard. But now, when the trainer asks the horse to walk on, the signal is given with the lunge whip and the voice – the most important aid in lungeing.

Gradually, the helper moves away from the horse towards the trainer at the centre of the circle. Success is achieved when the youngster walks willingly around the trainer at the end of the lunge rein. Lunge work can

Above *A mouthing bit*

then start at the trot. The horse now realizes that the control is coming from one central point and is receptive to the commands being given.

The breaking roller

The first purpose of the roller is to familiarize the youngster with the feel of a girth; later, it is necessary for the fitting of side reins. A breast plate should be used to keep the roller in place at first as otherwise it will be much too tight. The plate can be dispensed with when the roller can be tightened without the horse bucking. One of the ways of helping both trainer and horse is to place a stable rubber under the roller and to attach some pieces of cloth to the side-rings of the roller (two rubbers do the job well). These will help the horse to begin to understand the feeling of the saddle and the rider that will follow later. If the horse has been handled confidently and quietly, it will not object to this. If it does seem nervous, put the cavesson on, then the roller with the rubbers, and turn the horse loose in the school. The shrewd trainer who wants to produce really good horses will use every opportunity to let the horse learn for itself.

Mouthing

The secret of making a good mouth is to encourage the horse to accept the bit as a 'natural' part of its mouth. This takes time and patience. To accept the bit, the horse must learn to swallow and produce its normal saliva with it in his mouth. A wet mouth, within reason, is a sign of a sensitive mouth, and a dry mouth a sign of an insensitive one.

Mouthing is accomplished by leaving the mouthing bit in the youngster's mouth for short periods each day. The trainer should watch for any sign of objection; at the slightest sign of this, the bit should be removed, and the process repeated the following day. The same routine is followed until the horse accepts the bit completely. Take care, however, not to encourage the development of vices, such as putting the tongue over the bit. During this process, the horse should be worked on the lunge with a bridle fitted under the lunge cavesson and the lunge rein still attached to the centre 'D' ring.

Introducing the saddle

The saddle can now be substituted for the roller. This should ideally be done in an enclosed space. Having removed the stirrup leathers and irons, let the horse have a look at it first, say, after a lungeing session. A helper stands at the horse's head while the trainer lifts the saddle up and down just above the horse's back until the animal stands quite still and calm, showing no fear of the saddle at all. Then the trainer gently places the saddle over the back.

Once the saddle is in place, the horse should be thoroughly petted. The next day, the process is repeated and the girth secured. Once the horse has worked on the lunge quietly with the saddle, the leathers and irons can be put back on it. Work should now continue with these pulled down.

Long reins and side reins

Before backing, there is one final stage of training to accomplish – the introduction and use of the reins. There are two methods – long reining and side reining – but the former should be left to real experts. The use of side reins should be combined with that of a dropped noseband. With the horse in a simple snaffle bridle and drop noseband, the lunge cavesson goes over the top again and the lunge rein is once more attached to the centre 'D' ring. The side reins are then hooked to the rings of the bridle and buckled by a loop through the girth straps.

Allow the horse to relax thoroughly and just saunter around on the lunge at a slow walk. Eventually, it will 'reach' to make contact with the bit itself, and the process can then be repeated at the trot. The trainer should be able to tell when the time is right to start shortening the side reins until they finally reach a length corresponding to that which a rider would use on the horse. The art here, as in the entire programme, is to get the horse to learn from experience.

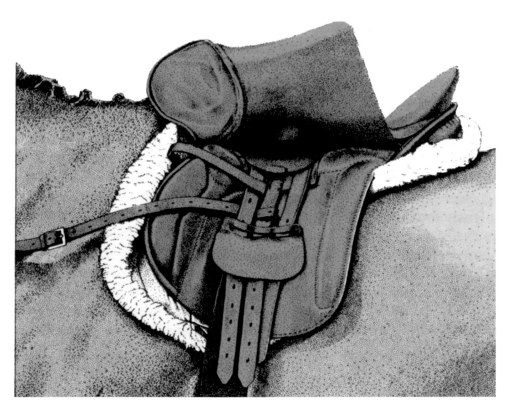

Left How side reins are attached to the saddle for lungeing

Backing

There are many different schools of thought on backing, but the essential part is to remember that, as in the introduction of the saddle, the rider must be introduced in stages. For this, two competent helpers are required; the trainer's job is to hold the horse's head to keep the horse calm and for safety, while one helper actually mounts the horse.

First, the helper stands next to the youngster and reaches up and touches the saddle. Then he or she is given a leg-up so that their body is simply resting over the saddle, and, finally, completes the task by putting the leg across the horse and sitting down in the saddle. Once there, the helper should sit quite still, with the feet out of the irons, holding a neck strap or the saddle's pommel for security. All the time both trainer and helper should be talking to the horse, and petting it when backing has been successfully completed.

Schooling under saddle

The prime aims of the trainer should now be to produce (1) a horse that goes forward freely with a balanced rhythm; (2) a horse with a steady head-carriage; (3) a horse that is balanced in all gaits; (4) a horse that moves 'straight'; (5) a horse that is supple and confident of its physical ability; and (6) a horse that willingly obeys the rider's aids. Once again, it must be remembered that these processes take time. Horses learn through routine, repetition and reward.

Moving forward freely

The first step in showing the horse that it must learn to await the rider's instructions is to teach it to stand still when being mounted. The trainer can achieve this by getting a helper to stand by the horse's head while he gets on and off several times. The horse will soon realize that it must stand still and await the command to move forward. It is worth doing this from both sides of the horse, as this will encourage the animal to remain calm and help it to keep its balance under the weight of the rider.

The horse is now ready to learn the first leg aid to walk on. The trainer asks the horse to walk forward with the leg aid, backing this up with a light touch of a dressage whip on the hindquarters, if necessary. As soon as the horse understands the signal, the whip can be dispensed with. The same process is repeated for the trot, but the canter should not be attempted until the horse is ready for training in balance and collection. Changes of direction should be quite simple at this stage, with, again, no collection being asked of the horse but only free forward activity. The aim is to educate the animal to the squeeze of the rein and to get it to bend its body in the direction it is travelling. At first this can be done at the walk by simply raising and squeezing the 'asking' rein, closing the inside leg to the girth, and positioning the outside leg slightly behind it, to get the horse to move out of one corner of the school and walk across to the one diagonally opposite for another change of direction.

Checking the pace

To teach the horse to check its pace, the animal should be walked in a straight line. About a third of the way along this, the trainer closes the hands to resist the forward movement, and, with the voice, encourages the animal to check its walk. Then, after a couple of yards, he or she opens the fingers, closes the legs to the girth, and encourages the horse to walk forwards again in an active rhythm. At first, the horse may resist, but, if the trainer shows patience and understanding, it will soon realize what is wanted and begin to enjoy it.

Once the horse has understood the signals at the walk, the same exercise is repeated at the trot. It will not be long before the youngster has an active, forward movement.

The head, balance and collection

The chief reason for teaching a horse to carry its head correctly is the additional weight and movement of the rider on its back. Running free, a horse will alter the position of its head and neck according to the pace or direction in which it is moving. With a rider, however, a new balance has to be learned.

There are two dangers which must be avoided during this stage of training. The first is that the horse's head must not be allowed to go up; a high head-carriage will force the horse to hollow its back, affecting balance and decreasing the activity and length of stride of the hindlegs. In addition, once the horse gets into this habit it will realize that control from the bit and the hands can be evaded.

Likewise, the horse's head must not get too low for exactly the same reasons. If this happens, the horse will round its back and be encouraged to stiffen the jaw and set the neck muscles against the pressure of the bit.

Another problem at this stage can involve what are termed the stiff side and the soft side of the horse. Just as people are left handed or right handed, so the vast majority of horses tend to favour one side of their body at the expense of the other. The side that the horse favours is known as the soft side; the hard side is the one on which the horse resists. The trainer must correct this to bring the body back into balance, and to 'straighten' the horse. At the same time, he or she should take advantage of the situation to get the horse to 'give' its jaw.

To find out which side is which, walk the horse on a free rein. Quietly pick up the left rein only and ask the horse to move to the left. If there is immediate response – the horse turning its head, neck and body to the directing rein – the left is the soft side. Confirm this by following the same procedure to the right. The horse should resist, first with its mouth and then with its body.

Once this has been established, the processes of 'straightening' and bringing to full collection can begin. The trainer first puts his other horse into a steady, even trot. Once the horse is relaxed, a firm, but light, contact is taken on the soft side rein. If the horse's soft side is its left, the animal is ridden clockwise around the school – vice versa if the right. The trainer then closes the fingers of the right hand in a squeezing action and slightly raises the right rein hand, so bringing pressure to bear on the right side of the horse's mouth and the corner of the lips. This is a request for the horse to 'give' (relax) its jaw from the hard side, where it would normally resist. The horse's response should be to give its jaw and lower the head; the trainer will feel this through a lighter contact on the right rein hand. The signals are backed up with the leg aids to maintain activity and bring the horse down on to the bit. This exercise should only be carried out for short periods, say, at the beginning of a training session, but repeated over the following days until the horse understands what is required of it. Throughout the process, the aim is to bring the horse into what is termed full collection, with the head carried 'naturally' just behind the perpendicular. Once success has been achieved, the horse can go on to more advanced work, such as circles and transitions.

Work at the canter

Work at the canter is one of the last stages in schooling the horse on the flat. The important thing here is to get the horse to follow the correct sequence of leg movements, so that it remains balanced.

If the horse is cantering to the left, the leading front leg must be the near-fore; to the right, the off-fore. This must be achieved without any loss of impulsion or change in the head carriage. The body must be 'bent', too; if the animal is on the left rein, then the body must curve to the left so that the horse will naturally go into a left-lead canter balance and with what trainers term cadence. The horse must not be allowed to lead from the shoulder; it should bend into its turn all the way from nose to tail.

To establish this, trot down the long side of the school, keeping the horse trotting evenly and relaxed at the jaw. On approaching the corner, ask for the bend to the left, with the left hand closed and left leg close to the girth. Simultaneously, sit down in the saddle, close both legs to the horse's flanks, with the right leg slightly behind the girth, and, with the seat aid, ask the horse to canter. If the horse does not strike off with the correct leg, come back to the trot and start again. The process should be repeated until the horse changes its pace correctly.

Once this has been achieved consistently, the horse

can start working in circles. Finally, comes the advanced stage of changing from one leading leg to the other. The first step in this is to ride in two circles, the first on the left lead. Then slow down to a trot for a few paces, and then ride into the canter again on a right-hand circle, this time with the right lead. The trotting period can be shortened with each session, until, eventually, the horse will change its leg while still in the collected canter.

Further exercises

At this stage, the trainer can start such exercises as the turn on the fore-hand, the shoulder-in and the haunches-in. The first gives the horse practice in obeying the trainer's aids; the other two help to supple its body.

The best method of training the horse to lengthen and shorten its stride, while preserving its balance and energy, involves the use of cavalletti. These are to the horse trainer what wall bars are to the gymnastics coach. Their use also helps to build up body muscle, as well as extending the horse's mental powers and making it calmer under the concentrated control of the rider, preparing it for the stress of jumping.

Two sets of cavalletti should be laid out in the school – one set to short strides (about 1m apart), and the other to long strides (about 2m apart). Start off with the poles in their lowest position and simply walk the horse over them to gain confidence. Then, work at the trot, allowing the horse to teach itself how to shorten and lengthen its stride, but making sure that it maintains energy and collection. Gradually, the cavalletti can be raised; this enables the horse to exercise its muscles and brings its joints to maximum flexion.

Learning to jump

When schooling a horse to jump, the same principles apply as those involved in schooling on the flat – that is, to encourage the horse to perform as naturally as possible while coping with the weight and signals of a rider.

During basic training, the young horse has learned to trot over poles in cavalletti work, so these can now be brought into use in elementary jumping training.

Again, two sets are used; this time, however, the last cavalletti are raised to represent a jump – a vertical jump on one side of the school, and a spread jump on the other. The young horse is started off on the lunge and trotted down the two grids and over the jumps. If possible, this should be done on both reins to give the horse confidence.

The technique is exactly the same with a rider; the trainer rides the horse on a free rein and virtually allows it to teach itself. The more the trainer can encourage this, the better competition jumper the horse is likely to become.

Following this, schooling can take place in the jumping lane and, finally, over practice fences.

The secret of success

Work, perseverance and patience are the secret of successful horse-training. The schooling figures – circles, figures of eight, and so on – are the tools of the trade and not an end in themselves. The aim is to control the horse as sensitively as possible, so that it seems as if it is performing entirely on its own – gracefully and independently, with the minimum of interference from its rider.

Anticipation is the hallmark of the artist in the saddle. In addition, the discipline that a good system of training demands to produce successful results brings a understanding between rider and horse – the partnership which forms the basis of the sport of equitation at all levels.

Here the horse is showing its natural movement in free canter.

BASIC RIDING

The key to learning to ride is basically one of confidence. The rider must have faith in his or her ability to communicate with, control and work with the horse; equally, the horse must have confidence in its rider. The only way to achieve this is to find a good instructor, who has the knack of encouraging his or her pupils to approach their lessons in a calm and relaxed manner. Riding is supposed to be a pleasure, so do not go to a hectoring instructor or trainer, who may turn this wonderful sport into a weekly nightmare.

The search can be a bewildering one, as level, competence and type of instruction often varies. Approval by a recognized riding association is always a sign of quality. In the UK, the British Horse Society (BHS) and the Association of British Riding Schools both publish a list of stables that have been inspected and approved; in the USA, the American Horse Shows Association does the same. In Australia, though there is no national system of assessment as such, the magazine Australian Horse and Rider publishes similar surveys.

The clothes to wear

At first there is no need to spend money on a full riding kit, but certain items are essential for both safety and comfort. A hard riding hat, or, better still, a racing-style crash helmet, is one of them, but make sure that the brand you buy meets national safety requirements. Jodhpur boots, western riding boots, or rubber riding boots (these are far cheaper than leather ones) are also vital. Trainers can slip through the stirrup irons and rubber wellingtons are not really the right shape.

At shows, it is important to be smart with dark jacket, collar and tie, breeches, hat and boots.

- Riding hat
- Shirt and tie
- Show jacket
- String and leather gloves
- Breeches
- Leather boots

Riding clothes must be practical, like this warm jacket, close-fitting trousers, boots and hat.

- Well-fitting riding hat
- Weatherproof jacket
- String or leather gloves
- Well-fitting jeans
- Rubber riding boots

- No hat
- Scarf
- Woollen gloves
- Baggy trousers
- Flapping coat
- High-heeled shoes

Flapping clothing which can distract a horse and get tangled in trees and bushes is not suitable.

Holding the headpiece in the left hand, put the reins over the horse's head and neck first. The horse will then be under control while the headpiece is being fitted. Make sure that no part of the bridle trails on the ground.

Hold the headpiece up in the right hand and cradle the bit on the thumb and forefinger of the left. Then slip the left hand under the horse's muzzle and insert a finger between its front and back teeth on the offside to open the mouth.

Having slipped the bit into the mouth, use both hands to bring the headpiece over its ears, one at a time. Smooth the forelock down over the browband and check that this is clear of the ears. See that no part of the headpiece is twisted.

Then fasten the throatlash and nose band. There should be a hand's width between throatlash and jaw and noseband. See that the bit is not low enough to rest on the teeth, or high enough to wrinkle the horse's lips.

With the horse tied up, smooth the saddle area of the coat before picking up the saddle by its front arch and cantle, and placing it lightly but firmly on the horse's withers. Then slide it back enough to let the horse's shoulders move freely.

Check that all is smooth under the saddle flap, then move to the offside and let down the girth, which has been lying over saddle. Return to the nearside and buckle the girth firmly, so that a hand can just be slipped beneath it. Saddling can be done in one operation.

Handling, mounting and dismounting

At first, the horse should be 'made ready' for you, but it is a good idea to ask if you can bring your mount out of its box and into the yard to get used to being around such a big animal. Greet the horse calmly and move to its shoulder, talking to it as you do so. Then, run your hand down the shoulder and give it a pat. Move to its head, undo the headcollar and lead the horse out of the box.

The next stage is to mount the horse – either unaided, or assisted by a leg-up. Beginners should always have a groom standing at the horse's head to ensure that the animal stands still while being mounted.

Always mount a horse from the near (left) side. Before doing so, check the girth for tightness; if it is too loose, the saddle may slip as the rider's weight comes on to the stirrup. Gather the reins in the left hand, maintaining a light contact with the horse's mouth. Take care not to keep the left rein too short, or the horse may start to circle as you mount.

Place the left hand on the pommel of the saddle and then turn the body so that your back is to the horse's head with the left shoulder parallel with the horse's left shoulder. Take the left stirrup iron with the right hand, turn it clockwise towards you and place the ball of the left foot in the iron, keeping the toe as low as possible. If it digs into the horse's flank, it will act as a signal to the horse to move forwards.

Otherwise clothes can be adapted to purse and needs. A thick, close-fitting pair of jeans (not the 'flared' variety), or a pair of 'chaps', worn cowboy-style over a pair of trousers, can take the place of breeches or jodhpurs at first. These should be worn with a thick sweater or windcheater in winter, or, in hot weather, a tee-shirt or sports shirt. A riding mackintosh is a good investment, as is a pair of string gloves. Wet reins, especially if also slippery with sweat, can be almost impossible to grip.

Place the right hand over the waist of the saddle, and, with the weight of the body on the left foot, spring upwards from the right foot, using the right hand as a lever. Bring the right leg over the saddle and then gently lower yourself into it. Place the right foot in the offside iron and take up the reins with both hands.

To dismount, take both feet out of the irons and collect the reins in one hand. Then, swinging the right leg well over the cantle of the saddle, gently, but briskly, vault off, landing on both feet.

Adjusting the stirrups

Once in the saddle, the next thing to do is tighten the girth again and then adjust the stirrup leathers to the correct length. The initial temptation at the start of a ride is to have the leathers too short. As the ride progresses, and the seat comes properly down into the saddle, it will be necessary to lengthen them.

To establish the correct length, take the feet out of the irons and let them hang down naturally. The iron should just touch the inside point of the ankle bone. Adjust the leathers accordingly, making sure that they are both the same length.

The seat

The seat is the rock on which all good riding is founded; without a correct position in the saddle, no pupil can hope to go on to advanced equitation successfully. A correct seat means that the rider is in balance – secure, light, and responsive to the horse's every movement. It is used in rhythm with the animal's action; the pushing down of the seat bones on the horse's back encourages it to lengthen its stride.

The rider sits into the middle and lowest part of the saddle, the body position being upright and free from stiffness, especially round the waist. The rider is in fact sitting on a triangle, two points being the seat bones and the third the crotch of the body.

The back should be straight, but relaxed and supple, with the shoulders held square. The head should always be held up and looking to the front. Never look down, or the back will become rounded and the chest hollowed.

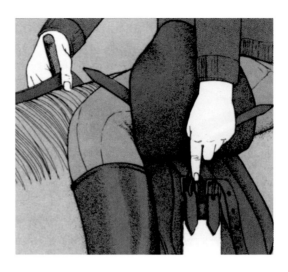

After riding for a few minutes, the girth will usually need a further tightening. There is no need to dismount as this can be done in the saddle. Take the foot from the nearside stirrup iron and move the leg forwards, so that the saddle flap can be lifted and tucked under the thigh, out of the way. Adjust the girth strap in the same way as a stirrup leather, tightening it by a hole or two while keeping a finger on the buckle prong. Then release the flap and replace the foot in the stirrup iron.

As a guide, place a hand behind you flat on the saddle. There should be room for the flat hand between you and the cantle.

The temptation to grip with knees and calves must be avoided. Otherwise the body will be stiffened, the seat raised out of the saddle and the position made rigid. The thighs and legs should wrap around the horse and mould themselves to the correct position. A simple routine to help achieve this is to open the legs away from the horse's flanks and then draw the thighs into position from behind. This will bring the large inside-thigh muscle under and to the back of the thigh, flattening the area and allowing it to rest close to the saddle and the horse. Then, by pushing the weight down on the ankles, the rider will feel the seat lower into the saddle.

The lower leg should hang down to rest lightly against the horse's sides, just behind the girth with the heel pressed down. This is where the rider's weight is balanced. Holding the lower leg too far forward or too far back must be avoided, because it affects the position in the saddle and makes it difficult to apply the leg aids correctly. Only the ball of the foot should rest in the stirrup iron, and both feet should be held parallel with the horse's sides.

When mounting, place the left hand on the saddle pommel and put the ball of the left foot into iron with the right hand, keeping the toe low.

Next place the right hand over the waist of the saddle and, keeping the toe under the horse against the girth, spring smoothly and lightly up.

Bring the right leg over, keeping it well clear of the saddle and the back of the horse. This should be done in one smooth movement.

Dismounting. First take both feet from the stirrup irons, transfer the reins to the left hand and grip pommel with the right hand.

Next, leaning forward lightly swing both legs clear of the horse, keeping weight on the right hand and holding the reins with the left.

Land lightly on both feet, facing the saddle and still keeping control with the reins in gentle contact with the horse's mouth.

If the position is correct, the rider's ears, shoulders, hips and heels should be in line with each other. The stirrup leather should be at right angles to the ground when the rider is mounted.

The arms should hang down naturally to the elbow. The hands, with thumbs uppermost, are held as if carrying two glasses of water. The rider should not get into the habit of bending the wrists inwards or of flattening the hand. A straight line should run from the elbow through the hand to the bit in the horse's mouth.

The best place to work on the correct saddle position is on the lunge rein, where most of the student's early work is usually done in any case. When working on the lunge, the rider should be holding a neckstrap, and not the reins. The horse is being controlled from the lunge; two people trying to direct it, one with the lunge and the other from the bridle, will only confuse the animal.

A strong independent seat can only be achieved by regular active riding, assisted by suppling exercises and riding without stirrups. These are essential for developing balance and confidence.

The aids

The aids are the system of signals used to control the horse. They fall into two categories; first come the natural aids of hands, legs, seat and voice, and second are the artificial aids of whip, spurs, draw reins, drop nosebands, martingales and so on. The only one a beginner should use is a whip.

All riding is based on controlling the natural impulsion of the horse. This is achieved by combined use of the rider's legs and seat. The aim is to get the horse moving freely and actively forward in the desired direction, and not evading the aids when they are applied. The rider can usually tell this through the hands; if the horse is resisting, there will be little 'feel' on the reins when activity is being asked for, and 'pull' if the horse is being checked. The legs are used in a squeezing action just behind the girth. A quick, light squeeze, repeated if necessary, is more effective than prolonged pressure. Use of the heels should be avoided.

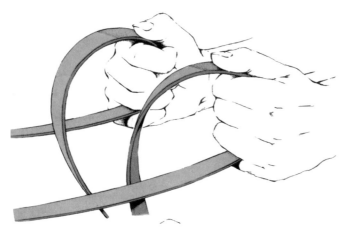

Above Single-rein bridle. The reins are held gently 10cm (4in) apart between the third and little fingers, with the slack held by thumbs.

Above With the double bridle, the reins are separated by the little fingers. The bridoon rein is on the outside.

Left When mounted adjust the stirrups by pulling the top leather up against the buckle under the saddle skirt. Keep a finger on the buckle spike – the leather can then be easily adjusted up or down.

Below left The iron should hang level with the point of the ankle bone.

Below right Secure the top leather through keeper on the saddle.

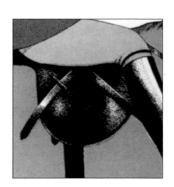

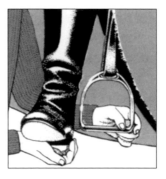

If the horse does not respond to the legs, the whip can be used to reinforce the aid. A tap on the horse's ribs, just behind the rider's leg, is usually adequate. Note that the whip is only an extension of the aid. It should not be used as a punishment except in extreme cases of disobedience.

Use of the hands

The hands control, never create, pace and direction through the use of the reins. Contact with the mouth should therefore be light and steady; pulling on the reins will only hurt and upset the horse. The wrists should be supple and flexible enough to follow the horse's natural rhythm; the aim is to achieve a passive hand, not a rigid one with the wrists set in a fixed position.

It is essential therefore to hold the reins correctly. With a single-rein bridle, the reins should pass between the little finger and the third finger of each hand. The remainder of the reins pass through the finger and thumb, with the thumb on top of the rein to aid the grip. Double bridles, however, can be held in several different ways. One of them is to divide the reins with the little finger of each hand, with the curb (lower) rein crossing inside to pass between the third finger and little finger. Again, the reins pass out through the index finger and thumb, with the remainder crossing over to the left.

The walk

All early work should be done at the walk until the pupil has established the basic confidence required to move on to the other paces. Take up contact with the mouth and apply the aids to make the horse walk on. Keep the hands relaxed when the walk has been established, however, or the horse may be tempted to go into a trot.

Right *A good seat is the basis for proper riding. The aim should be perfect balance and control. The rider's seat bones are pressed well down into the lowest part of the saddle and the calves are held closely to the horse's sides.*

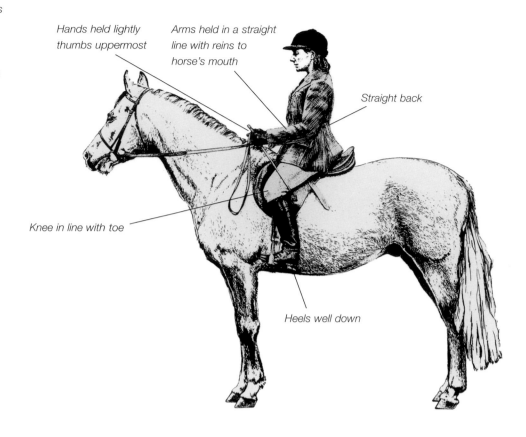

Hands held lightly thumbs uppermost

Arms held in a straight line with reins to horse's mouth

Straight back

Knee in line with toe

Heels well down

Right *The natural aids are the movements which communicate the rider's intentions to the horse. The body, legs and hands work together in complete harmony. If the horse is positioned and prepared correctly it can obey the rider's instructions more easily.*

The back muscles affect the seat. They make it more secure and enable the rider to maintain balance. Straightening the spine, combined with corresponding leg and hand actions conveys the rider's intentions to the horse.

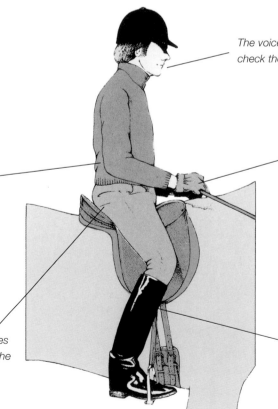

The voice can be used to soothe or check the horse.

The hands should be light and responsive, being used in a give-and-take action. They regulate the energy created by the calves, and control the forehand.

Pressure from the seat encourages the horse to move forward from the hindquarters. A firm, deep seat enables the rider to use the legs correctly.

The calves control impulsion and energy in the hindquarters and guide their direction.

Above Exercises strengthen the muscles and improve the rider's seat. They help the inexperienced rider gain confidence. The rider leans forward and down over the horse's neck to touch the left toe with the right hand. Then the rider sits upright and repeats the process on the other side.

Above With arms outstretched outwards, head up and back straight the rider turns as far as possible in each direction, twisting the body from the hips. This improves the suppleness of the back and waist. This exercise can be practised at the halt or when the horse is moving at a walk.

Any unwanted increase in pace should be checked by closing the hands to resist the forward movement, closing the legs to the sides and pushing down in the saddle with the seat bones. In response, the horse checks its pace. After a few strides, the rider should give with the hands, increase the pressure of the leg and seat aids and ask the horse to walk on again.

To ask for the halt, the rider applies both leg and seat pressure at the same time as lightly resisting the forward movement with the hands. The horse should stand still on all fours when it comes to the halt.

Changes of direction should also be learned and practised at the walk. The inside leg and hand ask for these, while the outside hand and leg control the pace. To go to the right, ask with the right hand, keeping the left one passive. Both legs should be closed to the horse to maintain the walk, but apply the left leg more strongly to prevent the swing of the quarters. To turn to the left, reverse the procedure.

The rider should make a conscious effort to think right or left. This concentration can act as a reinforcement to the physical aids being applied.

Above With arms folded, the rider leans back to rest on the horse's quarters, then sits upright again. The legs should remain in the correct riding position during the exercise. Do not attempt this, or any other, exercise on an inexperienced horse which may be frightened by the movements involved.

Right These diagrams show exercises involved in basic riding training. The rider can use the full area of the arena and combine work in circles and straight lines. By making frequent turns and changes of direction, with upward and downward transitions of pace, the rider learns to give clear, accurate aids. The exercises supple the horse and accustom it to bending on both sides.

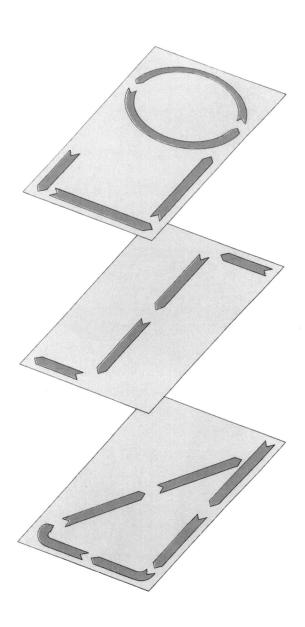

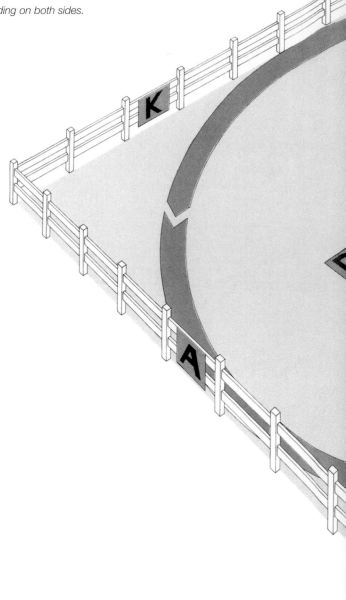

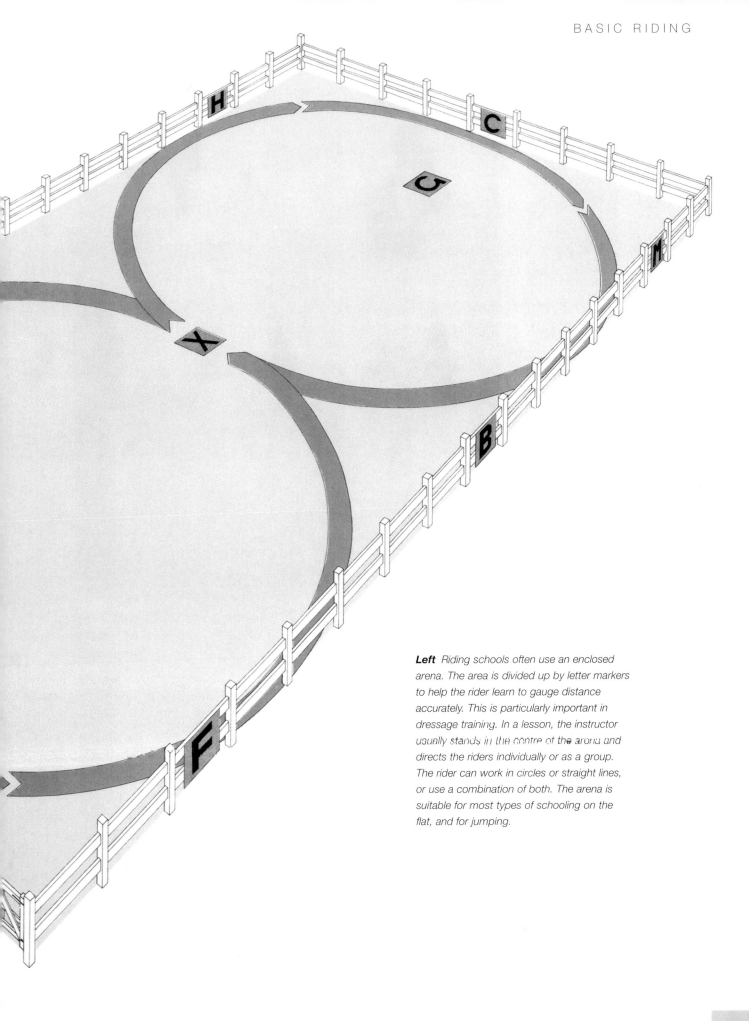

Left Riding schools often use an enclosed arena. The area is divided up by letter markers to help the rider learn to gauge distance accurately. This is particularly important in dressage training. In a lesson, the instructor usually stands in the centre of the arena and directs the riders individually or as a group. The rider can work in circles or straight lines, or use a combination of both. The arena is suitable for most types of schooling on the flat, and for jumping.

171

Right *To rise to the trot the rider leans slightly forward and eases the seat from the saddle to go with the movement of the horse.*

Far right *The sitting trot is used particularly during schooling. The rider does not rise to the trot but sits deeply, absorbing the bumps with the small of the back.*

Below right *Three common faults in the trot. In the first diagram, the rider is exaggerating the rise; this stiffens the position and leads to loss of balance. Rising with a hollowed back throws the shoulders forward and the seat back. A slouched back is equally bad, the spine should be straight.*

The trot

This is a two-time gait, in which the horse moves its legs in a diagonal sequence of near-fore, off-hind, off-fore and near-hind. Near-fore and off-hind make up what is known as the left diagonal; off-fore and near-hind the right. The rider can either sit in the saddle and follow the natural rhythm of the trot, or rise (post) slightly out of the saddle for one beat of the gait.

To achieve the transition from walk to trot, sit down in the saddle, close the legs and feel the inside rein. As the horse gets into its trot, sit into it for a few strides, using the legs to maintain the activity.

In the rising trot, the rider rises out of the saddle on one beat of one diagonal and descends on the other, with the weight of the body supported by the ankles, heels and stirrup irons, but not by the knees. These must act purely as a hinge. Rise from the hip, keeping the lower leg still. The thigh and body should remain at the same angle. Keep the horse moving forward and a light and even contact with the animal's mouth.

The seat should never be allowed to come completely out of the saddle and the reins should never be used as a lever when rising. In addition, always regularly change from one diagonal to the other. Like human beings, horses tend to favour one side of their body over the other, and this means that it is very easy to always remain on, say, the left diagonal during a prolonged period at the trot. This is bad for the horse as well as for the rider. To change diagonals, simply sit down in the saddle for two beats, and then start rising again on the other diagonal, using the leg to give added impulsion if there is resistance.

Diagonals should always be changed with each change of direction. For example, if trotting to the right on the left diagonal and then changing the rein to the left, the rider should shift his or her weight to the right diagonal. This keeps the horse level, balanced and gives it a 'breather'. In long-distance riding, or hacking, the diagonal at the trot should be changed regularly.

To return to the walk, sit well down in the saddle, close the hands firmly and apply the leg aids until the horse walks forward freely. Give with the hands but keep applying the leg aids until the momentum of the walk is firmly established.

Above In the trot the horse moves on alternate diagonal pairs of legs. Here the off-fore and rear hind legs move together, followed by the near-fore and off-hind.

Right On a bend to the right the rider rises as the outside foreleg and inside hind are coming to the ground, and sits as the other diagonal pair moves. The rider should change the diagonal with every change of the rein, by sitting for an extra beat, The diagonal can be checked by glancing down at the forward movement of the horse's shoulder.

The canter

The canter is a three-time gait, with one beat coming from each of the forelegs and the third from the hindlegs. The rider relaxes with this rhythm, keeping a steady, even contact with the mouth. Sit deeply into the saddle, allowing the back to follow the movement from the hips, and avoid the temptation to be tipped forward. Over excitement – and kicking hard with the heels – will only lead the horse to increase the speed of its trot.

The horse should always lead off into the canter with the correct leg. The sequence always begins with a hind – off-hind if going to the left and near-hind to the right. The near-fore and off-fore are the two leading front legs respectively. A horse that starts to canter with the wrong lead is said to be cantering 'false'.

Above and below When making the transition from the trot to a canter, the rider should ensure that the horse leads on the correct leg. This will give a balanced and flowing movement. The rider should sit deeply into the saddle and feel the rein in the direction the horse should lead. The rider squeezes with both legs. The outside leg presses behind the girth – this instructs the horse that its outside hind leg should be first to leave the ground as it changes to the canter. The inside leg is placed on the girth to maintain impulsion.

The rider should sit still and follow the natural movement of the canter with the back and hips. The position should be relaxed, but not loose in the saddle. The pace of the canter should always be steady and controlled.

Right *To reduce pace from a gallop to a walk, the rider should slow gradually, sitting upright and moving against the horse's forward impulsion with the seat and back, resisting and easing on the reins and closing both legs.*

It is easier to establish the correct lead if the aids for the canter are applied on a bend, when the horse's body should be bent in the direction it is going. Thus, it usually balances itself naturally to take up the canter on the desired leg. The best way to establish a good canter, therefore, is to work in a large circle. The horse should maintain an active, rhythmic trot, flexed slightly in the direction it is turning. Then, if going to the left, sit down in the saddle, feel the left rein, close the legs, the right leg controlling the quarters and the inside leg on the girth, and ask the horse to strike off into the canter. If the horse continues to trot, apply the aids again, reinforcing with a light tap of the whip on the inside if necessary.

The gallop

The gallop – the horse's fastest pace – is, like the walk, one of its most natural gaits. It should always be controlled and it is advisable to shorten the stirrups slightly to allow for the special riding position the pace requires.

At the gallop, the rider brings the seat out of the saddle, keeping a straight line between hand and elbow. The upper part of the body comes slightly forward, flexing from the hip, not collapsing the back, with the weight supported by the thighs and ankles. The knee and calf should remain close to the saddle. The faster the pace, the more forward the upper part of the body should lean, as the horse's centre of gravity also moves forward. Keep as still as possible to help the

horse maintain its balance. Give with the hands to allow the horse a comfortable length of rein, but always keep contact with the mouth.

For a change of direction, the rider lowers the seat into the saddle, steadies the pace slightly, and asks, as in the other paces, for the turn. If the horse refuses to check its pace, the best course of action is to sit upright and turn the horse in a circle. Above all, never pull – the horse will only pull back.

Jumping

Riding over jumps is just as much a matter of confidence as the basic process of learning to ride. All elementary jumping techniques should therefore be learned and practised at the trot, before increasing the pace to a controlled canter. With full confidence and control, jumping comes easily; the basic rule is to aid the horse as much as possible and not to hinder it. When jumping, the stirrups should be slightly shortened.

There are many exercises which can be practised by novice jumpers to help them to learn to jump correctly. For the first lessons, the rider should use a neck strap; this lessens the risk of a nervous pupil pulling on the reins and so jabbing the horse in the mouth with the bit. Jumping without stirrups is also an excellent way of improving balance and developing muscles.

The first step to practise is the approach. Sit well down in the saddle, keeping a very close contact with the horse with thighs, knees and calves, and use the

Above The rider should aim at the centre of the fence and keep the horse travelling in a straight line, controlling with the reins and driving with the legs and seat to create power in the hindquarters.

seat and legs to build up impulsion. Support the weight of the body by thighs and ankles – not by the hands – and bring the upper part of the body forward so that it is just off the perpendicular. Never look down, always ahead, and ride for the middle of the obstacle, keeping a light even contact on the reins. The rider must allow the horse freedom of the head and neck.

As the horse starts to leave the ground, bring the hands well down on either side of the neck to allow it to lower and stretch, while bending the body forward from the hip upwards over the centre of gravity. The weight of the body comes slightly out of the saddle. Keep the thighs as close to the horse as possible and the lower leg and feet in the same position as for riding on the flat, making sure that they do not go back in the air.

Once in the air, the rider should give the horse the maximum freedom to complete its jump. Follow the horse's mouth with the hands, but maintain contact. Bring the body well forward from the hip and down close to the horse. As the horse starts to come down to land, begin the return to the normal riding position to balance the animal.

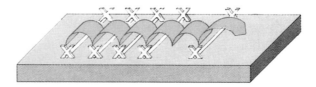

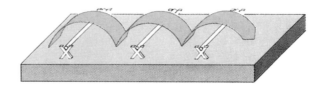

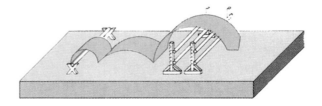

Above Schooling over cavalletti strengthens the seat and helps the horse develop a balanced rhythm. The spacing can vary according to the exercise.

One useful exercise to help achieve a good position is to work with cavalletti in the school. The idea is not to present the rider with real fences, but to simulate them, so that he or she can concentrate on position in the saddle and learn to regulate the horse's stride and direction. The cavalletti can be arranged as a box in the centre of the school, or down one side of it.

Trot around the school in the sitting-jumping position – this means sitting in the same way as for riding on the flat, but with the upper part of the body bent slightly forward. From any corner of the school, turn to approach the box, coming up into the poised jumping position as you do so. This means that the rider raises the seat out of the saddle, taking the weight on thighs, ankles and heels, without using the reins for support. Then, looking directly ahead, ask the horse to trot

through the box. On reaching the other side, return to the original position and trot on around the school on the opposite rein to the one first used.

This exercise enables the rider to practise various angles of approach. It also enables the pupil to control the pace of his or her mount while concentrating on developing the right position in the saddle.

Another, more advanced, exercise with cavalletti helps improve rhythm and timing. Cavalletti are placed at various intervals down one side of the school, one set being combined to create a spread element. The rider soon learns to use the leg and seat aids to lengthen and shorten the horse's stride as necessary.

Through the use of such jumping exercises, a good basic technique can be developed. This is essential before going on to more advanced forms of jumping.

Right As it approaches the jump the horse lowers its head and neck, to balance its take-off The rider should keep the seat in light contact with the saddle.

On take-off the horse shortens its neck, raises its head and lifts the forehand. It springs up and forward off its hocks, head and neck stretched out. The rider should adopt the jumping position shown.

In suspension over the jump the horse's neck and head are stretching forward and down, the hind legs gathered under the belly. The rider should go naturally with the horse.

The horse lands on its forefeet, then the hind legs follow. The head comes up and the neck shortens. The rider must avoid being left behind and jerking the horse's mouth.

BASIC CARE

Looking after and caring for a horse or pony is perhaps the greatest responsibility any rider faces. Having learned to ride, many riders aim at eventually having a horse of their own. It is worth remembering, though, that looking after a horse unaided – especially if it is stabled – can be a full-time occupation. One answer is to board the horse out at livery, which can be very expensive. Another is to get someone to help out during the day. Most of the other factors involved, such as feeding, watering, exercising and grooming, are mainly matters of common sense, combined with willingness to ask for and take expert advice whenever necessary.

Horses can either be stabled, kept at grass or the two systems can be combined. This means that the horse can run free during the day and have the shelter of a stable by night – except in hot weather, when the procedure should be reversed. Which system is adopted is a matter of choice, practicality, and the type of horse concerned. Ponies, for example, are usually sturdier and more resilient to extremes of climate than horses, particularly thoroughbreds and part-breds. Some thoroughbreds, for instance, should not be left out over the winter. Nor can a horse being worked hard in, say, competitions be really kept fit enough except by being cared for in a stable. At the very least, it must be fed extra food in the field. The amount of extra feeding required should be worked out using the same guidelines as those for a stabled horse. In the case of

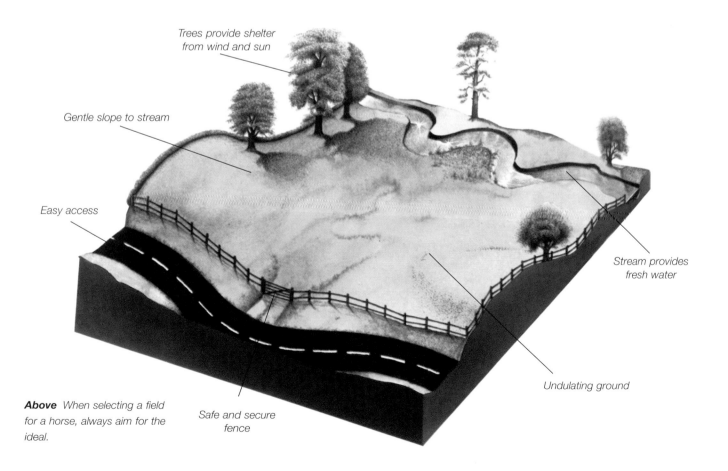

Trees provide shelter from wind and sun

Gentle slope to stream

Easy access

Stream provides fresh water

Undulating ground

Above *When selecting a field for a horse, always aim for the ideal.*

Safe and secure fence

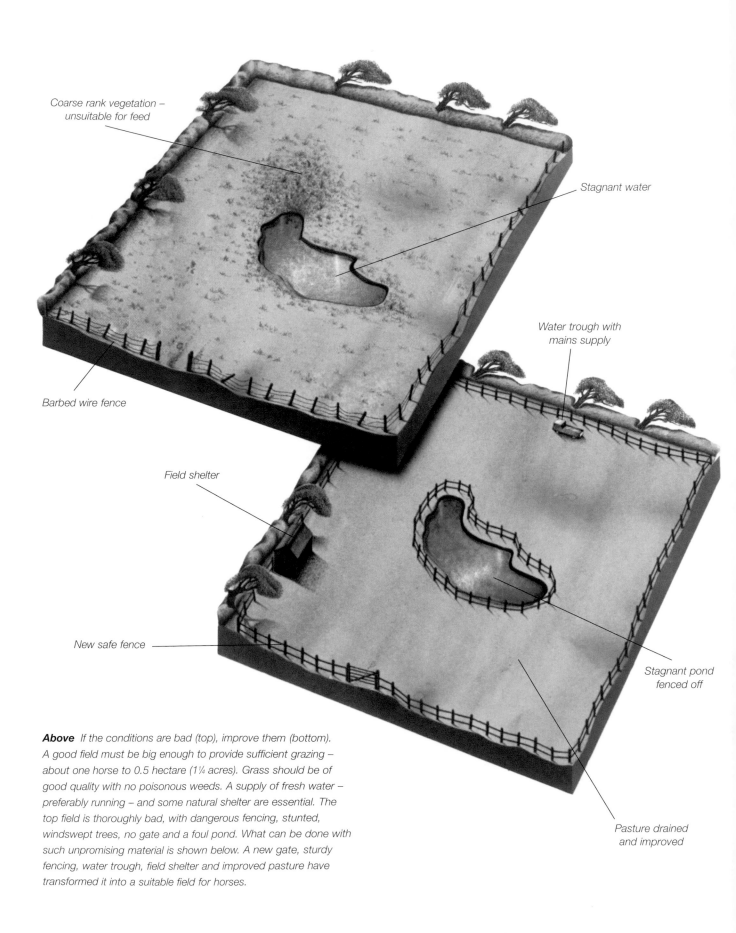

Coarse rank vegetation –
unsuitable for feed

Stagnant water

Barbed wire fence

Water trough with
mains supply

Field shelter

New safe fence

Stagnant pond
fenced off

Pasture drained
and improved

Above If the conditions are bad (top), improve them (bottom).
A good field must be big enough to provide sufficient grazing –
about one horse to 0.5 hectare (1¼ acres). Grass should be of
good quality with no poisonous weeds. A supply of fresh water –
preferably running – and some natural shelter are essential. The
top field is thoroughly bad, with dangerous fencing, stunted,
windswept trees, no gate and a foul pond. What can be done with
such unpromising material is shown below. A new gate, sturdy
fencing, water trough, field shelter and improved pasture have
transformed it into a suitable field for horses.

a field-kept animal, however, the total amount involved should be divided into three, rather than into four.

The combined system can also be adapted to suit the needs of a rider who is using his or her horse frequently, but cannot spare the time to keep it fully stabled. If the horse is being worked regularly in the spring or summer, say, it is a good idea to bring it into the stable first thing in the morning for the first extra feed that will be required. If the horse is to be ridden more than once that day, the same routine is followed as for the stabled horse until the afternoon, when the animal can be turned out for the night. If only one ride is possible, it can be turned out after the second feed, or, if it cannot be exercised at all, it can be turned out after the first.

Keeping a horse at grass

Looking after a horse kept at grass is less time-consuming than looking after one kept in a stable. Among the pluses are the natural vitamins and the exercise the horse gets, but equal responsibility is still demanded from the owner. Statistics show that more accidents happen to horses left unattended in a field than those in a stable. They can kick each other, get tangled up in fences or gates and quickly lose condition through either illness or just plain bad weather. Also, a horse should be visited every day, even if it is not being ridden. Horses are gregarious creatures – ideally, a horse should be kept in company with others – and require affection. Neglect will only make them difficult, if not impossible, to catch.

The ideal field is large – between 6 and 8 acres. It should be undulating, well-drained, securely fenced by a high-grown hedge reinforced by post-and-rail fencing, with a clump of trees at one end and a gravel-bedded stream to provide fresh water. But this situation is often hard to achieve. It is usually considered that about 1 to 1½ acres per pony is adequate, provided that the grass is kept in good condition. Because horses are 'selective grazers' – that is, they pick and choose where and what they eat – a paddock can become 'horse sick'. Some places will be almost bare of grass, while others will be overgrown with the rank, coarse grasses the horses have found unpalatable. In addition, the ground will almost certainly be infested with parasites, the eggs of which horses pass in their dung. If action is not taken, the horses are sure to become infected with worms. These fall into two categories, of which roundworms are by far the most important and potentially destructive. Of these, the most dangerous are red worms (*Strongyles*), which, untreated, can lead to severe loss of condition. Even though the horse is well-fed, it looks thin and 'poor', with a staring coat; in the worst cases, anaemia may develop or indigestion, colic and enteritis.

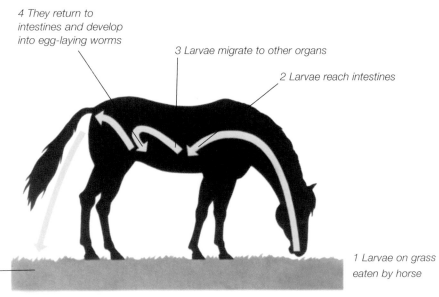

Right The life cycle of the redworm, or large Strongyle. The eggs are dropped in the dung of infected horses. Larvae hatch when conditions are warm and moist to be absorbed during grazing. Inside the horse they reach the gut. Piercing the gut wall, they migrate through the internal organs and blood vessels, returning to the gut to mature and lay eggs, which are passed out in the dung to repeat the cycle.

4 They return to intestines and develop into egg-laying worms

3 Larvae migrate to other organs

2 Larvae reach intestines

5 Eggs passed out, in droppings onto pasture

1 Larvae on grass eaten by horse

Below Pastures vary according to area, but good grazing should include some of these grasses and weeds. Perennial Rye Grass, Timothy and Cocksfoot are the most nutritious and are readily sought out. Sainfoin, Dandelion and Ribgrass are weeds with valuable mineral content. As horses are selective feeders and tend to overgraze, the various sections of the paddock need resting in turn through spring and summer to allow fresh growth. Grazing cattle or sheep on pasture ensures even grazing and will reduce worm infestation.

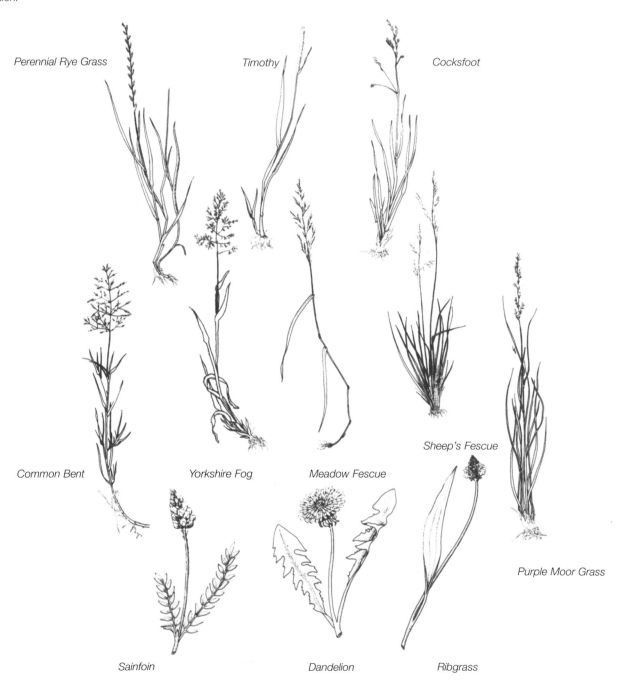

Perennial Rye Grass

Timothy

Cocksfoot

Common Bent

Yorkshire Fog

Meadow Fescue

Sheep's Fescue

Purple Moor Grass

Sainfoin

Dandelion

Ribgrass

As far as an infected horse is concerned, the treatment is regular worming, but it is far better to tackle the problem at source by making sure that the field is maintained properly. A large field should be subdivided so that one area can be rested while another is being grazed. Ideally, sheep or cattle should be introduced on the resting areas, as they will eat the tall grasses the horses have rejected. They will also help reduce worm infestation, as their digestive juices kill horse worms. Harrowing is also essential as it aerates the soil, encouraging new grass to grow, and also scatters the harmful dung. Failing this, the manure must be collected at least twice a week and transferred to a compost heap.

Mowing after grazing, coupled with the use of a balanced fertilizer, also helps keep a field in good condition, but horses should not be returned to their grazing too soon after it has been so treated. If in doubt, allow three weeks.

Bots are another problem for field-kept horses, for which veterinary treatment is necessary.

Below Self-filling trough with automatic valve in enclosed section and (left) trough with inlet pipe close-fitted and tap recessed beneath. Both are of safe design with no sharp edges or projections. Site a trough on well-drained ground to avoid churned mud and away from the falling leaves of trees. Troughs should be emptied and cleaned regularly. If ice forms in the winter it should be broken daily.

Food, water and shelter

All grassland is composed of a mixture of grasses and other plants. Some have little nutritional value, though the horse may well like them, but the three most important are Perennial Rye Grass (*Lolium perennae*), Cocksfoot (*Dactylis glomerata*) and Timothy (*Phleum pratense*). Some White Clover (*Trifolium repens*) is useful, but beware of a heavily-clovered pasture. This may prove too rich and lead to digestive problems. Even if clover is not present, grass itself can cause problems. This is especially the case in the spring when excessive greed can lead a horse to put on too much weight, and sometimes to the painful disease called laminitis, or founder. Also, a horse or pony can only exist on grass alone for the summer months – from about the end of April to the beginning of September. By October, supplementary feeding becomes essential. Start off with hay and then provide oats or beans, if required. The more refined the breed, the more extra feeding that will be necessary.

Water is another essential; field-kept horses must have easy access to a plentiful supply of fresh water. Remember that a horse drinks about 35 litres (8 gal) a day. If the water supply is in the form of a stream, check that it can be reached by means of a gentle slope; if the banks are steep or muddy, it is safer to fence the stream off and provide a water trough instead. Similarly, always fence off stagnant pools and ponds.

The most convenient form of trough is one connected to a mains water supply, controlled by either a tap or automatic valve. Custom-made troughs are on the market, but cheaper alternatives are an old domestic cistern or bath. Remember to remove all sharp projections, such as taps, and to give the inside a thorough cleaning before putting into use. If there is no piped water supply, use a hose or fill the trough with buckets. Buckets alone are totally insufficient. A horse can easily drink a whole bucket of water at one go, and, in any

Left *A shelter is an essential addition to any field – even one with trees and hedges – as horses need one to escape from wind and cold in winter. In summer it provides shade, coolness and protection from insects. In cold or wet weather, hay can be conveniently fed in a rack or hay-net within the shelter.*

Below *Suitable types of fencing. From the left: post and rail, post and wire, rail and wire combined and dry stone wall. Check the tautness of wire fences regularly and inspect walls for damage after frosts.*

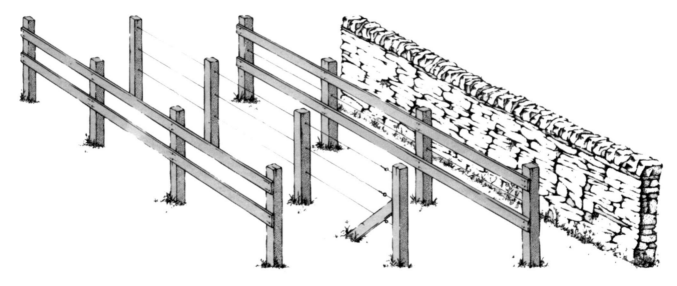

case, a bucket can all too easily be kicked over. Daily checks of the water supply are vital, especially in winter, when ice may form and must be broken. A child's rubber ball left floating on the surface of a trough will help to keep the water ice-free, except when frosts are severe, when the ice must be broken daily. Winter and summer also bring the problem of shelter. From a horse's point of view, the worst elements are wind, rain and sun. Even if the field possesses a natural windbreak, an artificial shelter is a good addition. It need not be complicated – a three-sided shed the size of a large loose box is usually adequate. Make sure that the open side does not face the sun.

Fencing and gates

Sound and strong fencing is essential for safety. A fence must be high enough to prevent horses from jumping over it – 1.3m (3ft 9in) is the absolute minimum. Bars must also be fitted; two rails are usually adequate for containing horses, with the bottom one about 4.5cm (18in) from the ground. Small ponies, however, can wriggle through incredibly small gaps, so a third or even a fourth rail should be added for them. This type of fencing is known as post-and-rail, or 'Man 0' War'.

Of all the types of fencing available, timber is the safest but most expensive. Hedges run a close second, but should be regularly checked, as otherwise a determined pony might well push his way through. Gaps can be reinforced with timber, but avoid filling a gap with wire. Concealed by a hedge in summer, it could be hard for a horse to see and so could lead to accidental injury. Stone walls are also attractive, but they, too, will need regular checking, especially after a hard winter when frost may have loosened the mortar.

However, wire is perfectly adequate as fencing on its own, as long as the correct type of wire is used. Avoid barbed wire, chicken mesh or sheep wire and use a plain heavy gauge galvanized wire instead. For safety and effectiveness, the strands must be stretched so that they are evenly taut and then stapled to the inside of the posts. Strong stretcher posts should be positioned at regular intervals. Check regularly for signs of weakness, such as loose posts, broken wires or sprung staples. If each strand of wire ends in an eyebolt attached to the end posts, the wire can be tightened from time to time.

Left Four typical gates. The first two, the hang gate and slip rails are the simplest to fit and the cheapest. They are lifted away, not swung open. The other two are a traditional wooden five-barred field gate and a modern half-mesh metal gate. Metal gates can be galvanized or painted. Wooden ones are painted or treated with a wood preservative.

Gates are another safety factor. The only criterion is that they should be easy for people to open and close, but that it should be impossible for the horse to do so. A five-barred farm gate, hung just clear of the ground so that it swings freely when unlatched, is ideal. It should be fitted either with a self-closing latch, or with a simple chain fitted with a snap lock and fastened to the latching post. Slip rails and hang gates are cheaper alternatives.

*Right Gate fastenings must be impossible for horses to open, but simple for human beings. Here are three secure kinds. **Top** A simple catch with a lug held in a notch. **Centre** A catch with a release mechanism. **Below** A spring catch with a bar held forward against a retaining hook.*

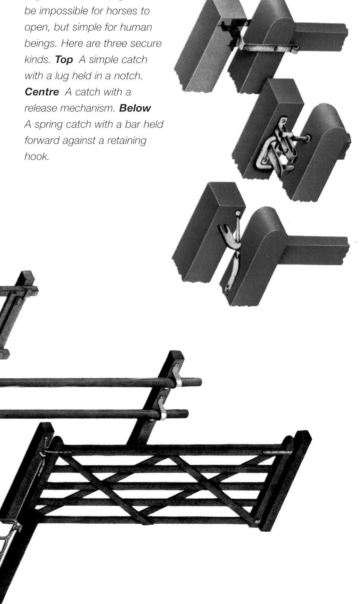

Yew

Privet

Tutu

Castor oil plant

False acacia

Horsetail

Deadly
nightshade

Ragwort

Hemlock

Ngaio

Purple
milk-vetch

Avocado

Rangiora

Yellow
star-thistle

Oleander

Buckthorn

St. John's wort

Many trees, shrubs and plants are poisonous to horses. Above are some commonly found in various parts of the world. Great care should be taken to check the pasture and to eradicate any that may appear in fields where horses are kept.

Some plants remain poisonous even when the plant itself dies. Sprayed and uprooted plants should not be left to wither in the field, but should be removed and burned. Many plants are just as poisonous after drying and long storage.

Hay and bedding should, therefore, be examined and any harmful plants removed. Horses will eat a toxic plant, like ragwort, when it is fed to them dried in hay, although they will not touch it growing in the field because of its bitter taste, which, however, disappears with drying.

Fortunately, horses are not attracted to some of the most toxic plants. They will only eat deadly nightshade, for example, if virtually starving. However, some equally poisonous ones, like yew and privet do get eaten occasionally.

Garden hedges and their clippings can also be a source of poisoning. Make sure that a horse does not snatch at them while out riding. Poisonous, exotic plants, less easy to identify than familiar native ones, may grow in gardens and parks too.

Poison can be quickly fatal, or it may take as long as a month to work. Symptoms include loss of condition, lack of appetite, jaundice, staggering and nervous spasms. The horse may have a normal temperature throughout the period.

'Turning out', exercise and grooming

Before a pony or horse is turned out into a field, always check it carefully. Inspect the gate and fencing, strengthening any weak points. Make certain that there are no poisonous plants either in the field or within reach of the fence. See that there is an adequate supply of water, and check that there are no man-made hazards, such as broken bottles, tin cans and plastic bags lying about, which could injure the horse; a pony can die if it swallows a plastic bag, for example. Have any rabbit holes filled in to avoid the risk of a cantering horse catching its feet in one, falling, and perhaps breaking a leg.

When you are satisfied with the state of the field, turn the horse out. If it is not to be ridden for some time, say over the winter, have the shoes removed. This will lessen the danger of injury in the event of any kicking contest with other horses kept in the field.

Before exercising, always check the horse for cuts, bruises and other injuries. This procedure should also be carried out during the daily visits. Pick out the feet, noting the condition of the shoes. Also check the teeth regularly. Left unattended, they can develop rough edges, which make eating difficult. If this happens, they will need to be filed.

Remember, too, that the horse will be in what is known as 'grass condition'. Its soft muscles and its extra layers of fat will make it incapable of any prolonged period of hard work, without sweating heavily and exhibiting other signs of distress. Forcing a horse to do so will only damage wind and limbs. If, as at the start of the school holidays, say, the horse is being ridden frequently for the first time in some months, it is a good idea to start a supplementary feeding programme a few weeks before, as grass is not a high-energy food. In any case, exercise should always be gradual, slowly building up from walking to a full exercise programme.

After exercise, the horse may well be sweaty, particularly if the animal has a long, shaggy coat. It is best to turn it out immediately and not to wait until the sweat has completely dried, or there is the danger of colds or, in extreme cases, colic. Conversely, in winter remember that the grease in a horse's coat helps to keep it warm, so restrict after-exercise grooming to remove any mud. A clipped horse should always wear a New Zealand rug in the field in the winter.

Groom with a dandy brush, taking care to get rid of all dried and caked mud and any sweat marks. Groom the mane and tail with a body brush and, finally, sponge out eyes, nostrils and dock.

The stabled horse

There are two main reasons for keeping a horse in a stable. The first is that the horse may be too well-bred to live out in all weathers, without seriously losing condition. The second is the amount of work the rider requires the horse to do. If a horse is being ridden a great deal, it must be fit enough to cope with its rider's demands without showing signs of distress, such as excessive sweating and blowing. Such a degree of fitness takes time to achieve and can only be maintained in a stable.

The ideal stable is also often easier to provide than the ideal field. It should be roomy, warm, well-ventilated yet draught-free, easy to keep clean, have good drainage and be vermin proof. It should face away from prevailing winds and have a pleasant outlook – preferably on to a stable yard or at least an area where something is often going on. The horse could be spending some 22 hours a day in the stable and unless there is something to hold its attention, it may well become bored. This can lead, in turn, to the development of vices, such as weaving (rocking from side to side), box walking (a constant restless wandering around the box), or crib-biting (gripping the manger or stable door with the teeth and drawing in a sharp breath). The first two vices may lead to loss of condition, the third to broken wind.

Buying, renting or building

Any stable, whether it is bought, rented, converted or specially built, must conform to certain basic standards. If a stable is being converted, say, from a garage or barn, or being built from scratch, make sure that these standards are followed.

Right Inside and outside views of two loose boxes planned with the comfort of the horse and ease of maintenance as the first considerations. An ideal loose box should be strongly built of good quality materials to keep it warm and draught-free, but still light and airy. It should be large enough to allow a horse freedom of movement – say 3.5m x 3.5m (12ft x 12ft) for a 14.3 to 16.2hh horse. Non-slip flooring is essential for safety and self-filling drinking bowls cut down on labour and spillage. The half-door should face something interesting to prevent boredom.

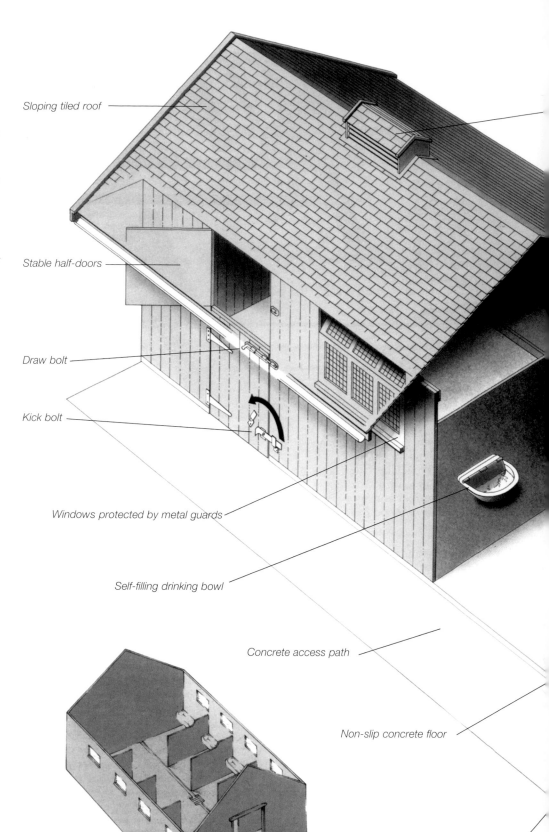

Sloping tiled roof

Stable half-doors

Draw bolt

Kick bolt

Windows protected by metal guards

Self-filling drinking bowl

Concrete access path

Non-slip concrete floor

PVC gutters and drainage pipes

Right Traditional stalls take up less room than loose boxes and are, therefore, cheaper to keep and quicker to clean. They are often used in riding schools where many ponies are kept. A stall must be wide enough to let a horse lie down comfortably.

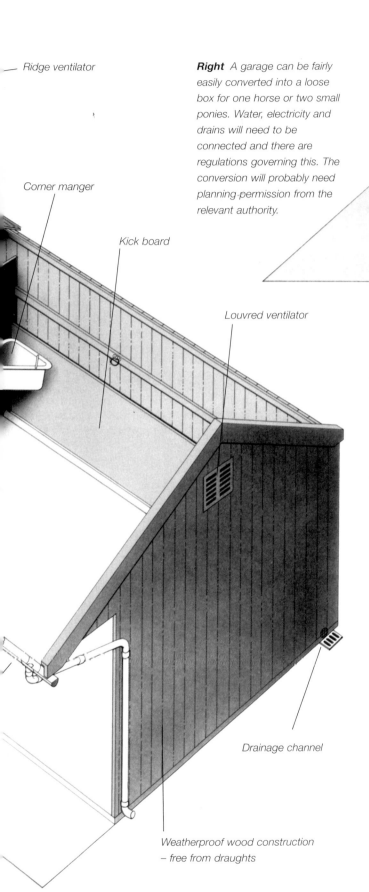

Ridge ventilator

Corner manger

Kick board

Louvred ventilator

Right A garage can be fairly easily converted into a loose box for one horse or two small ponies. Water, electricity and drains will need to be connected and there are regulations governing this. The conversion will probably need planning permission from the relevant authority.

Drainage channel

Weatherproof wood construction – free from draughts

In the latter case, either an architect can design a stable to your individual specifications or one can be bought ready-made. This type of stable is usually delivered in sections and erected on a pre-prepared concrete base. But, before committing yourself, always check your plans out with the local authority concerned. They may well have to grant planning permission, and will certainly have regulations governing such crucial health factors as drainage.

The choice of site is very important. As far as possible, it should be level and well-drained, with easy access to the electricity and water supplies. The stable itself should be situated with the doorway facing the sun and the general lay-out should be planned to have all the essential elements – stable, feed room, tack room and manure heap – conveniently close together.

The stable can either be a straight stall or a loose box; the latter is much more commonly used today, particularly in the UK and USA. The chief advantage of a stall is that it can be relatively small, so making cleaning easier. But, as it is open at one end, the horse has to be kept tied up. The usual method is known as the rope and ball system, where the halter rope is passed through a ring on the manger and attached to a hardwood ball resting on the horse's bed. This helps to safeguard the horse against possible injury, while still allowing it some freedom of movement.

Above *The 'rope and ball' method is a safe way of securing a pony in a stall. The headrope passes through a metal ring and a heavy wooden ball is attached to the free end. The rope must be long enough to let the horse lie down comfortably.*

Most horse owners prefer the loose box, as it allows the horse far more freedom to move around and so more comfort. Size is here all-important; cramming a l6hh hunter into a loose box built for a Shetland pony can only lead to trouble. As a rough guide, 3.5m (12ft) square is probably the optimum size, rising to 4m (13ft) for horses over 16hh. It is worth bearing in mind that a child's first pony, say, will be outgrown in time, so the bigger the box the better.

Boxes should be square rather than oblong, so that the horse can more easily determine the amount of room it has to lie down or to roll. The box must be big enough to minimize the risk of the horse being 'cast' – that is rolling over and being trapped on its back by the legs striking the wall. If it struggles to get up, the horse may injure itself severely. The ceiling height should allow plenty of clearance for the horse's head; 3m (10ft) is the bare minimum.

Brick and stone are both durable and attractive building materials, but breeze blocks, solid concrete blocks or timber may be cheaper. Both walls and roof should be insulated, which will keep the stable warmer when the weather is cold and cooler when it is hot.

The floor must be hard-wearing, non-absorbent and slip-proof. A well compacted concrete base is perfectly adequate, provided that it is made with a loam-free aggregate and treated with a proprietary non-slip coating after laying. Alternatively, roughen the surface with a scraper before the concrete sets. Make sure that the floor slopes slightly – a slope of about 1 in 60 from front to rear is ideal – so that urine can drain away easily. An alternative is to cut a narrow gulley along one inside wall leading to a channel in the wall and so to an outside drain. The channel should be fitted with a trap to stop rats getting in and cleared of dirt and debris daily.

The usual type of stable door is made in two halves, the top half being kept open for ventilation. This should be planned to ensure that the horse gets plenty of fresh air but no draughts, as these can lead to it catching colds and chills. The best position for a window is high on the wall opposite the door so that sufficient cross-ventilation can be provided. Make sure it is fitted with shatter-proof glass, and covered with an iron grill. Otherwise, vents can be built in the roof to allow stale air to escape. They should be protected by cowls.

Doors must be wide and high enough for a horse to pass through without the risk of injury; 1.5m (4ft) is the minimum width, 2.25m (7½ft) the minimum height. Make sure that the door opens outwards so that access is easy and that strong bolts are fitted to both halves of the door. On the lower door, two bolts are necessary – an ordinary sliding bolt at the top and a kick bolt, operated by the foot, at the bottom. The top half needs only one bolt. Remember that the material used must be strong enough to withstand the kicking of a restless horse. Inside the stable, kicking boards, usually cut from hardwood and some 1.8m (5ft) high, will help with this problem.

Electricity is the only adequate means of lighting. The light itself should be protected by safety glass or an iron grill and all wiring should be housed in galvanized conduits beyond the horse's reach. Switches must be waterproof, properly insulated, and, whenever possible, fitted outside the stable.

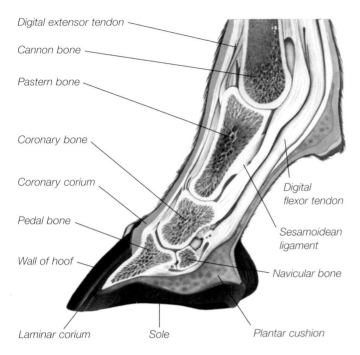

Digital extensor tendon

Cannon bone

Pastern bone

Coronary bone

Coronary corium

Pedal bone

Wall of hoof

Laminar corium   Sole

Digital flexor tendon

Sesamoidean ligament

Navicular bone

Plantar cushion

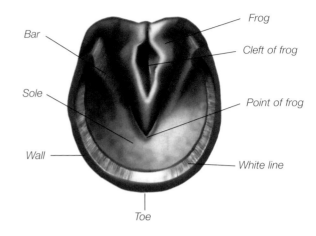

Bar

Sole

Wall

Toe

Frog

Cleft of frog

Point of frog

White line

Left A section down the mid-line of a horse's foot, showing the outer layer of shock-absorbing horn and the sensitive internal structure it protects. Nourished by secretions of the laminar corium, a hoof constantly replaces worn-away horn. **Right** Sole of an unshod hoof. The concave shape gives grip and the wedge of the frog is grooved for extra purchase.

Shoeing the horse

Any horse being ridden regularly on a hard surface, such as a road, must be shod, or the wall of the hoof will be worn down quicker than it can grow. This will cause friction, soreness and lameness. Hardy ponies, working lightly and solely on grass, can do without shoes, but their hooves should still be looked at regularly by a blacksmith.

Inspections should take place at regular four to six week intervals. The signs that a horse needs to be reshod are a loose shoe; one that has been 'cast' (lost); a shoe wearing thin; one in which the clenches (securing nails) have risen and stand out from the wall; and if the foot is overlong and out of shape.

Horses can be either hot-shod or cold-shod. In hot-shoeing, the red hot shoe is shaped to the exact size of the hoof. In the latter, the shoes are pre-cast and fitted cold. Whichever method is used by the blacksmith, always check the following points after shoeing has been completed.

Make sure that the shoe has been made to fit the foot – not vice versa. Check that the shoe is suitable for the work you want the horse to do, and that the weight

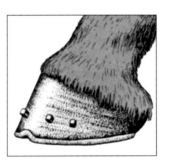

Re-shoeing is needed when the clenches have risen through the hoof wall.

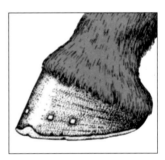

Here the shoe has worn extremely thin and should be replaced.

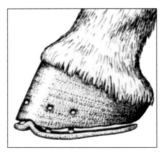

This shoe is loose and likely to be cast. The hoof must be re-shod.

A newly-shod hoof showing well-positioned clenches and a close-fitting shoe.

of the shoes is in the right proportion to the horse's size. As a rough guide, a set of shoes for a horse should usually weigh around 2kg (4½lb). Look at the heel and toe of the foot to make sure that its length has been reduced evenly. See that the foot is in contact with the ground. Check that the right size and number of nails have been used and the clenches are correctly formed, in line and the right distance up the wall. Finally, make sure the clip fits securely and that there is no gap showing between the newly-fitted shoe and the hoof.

Fixtures and fittings

The basic rule to follow is the fewer fittings the better, to minimize the risk of possible injury. The only essential is a means of tying the horse up. Normally, this consists of two rings, fixed to bolts which pass right through the stable wall. One ring should be at waist height and the other at head height. All other fittings and fixtures are a matter of individual preference.

Fixed mangers positioned at breast level and secured either along a wall or in a corner of the loose box are found in many stables. They should be fitted with lift-out bowls to facilitate cleaning and have well-rounded corners. The space beneath should be boxed in to prevent the horse from injuring itself on the manger's rim – this space makes a good storage place for a grooming kit. However, a container on the floor, which is heavy enough not to be knocked over and which can be removed as soon as the horse has finished its feed, is adequate.

Fitted hay racks are found in some stables, but they are not really advisable. They force the horse to eat with its head held unnaturally high and hayseeds may fall into its eyes. The best way of feeding hay is to use a haynet. It is also the least wasteful, as haynets permit accurate weighing. The net should always be hung well clear of the ground and be fastened with a quick-release knot to one of the tying-up rings.

Water is as essential to the horse in the stable as for a horse in the field. Automatic watering bowls are one way of providing a constant supply – but never position them too close to the haynet and manger, or they may get blocked by surplus food. Buckets are satisfactory, provided, again, that the bucket is heavy enough not to be accidentally upset. Use of a bucket means that it is possible to control the amount of water the horse drinks – important after exercise, for instance, when a 'heated' horse must not drink too much – and also to check how much it is drinking more easily. This is especially useful in cases of suspected illness.

Stable routine

The daily programme for looking after a stabled horse takes up a great deal of time. All the stages have to be carried out, though some, such as the number of feeds, will vary from case to case. Skimping will only lead to problems later.

1. Tie up the horse and check over for injuries which may have occurred during the night. Replenish its water, if necessary, and fill the haynet. Muck out the stable. Quarter the horse thoroughly. Pick out feet with a hoof pick. Lay the day bed.
2. First feed.
3. Allow the horse time to digest – at least 1¼ hours – and then saddle up and exercise. On returning to the stable, refill water bucket and remove droppings.
4. Tie up and groom thoroughly. Put on day rug (blanket) if used. Check water again and refill the haynet. Give the second feed.
5. Pick out feet again and remove droppings. Shake up bedding, replace the day rug (blanket) with a night rug, and replenish water.
6. Third feed. Clean tack.
7. Remove droppings, and lay the night-bed. Replenish the water and re-fill the haynet. Final feed. Put on a night rug (blanket), if worn.

The only way of short-circuiting this routine is to adopt the combined system of care. This has considerable advantages in time and labour, but is not suited to all horses, especially those being worked hard. Otherwise, board or livery is the only alternative. Some riding schools offer what is termed half-livery; this means that the horse gets free board in exchange for use as a hack. The risk is that the horse may be roughly treated by inexperienced riders even in a supervised lesson. Full livery is extremely expensive; in the UK it can cost as much as £30 a week. In either case, always check that the stable you choose is officially approved by a recognized riding authority.

The principal areas of a horse-owner's day, however, are not as complex as they seem. They can be broken down into various tasks, all of which are relatively simple to carry out.

Bedding down and mucking out

The purpose of bedding is to give the horse something comfortable to lie on, insulate the box, absorb moisture and prevent the horse's legs jarring on the hard stable floor. It must be kept clean – hence the daily task of mucking out. This is usually done first thing in the morning, and, with practice, can be carried out quite quickly.

Straw is the best possible bedding material, though other kinds can be substituted. Wheat straw is excellent, because it is absorbent and lasts well. Barley straw may contain awns, which can irritate the horse's skin. Oat straw should be avoided, because horses tend to eat it and it tends to become saturated.

Of the substitutes, peat makes a soft, well-insulated bed; it is also the least inflammable of all bedding materials. However, it is heavy to work. Damp patches and droppings must be removed at once, replacing with fresh peat when necessary. The whole bed requires forking over and raking every day, as the material can cause foot problems if it becomes damp and compacted.

Wood shavings and sawdust are usually cheap but can be difficult to get rid of. Both need to be checked carefully to see that they do not contain nails, screws, paint, oil or other foreign matter. Wood shavings can be used alone, but note that, like peat, they can cause foot problems if they become damp and compacted. Sawdust is best used in combination with other materials.

Mucking out is the first job done each morning in the stable. Soiled straw and dung are separated from the cleaner portions of the night bedding by tossing with a fork. The cleaner straw is then heaped at the back of the stall to be used again.

The soiled straw and droppings are put into a barrow for removal to the manure heap. In fine weather much of the night bedding can be carried outside to air in the sun. This will freshen it up, restore its springiness and make it last longer.

When the bulk of soiled straw has been removed and the cleaner straw reserved, the floor should be swept clean of remaining dirt. It should be left bare to dry off and air for a while. The clean straw is then spread as a soft floor-covering for the day.

The soiled straw and dung are tossed on the manure heap. Take care to throw the muck right on to the top of the heap, as a neatly built heap decomposes more efficiently. beat the heap down with a shovel after each load to keep it firm and dense.

There are two types of bed – the day bed and the night bed. The first is a thin layer of bedding laid on the floor for use during the day; the second is thicker and more comfortable for use at night. With materials such as peat or wood shavings, laying the bed is very simple. Just empty the contents of the sack on the floor and rake them level, building up the material slightly higher around the walls to minimize draughts.

Laying a straw bed requires slightly more skill. As the straw will be compacted in the bale, it has to be shaken up so that the stalks separate, and laid so that the finished bed is aerated, springy and free from lumps. A pitchfork is best for the purpose.

Some owners prefer the deep litter method of bedding, where fresh straw is added to the existing bed every day, removing only droppings and sodden straw beforehand. After a time, the bed becomes as much as two feet deep, well-compacted below and soft and resilient on the surface. At the end of a month, the whole bed is removed and re-started. This method should be used only in loose boxes with first-rate drainage. In addition, the feet must be picked out regularly, as otherwise there is a major risk of disease.

Feeding and fodder

Heredity has given the horse a very small stomach for its size and the food it eats takes up to 48 hours to pass through the digestive system. This system is in itself complex. It depends not only on the right amounts of food at the correct time for smoothness of operation, but also on an adequate supply of water and plenty of exercise. In the wild, horses drink twice a day, usually at dawn and dusk. In between, their day is divided into periods of grazing, rest and exercise. Field-kept horses can duplicate this pattern to some extent, but stabled horses cannot do so.

It is essential to follow a basic set of feeding rules. Otherwise the horse's sensitive digestion may well be upset, encouraging the risks of indigestion, impaction, formation of gas in the stomach or sudden colic attacks.

Laying a night bed of straw requires some skill. First clean straw saved from the day bed is tossed and shaken well with a pitchfork before being spread evenly over the floor as a foundation.

Next new straw is taken from the compressed bale and shaken well to free the stalks and make the bed springy. The floor must be thickly and evenly covered to encourage the horse to lie down.

Last the straw is banked up higher and more thickly around the sides of the box. This cuts down draughts, keeps the horse warmer and gives the animal extra protection from injury during the night.

1. *Tongue*
2. *Soft palate*
3. *Gullet*
4. *Stomach*
5. *Small intestine*
6. *Caecum (concealed behind large colon in small diagram)*
7. *Large colon*
8. *Small colon*
9. *Rectum*

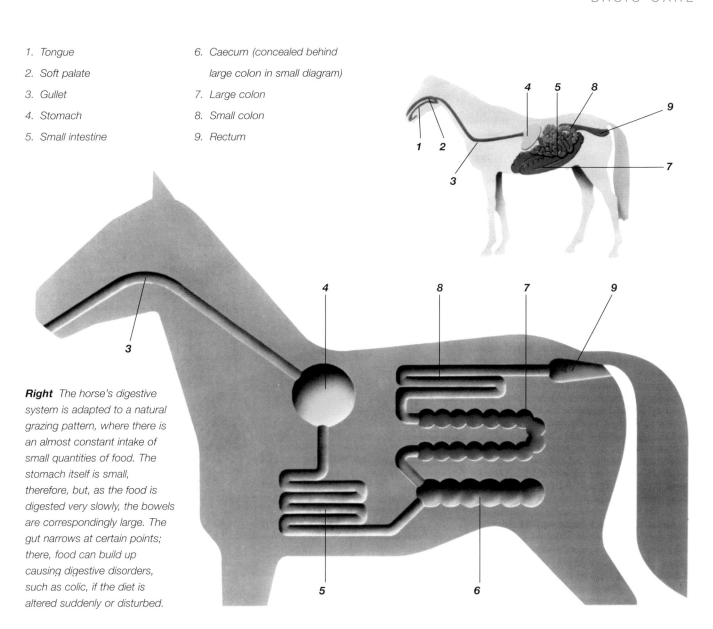

Right *The horse's digestive system is adapted to a natural grazing pattern, where there is an almost constant intake of small quantities of food. The stomach itself is small, therefore, but, as the food is digested very slowly, the bowels are correspondingly large. The gut narrows at certain points; there, food can build up causing digestive disorders, such as colic, if the diet is altered suddenly or disturbed.*

The basic rules are to feed little and often, with plenty of bulk food – grass or hay – and according to the work you expect the horse to do. Make no sudden change in the type of food, or in the routine of feeding, once the diet and time has been established. Always water the horse before feeding, so that undigested food is not washed out of the stomach. Never work a horse hard straight after feeding or if its stomach is full of grass. Let it digest for 1¼ hours or so, otherwise the full stomach will impair breathing. Similarly, never feed a horse immediately after hard work, when it will be 'heated'.

The staple diet of the horse is grass, or, in the case of a stabled horse, hay. The best type is seed hay, usually a mixture of rye grass and clover, which is specially grown as part of a crop-rotation programme. Meadow grass, also commonly used, comes from permanent pasture and so can vary in quality. The best way of judging this is by appearance, smell and age. Hay should smell sweet, be slightly greenish in colour and at least six months old. Blackened, mouldy or wet hay should never be used as fodder.

Of the other types of hay, clover is too rich to be fed to a horse on its own, and the same rule applies to alfalfa, or lucerne, common in the USA and Canada. Alfalfa is extremely rich in protein, so feed small quantities until you can judge how much is needed.

Concentrates for work

Ponies and horses in regular, hard work need additional food to keep them in a fit, hard-muscled condition. In other words, they need energy rather than fatness. This is provided by the feeding of concentrated foodstuffs, usually known as 'short' or 'hard' feeds. Of these, the best is oats, which can be bruised, crushed or rolled to aid digestion. Manufactured horse cubes or pellets are a useful alternative.

Oats have no equal as a natural high protein, energy-giving food and are an essential part of the diet for all horses in work. Good quality oats are plump and short, and pale gold, silver grey or dark chocolate in colour. They should have a hard, dry feel and no sour smell. Take care, however, not to feed too much, or a horse may speedily become unmanageable. This caution applies particularly to children's ponies, which are often better off without oats at all.

Cubes and pellets are manufactured from various grains and also usually contain some grass meal, sweetners such as molasses or treacle, extra vitamins and minerals. Their nutritional value is about two-thirds that of oats, but they are less heating and so ideal for ponies. Their chief advantage is that they

Below *Proper feeding with the correct balance of vitamins is essential for health. The diagram shows how particular vitamins work throughout the system and what effects they have. Any deficiency of these vitamins, A, B1, B2, B6, D and E, in the horse's diet, will lead inevitably to debility and general loss of condition.*

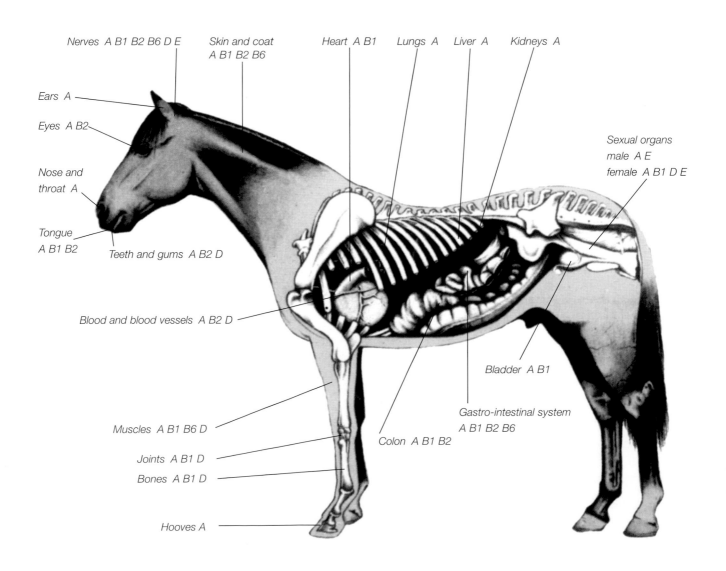

Nerves A B1 B2 B6 D E

Skin and coat
A B1 B2 B6

Heart A B1

Lungs A

Liver A

Kidneys A

Ears A

Eyes A B2

Nose and
throat A

Tongue
A B1 B2

Teeth and gums A B2 D

Sexual organs
male A E
female A B1 D E

Blood and blood vessels A B2 D

Bladder A B1

Muscles A B1 B6 D

Colon A B1 B2

Gastro-intestinal system
A B1 B2 B6

Joints A B1 D

Bones A B1 D

Hooves A

provide a balanced diet on their own, as they do not have to be mixed with other food-stuffs. However, they are expensive.

Other grains can be used in addition or as alternatives to oats, but they are all of lesser quality. Flaked maize (corn) is used in many parts of the world as a staple feed. It is high in energy value, but low in protein and mineral content. Like oats, it can be heating for ponies and is usually fed to animals in slow, regular work, such as riding school hacks. Boiled barley helps to fatten up a horse or pony in poor condition and is a useful addition to the diet of a stale or overworked horse. Beans, too, are nutritious, but, again, because of their heating effect, they should be fed sparingly, either whole, split or boiled.

Other useful foods

Bran makes a useful addition to a horse's diet, as it helps provide roughage. It is either fed dry mixed up with oats – the combined mixture should be slightly dampened – or in the form of a mash. This is a good 'pick me up' for a tired or sick horse. The mash is made by mixing ⅔ of a bucket of bran with ⅓ of boiling water and is fed to the horse as soon as it is cool enough to eat. Always remove any remains, as the mash can quickly go rancid.

Oatmeal gruel is an alternative. This is made by pouring boiling water on to porridge oats and leaving to cool. Use enough water to make the gruel thin enough in consistency for the horse to drink. Linseed, prepared as a jelly, mash or tea, is fed to horses in winter to improve condition and to give gloss to the coat. It must be soaked then well cooked to kill the poisonous enzyme present in the raw plant. Let the mix cool before giving it to the horse. Dried sugar beet is another good conditioner, because of its high energy content. Most horses like it because of its sweetness. It must be always soaked in water overnight before it is added to a feed. If fed dry, the beet is likely to cause severe colic, as it swells dramatically when wet.

Roots, such as carrots, turnips and swedes, again help condition and are also of particular value to delicate or fussy feeders. Always wash the roots first and then slice them into finger-shaped pieces. Small round slices may cause a pony to choke.

Molasses or black treacle can be mixed with food to encourage a finicky feeder. In any case, all feeds ideally should contain about 0.45kg (1lb) of chaff – chopped hay. Chaff has practically no nutritional content, but it does ensure that the horse chews its food properly, so helping to minimize the risk of indigestion. It also acts as an abrasive on teeth. Finally, a salt or mineral lick – left in the manger – is essential for all stabled horses. Field-kept animals usually take in an adequate amount of salt during grazing, but a lick is also a good safeguard.

Vitamins and minerals

An adequate supply of vitamins and minerals is vital in addition to the required amounts of carbohydrates, proteins and fat. Vitamins A, B1, B2, B6, D and E are all essential; otherwise the horse's resistance to disease will certainly be lessened, and actual disease may well result. Normally, good-class hay and grass, bran and carrots will contain most of the vitamins a horse needs; oats, barley, flaked maize and sugar beet pulp are also all useful. Vitamin D, however, can only be artificially administered through cod liver oil, or left to the action of sunlight on the natural oil in the coat.

The absence of a sufficient supply of minerals can be even more serious than a lack of vitamins, especially in the case of a young horse. The essential minerals required are: calcium and phosphorus, for the formation of healthy teeth and bones; sodium, sodium chloride (salt) and potassium, for regulation of the amount of body fluids; iron and copper, vital for the formation of haemoglobin in the blood to prevent anaemia; while magnesium, manganese, cobalt, zinc and iodine are all necessary. Magnesium aids skeletal and muscular development; manganese is needed both for the bone structure and for reproduction; zinc and cobalt stimulate growth; while iodine is particularly important in control of the thyroid gland.

However, of all these minerals, the most important is salt. This is why it is vital to provide a horse with a salt lick in either stable or field.

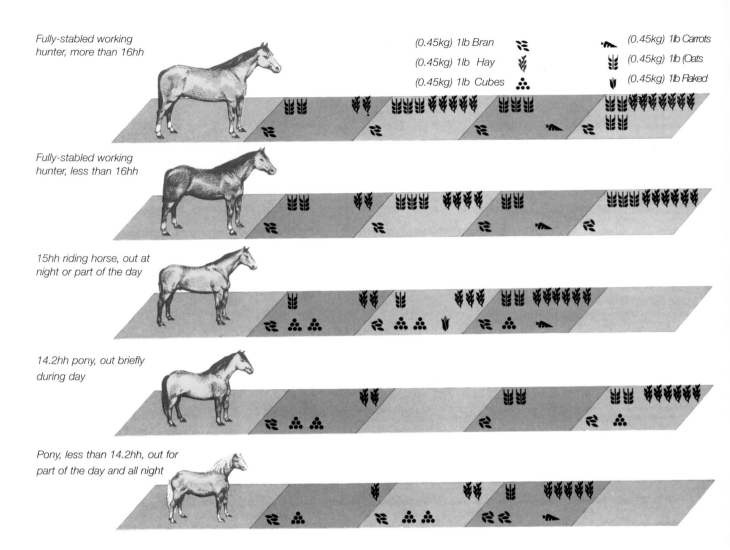

Fully-stabled working hunter, more than 16hh

Fully-stabled working hunter, less than 16hh

15hh riding horse, out at night or part of the day

14.2hh pony, out briefly during day

Pony, less than 14.2hh, out for part of the day and all night

(0.45kg) 1lb Bran
(0.45kg) 1lb Hay
(0.45kg) 1lb Cubes
(0.45kg) 1lb Carrots
(0.45kg) 1lb (Oats
(0.45kg) 1lb Flaked

Above *The amount of food a horse requires varies according to its size, temperament and the type of work it will be doing. This chart gives basic specimen diets for horses with an even temperament. The amount and type of food given to each individual horse should be adapted according to observation.*

As with vitamins, the chief source of these minerals is grass or hay, together with the other foods mentioned above. However, if the horse needs extra vitamins and minerals, always take the advice of a vet first – an excess of vitamins or minerals can be as dangerous as an underdose. These are many suitable proprietary products on the market. These usually come in the form of liquid, powders and pellets, designed to be mixed in with other food for ease of feeding.

Signs of lack of vitamins are usually seen on the skin and coat; examination of the teeth, gums and eyes can also give warning of possible deficiency. But, with sensible and controlled feeding, the problem should not arise.

Quantities to feed

There is no hard and fast guide to the exact amounts of food a horse should be fed, as much depends on the type and size of horse and the work it is expected to do. However, as far as a stabled horse is concerned, the amount should certainly not be less than the horse would eat if it was grazing freely.

If the horse concerned was 15.2hh, say, it would eat approximately 12kg (26½lb) of grass a day. Bigger horses require an extra 0.9kg (2lb) for every extra 5cm (2in) of height; smaller ones need 0.9kg (2lb) less.

With this basic total established, it is possible to plan a feeding programme, varying the amounts of bulk and concentrated food according to the demands being made upon the horse. Taking as an example a lightweight 15.2hh horse that is being hunted, say, three days a fortnight in addition to other regular work, the emphasis will be on an almost equal balance between concentrates and hay or grass. The horse should be getting some 6kg (14lb) of concentrates a day to some 7kg (15lb) of hay. If, however, the horse is being lightly worked – or not worked at all – the amount of hay will rise and the quantities of concentrates diminish.

Remember, too, that most horses feed much better at night, so it is important that the highest proportion of food be given in the final feed of the day. If the horse is being given three feeds a day, for example, the proportions are 10 per cent in the morning, 30 per cent at midday and 60 per cent at night.

The best guide of all is simple observation. If a horse is too fat, it will need its rations reduced; if too thin, it will need building up. Always reduce the amount if food is left uneaten.

Exercising the horse

All stabled horses must have regular and adequate exercise. Otherwise they can develop swollen legs, azoturia and colic – and will, in any case be spirited and difficult to manage when ridden. They can also become bored and develop bad habits. The amounts needed vary with the type and weight of horse and the work it is expected to do; a hunter needs more exercise than a hack.

As with feeding, there are a few basic rules to remember. Most importantly, never exercise a horse until 1½ hours after a heavy feed; 1 hour after a small one. In any case, always remove the haynet an hour before exercise. Horses full of hay find breathing difficult when being worked hard.

The point of exercise is to get and keep the horse fit enough for the demands being made on it. A horse brought up from grass, say, is likely to be in

'grass condition'. In such a case, fitness can be achieved only through a rigidly controlled programme of exercise and feeding. Restrict exercise to walking, preferably on roads, for a week. Then combine walking with slow trotting. Soon, work can start in the school, while the period of road work can also be extended. Increase the amount of grain fed in proportion to the extra in work. By the end of six weeks, the horse should be ready to be cantered over distances not exceeding 0.8km (½ mile). In the ninth week, it can have a gallop for up to 1.2km (¾ mile), but this should be strictly controlled so that the horse does not gallop flat out at full speed.

Indications of success are an increase in muscle and the disappearance of the profuse, lathery sweat of the out-of-condition horse. Never try to hurry the process; a horse cannot be conditioned through cantering and galloping, but only by slow, steady, regular work. This applies just as much to stabled horses and ponies.

Always aim to end the exercise with a walk so that the horse comes back to its stable or field cool and relaxed. Once the tack has been removed, inspect the horse for cuts and bruises, pick out its feet, and brush off the saddle and sweat marks. Then rug up or groom. If you have been caught in the rain trot the horse home so that it is warm on arrival. Untack, and then give the horse a thorough rubbing down, either with straw or a towel. When this has been completed, cover the back with a layer of straw or use a sweat sheet. It is vital to keep the back warm to avoid the risk of colds and chills.

A thorough drying is essential if the horse is very hot and sweaty, but it will need to be sponged down first with lukewarm water. Either restrict sponging to the sweaty areas – usually the neck, chest and flanks – or sponge the entire body. Then, scrape off the surplus water with a sweat scraper, taking care to work with, and not against, the run of the coat. Next, rubdown and, finally, cover with a sweat sheet. If possible, lead the horse around until it is completely dry.

Horses that have been worked exceptionally hard – in hunting, say, or in competitions – need further care. On returning to the stable, give the horse a drink of warm water. Then follow the procedures outlined above. Feed the horse with a bran mash and then leave it to rest. Return later to check that the animal is warm enough or has not broken out into a fresh sweat. Check for warmth by feeling the bases of the ears. If they are cold, warm them by rubbing them with the hand and then put more blankets on the horse. If the ears remain cold, rub down again and walk the horse around until it is completely dry.

Grooming the horse

The chief point of grooming is to keep the horse clean, massage the skin and tone up the muscles. Field-kept horses need less grooming than stabled horses, particularly in winter, but some must nevertheless be carried out.

A good grooming kit is essential. This should consist of a dandy brush, to remove mud and dried sweat marks; a body brush, a soft, short-bristled brush for the head, body, legs, mane and tail; a rubber curry comb, used to remove thickly-caked

To pick up a horse's foot, stand facing its tail. Warn it first by sliding a hand down from its shoulder to its fetlock. This can also encourage the horse to move its weight over to the other legs. It also helps to keep a young horse calm.

Working from the frog to the toe and concentrating on the edges first, use the point of the hoof pick to prise out any foreign objects lodged in the foot. Pebbles wedged between the frog and the bar can cause lameness. Take care not to push the point into the frog.

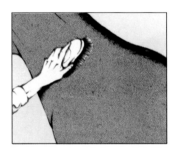

The dandy brush is used to remove heavy dirt caked mud and sweat stains, particularly from the saddle region, belly, points of hocks, fetlocks and pasterns. As it is fairly harsh it should not be used on the more tender areas, or on a recently clipped horse.

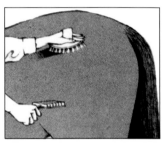

A body brush has short, dense bristles designed to penetrate and clean the coat. It should be applied with some pressure, in firm, circular movements. After a few strokes clear it of dust with a curry comb. A gentler brushing should be given round the head.

The body brush is also used to groom the tail. This should be brushed a few hairs at a time, starting with the undermost ones. Remove all mud and tangles, taking care not to break any hairs. Finally, the whole tail should be brushed into shape from the top.

Wring out a soft sponge in warm water and sponge the eyes first, wiping outwards from the corners. Carefully sponge round eyelids. Wring out the sponge and wipe over the muzzle, lips and nostrils. A separate sponge should be used to sponge the dock area.

The water brush is used to 'lay' the mane. The tip of the brush is dipped in a bucket of water and thoroughly shaken before it is applied. Keeping the brush flat, make firm, downward strokes from the roots. The mane should be left neat and slightly damp.

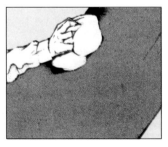

As a final touch to the grooming go over the whole coat with the stable-rubber to remove any trace of dust. This cloth is used slightly damp and folded into a flat bundle. Work along the lie of the hair. The stable-rubber leaves the coat gleaming.

mud or matted hair, and a metal one, for cleaning the body brush; a water brush, used damp on the mane, tail and hooves; a hoof pick; a stable rubber, used to give a final polish to the coat; and some foam rubber sponges, for cleaning the eyes, nostrils, muzzle and dock.

Where more than one horse is kept, each animal should have its own grooming kit, kept together in a box or bag and clearly marked. This helps to prevent the risk of infection in cases of illness.

Grooming falls into three stages, each of which is carried out at a different time of the day. The first of these is quartering, normally done first thing in the morning before exercise. Tie up the horse. Then, pick the feet out and, next, clean the eyes, muzzle and dock with a damp sponge. If worn, rugs should be unbuckled and folded back and the head, neck, chest and forelegs cleaned with a body brush. Replace the rugs and repeat the process on the rear part of the body. Remove any stable stains with a water brush. Finish by brushing the mane and tail thoroughly with the body brush.

Strapping is the name given to the thorough grooming which follows exercise, when the horse has cooled down. Once again, tie the horse up and pick out its feet. Follow by using the dandy brush to remove all traces of dirt, mud and sweat, paying particular attention to marks left by the girth and saddle and on the legs. Work from ears to tail, first on the near side and then on the off. Take care to use the brush lightly to avoid irritating the skin.

Next, comes the body brush. This must be used firmly for full effect. Start with the mane, pushing it to the wrong side to remove scurf from the roots. Brush the forelock. Then, start on the body, working from head to tail and grooming the nearside first, as before. Work with a circular motion, finishing in the direction of the hairs, and flick the brush outwards at the end of each stroke to push dust away from the body. At intervals, clean the brush with the curry comb, which is held in the other hand. It can be emptied by tapping on the floor at intervals.

Brush the head, remembering that this is one of the most sensitive areas of the horse. So use the brush firmly, but gently, and take particular care when grooming around the eyes, ears and nostrils. Finally, brush the tail – a few hairs at a time – so that every tangle is removed.

The next stage is wisping, which helps tone up the muscles and also stimulates the circulation. A wisp is a bundle of soft hay, twisted up to form a rope. Slightly dampen it, and use vigorously on the neck, shoulders, quarters and thighs, concentrating on the muscular areas. Bang the wisp down hard on these, sliding it off with, not against, the coat. Take care to avoid bony areas and the tender region of the loins.

Sponge the eyes, lips, and muzzle and nostrils. Then, with a second sponge to minimize the risk of possible infection, wash round the dock and under the tail. Lift the tail as high as possible, so the entire region can be adequately cleaned. 'Lay' the mane with the water brush. Then brush the outside of the feet, taking care not to get water into the hollow of the heel. When the hooves are dry, brush hoof oil over the outside of each hoof as high as the coronet.

Finally, work over the horse with the stable rubber for a final polish. The object is to remove the last traces of dust from the coat. Fold the rubber into a flat bundle, dampen it slightly, and then go over the coat, working in the direction of the lie of the hair.

Strapping takes from between ½ and ¾ with practice. It will normally take a novice slightly longer, largely because of the unaccustomed strain it imposes on the groom's muscles. 'Setting fair' – the last grooming of the day – takes far less time. Simply brush the horse lightly with the body brush, wisp and then put on the night rug (blanket), if one is normally worn.

Travelling with a horse

Careful planning when entering for a horse show, say, or going for a day's hunting, is essential if the horse is to arrive fit enough to undertake the tasks demanded of it. The first essential is to plan the journey; a fit horse can be hacked for up to 16km (10miles), walking and trotting at an average speed of no more than 10kp/h

(6mph) – a grass-kept pony's average should not be more than 6.5km/h (4mph). However, if the distance involved is greater than this, transport will be needed. Horse boxes or car-towed trailers are the usual method of transport over long distances. Apart from the obvious mechanical checks that should be carried out before each journey, the horse's own requirements, too, need attention. A hay net is one essential; this should be filled with hay and given to the horse during the journey, unless the animal is expected to work hard immediately on arrival. Others include a first aid kit; rugs (day and sweat); bandages; grooming kit; a headcollar; a water bucket and a filled water container. This last item is essential if the journey is to be a particularly long one, when the horse will need to be watered perhaps once or even twice en route. In some cases – when hunting, for example – the horse can travel saddled-up, with a rug placed over the saddle, but, in the case of competitions, a rug alone should be worn. Travelling bandages should always be used, as well as a tail bandage to stop the top of the tail from being rubbed. In addition, knee caps and hock boots should be worn as an added protection.

Preparation of the horse itself must start the night before, with an especially thorough grooming. Both mane and tail should be washed. A grass-kept horse should be kept in for the night, if possible. The next morning, follow the normal stable routine, with the addition of a drawn-out strapping. Remember that, in the case of a show, the mane should be plaited; this can be started the night before to ease the task of getting the mane into shape, but will need to be completed the following day.

Loading the horse

Getting a horse into a box or trailer is an easy enough task, provided that the process is tackled calmly and without undue haste. The simplest way is for one person to lead the horse forward, walking straight forward and resisting the temptation to pull at the head. A couple of helpers should stand behind the horse in case help is required, but out of kicking range.

The main reason for a horse showing reluctance to enter a box is usually its fear of the noise of its hooves on the ramp. This can be overcome by putting down some straw to deaden the sound. Loading another, calmer, horse first, or tempting a horse forward with a feed bucket containing a handful of oats, also act as encouragements.

A really obstinate horse, however, will have to be physically helped into the box. The way to do this is to attach two ropes to the ramp's rails, so that they cross just above the horse's hocks, with two helpers in position – one at each end of the ropes. As the horse approaches the ramp, they tighten the ropes to propel the animal into the box.

Tack – care and maintenance

Care of saddles and bridles is just as important as care of the horse itself. Ill-fitting, dirty or worn tack is not only unpleasant and uncomfortable for the horse; it can also be extremely dangerous for the rider. Therefore always keep tack clean and check it regularly for wear. With saddles this applies particularly to girths and stirrup leathers – a badly-worn girth is a potential killer. Bits should never be allowed to become worn and rough.

All tack should be stored in a cool, dry place – a purpose-planned tack room is the best. A warm, damp atmosphere will cause leather to crack, break or develop mould. Similarly, metal parts will tarnish or rust. Always hang bridles up on a bridle rack; saddles should be placed over a saddle horse, or on a wide padded bracket screwed firmly to the wall.

Tack should be cleaned daily; at the very least, sweat marks should be removed and the bit thoroughly cleaned. The equipment needed is as follows: a rough towel or large sponge for washing; a small, flat sponge; a chamois leather; saddle soap; metal polish or wool; a couple of soft cloths; a dandy brush; a nail, to clean curb hooks; a bucket; hanging hooks for bridle, girths and leathers; a saddle horse; and a vegetable oil.

When cleaning the saddle, place it on the saddle horse and remove all fittings, such as girths and

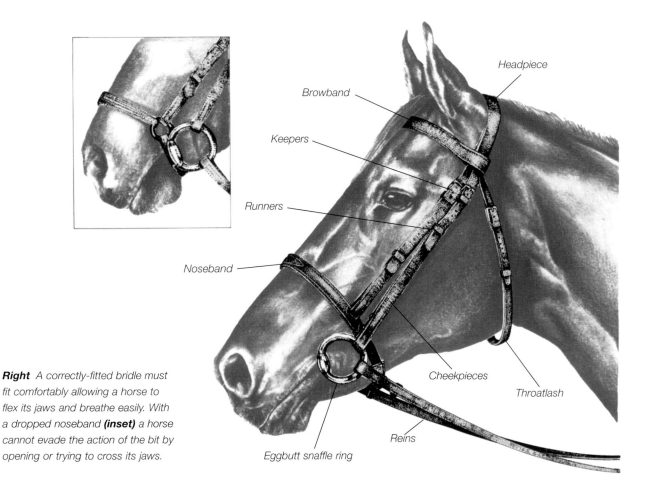

Headpiece

Browband

Keepers

Runners

Noseband

Cheekpieces

Throatlash

Reins

Eggbutt snaffle ring

Right *A correctly-fitted bridle must fit comfortably allowing a horse to flex its jaws and breathe easily. With a dropped noseband **(inset)** a horse cannot evade the action of the bit by opening or trying to cross its jaws.*

stirrup leathers. These should be cleaned separately. Wash the leatherwork with lukewarm water to remove dirt, dried sweat and grease – but take care not to get the saddle saturated. If the lining is of leather, it can also be washed. Otherwise scrub it down dry with a dandy brush.

With the chamois leather slightly dampened, dry the saddle off. Apply saddle soap liberally with the damp sponge, working it well into the saddle to get the soap into the leather without creating a lather. Allow some time for the leather to absorb the soap. Then rub over with a moist sponge and, finally, wipe down with the chamois leather. Clean the leather pieces that have been removed with saddle soap, and the metal ones with metal polish. Clean out the holes of stirrup leathers with a match or a nail. Leather girths should be oiled on the inside. Web string and nylon ones should be brushed down with a dandy

brush and washed occasionally, using pure soap. Then, reassemble. As a preliminary to cleaning, it is a good idea to take the bridle to pieces so that the stitching can be thoroughly checked for wear. Reassemble, and, starting with the bit, wash with lukewarm water. Dry, soap the leather and polish the metal in the same way as the saddle. If the leather needs oiling, take the bridle apart once cleaning has been completed. Oil each piece individually. Then fit the parts together again, taking care that the bit is in the correct position.

Bridles and bits

All commonly-used bridles have the same purpose – to hold the bit in the mouth. It is through use of this, in conjunction with seat and legs, that the horse is guided and controlled. There are two main types of bridle – the snaffle bridle, with one bit, and the double bridle, with two. The latter has two bits and two sets of reins.

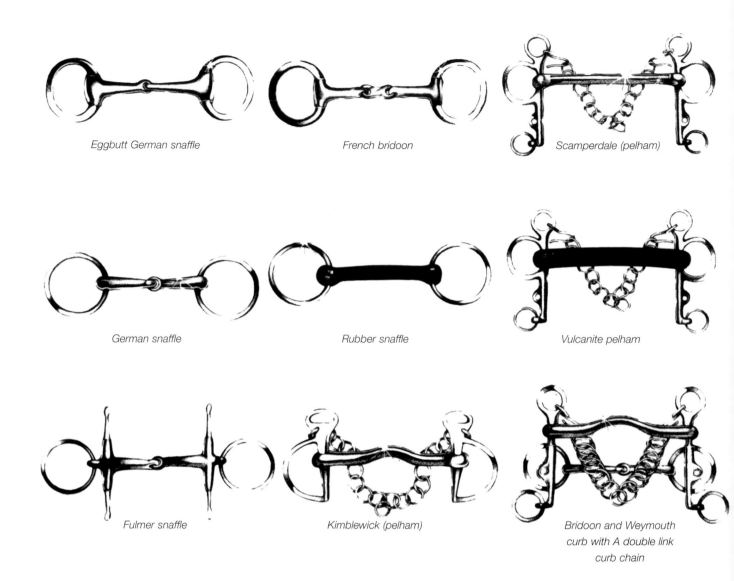

Eggbutt German snaffle

French bridoon

Scamperdale (pelham)

German snaffle

Rubber snaffle

Vulcanite pelham

Fulmer snaffle

Kimblewick (pelham)

Bridoon and Weymouth
curb with A double link
curb chain

All modern bits are based on one of two principles – either the snaffle or the curb. The snaffle is a mild bit. It consists of a metal bar, either jointed or plain, with a ring at either end to which the rein and headpiece of the bridle are attached. Pressure on the bit via the rein causes it to act on the corners of the horse's mouth, with a nutcracker action if the bit is jointed.

The curb is also of metal; it may have a hump, called a port, in the middle. It is fitted with shanks at either end, the cheekpieces being attached to the top of the shanks and the rein to rings at the bottom. The shanks are linked by a chain which lies in the chin groove.

Pressure on the rein has a leverage effect – the longer the shanks, the greater the leverage. This causes the bit to act in three ways. The mouthpiece presses

Above *Some typical bits. A bit applies pressure to the bars, the tongue and the corners of a horse's mouth. Jointed snaffles produce a squeezing or nutcracker action. Thick, straight snaffles are the mildest and are used on young or light-mouthed horses. Pelhams try to combine the curb with the snaffle. They are used with a curb chain and either single or double reins. The double bridle is a thin bridoon (or snaffle) and curb bit. Used together, these give the rider more precise control.*

downwards on to the bars of the mouth (the gap between the front incisors and the back molars), the top of the headpiece presses on to the poll, and the curb chain tightens in the chin groove. If the bit has a high port, the top of it will be brought into contact with the roof of the mouth.

There are many variations of these two basic types of bit. The double bridle, for example, uses a jointed snaffle bit (a bridoon) in combination with an English curb – a curb fitted with short, straight shanks and a lip-strap to keep the curb chain in the correct position. Always use the mildest bit possible. A severe bit often produces exactly the opposite result to the one intended, as the horse can easily become upset, excitable and harder to control. Above all, avoid using the bit insensitively, as this will only lead to the horse developing a hard mouth. Signs of this are the corners of the mouth and the tongue becoming calloused through constant pressure from the bit. If this happens, remedial action should be taken immediately.

Right (top) A double bridle is mainly used by experienced riders on well-trained horses in shows or for dressage. It is not for the novice.

Right (bottom)The headcollar should fit comfortably, and be mode of strong leather. It is used for leading a horse or tying it up.

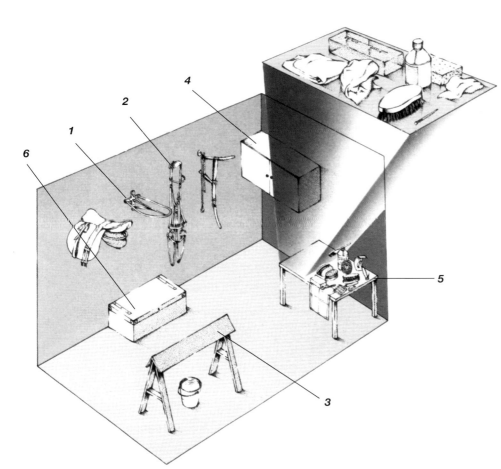

Left A well-equipped tackroom and above basic cleaning kit. A well-planned tack room should bo equipped with saddle and bridle racks (1, 2) while a saddle horse (3) and hooks for the bridle are also useful. The room itself should be clean and dry with enough space to hold the necessary materials; a first aid box (4), a grooming kit (5) and a chest for blankets and rugs (6). All tack must be cleaned regularly – daily, if possible – to keep it supple, and checked for wear, especially in places where leather is joined by stitching.

***Top** The deep-seated dressage saddle helps the rider keep a good, central seat. It is straighter cut to help the lengthened leg position.*
***Bottom** A jumping saddle is more forward cut and keeps the rider's seat and weight positioned in the deepest part of the saddle. Deep knee rolls give extra support.*

***Below** Girths should be chosen and checked carefully. From left: Lampwick, close-woven, leather-strapped girth. String; air gets through and so prevents chafing. Balding, leather girth, shaped to avoid galling. Three-fold, soft leather girth, kept supple with oiled cloth laid in fold.*

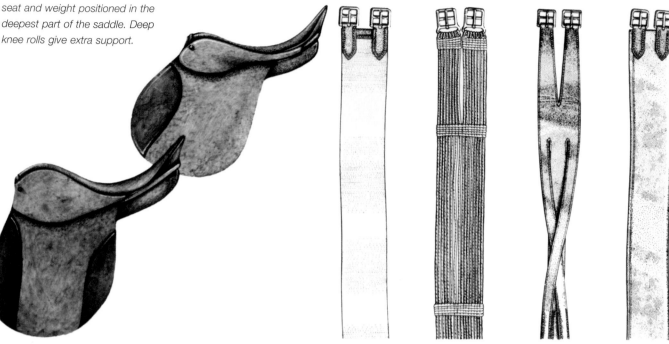

Selecting a saddle

As with bridles and bits, there are various types of saddle – some designed for a particular task, or, as in the case of the Western saddle, a specific style of riding. The most important thing to remember is that the saddle must fit the horse properly. An ill-fitting saddle will make the horse and rider very sore; and it will also make it impossible for the rider to position himself correctly.

The framework of the saddle is called the tree and determines the final shape, so it must be correctly made. Many riding associations, such as the Pony Club, have their own approved patterns and it is always safest to look for one of these. The commonest form in use today is the 'spring tree' – so-called because it has two pieces of light steel let into it under the seat to increase resilience. Treat the tree with care. If a saddle is dropped the tree may break. The saddle cannot then be used until it is professionally repaired.

The rest of the saddle consists of layers of webbing, canvas, serge, and finally, leather. The padded part, which rests on the horse's back, is usually made of felt or stuffed with wool. It is important that this padding is arranged so that the rider's weight is distributed evenly over the back and carried on the fleshy part rather than the spine. This helps to preserve the horse's strength and stamina and prevents sores from developing. If additional protection is necessary, a pad – known as a numnah – can be placed beneath the saddle.

Girths keep the saddle in place, so they must be strong. They should be inspected regularly for wear. They can be made of leather, webbing, or nylon string – in the case of webbing, two girths should be used for additional safety. Stirrup irons, too, should always be chosen with safety foremost in mind. Safety irons, often used by children, are specifically designed so that the foot will come free in a fall. Adults should always check that there is 12mm (½in) clearance on either side of the foot, measured at the widest place of the boot or shoe, so that it does not become jammed.